Domestic fortress

MANCHESTER
1824

Manchester University Press

Domestic fortress

Fear and the new home front

Rowland Atkinson and Sarah Blandy

Manchester University Press

Published by Manchester University Press
Altrincham Street, Manchester M1 7JA

www.manchesteruniversitypress.co.uk

British Library Cataloguing-in-Publication Data
A catalogue record for this book is available from the British Library

Library of Congress Cataloging-in-Publication Data applied for

ISBN   978 1 7849 95317   paperback

First published 2017

Typeset in 10.5 on 12.5 pt Bembo Std Regular
by Toppan Best-set Premedia Limited

Contents

Figures

Acknowledgements

This book is the product of our longstanding interest in the various themes represented here and several research projects funded by the UK government, British and Australian research councils among others. We would like to acknowledge the funders of those projects, and thank the colleagues whose responses to our work have challenged us and have enriched our theoretical approach as it developed. A particular debt of gratitude is owed to Lee Williams for his research assistance.

home

an ancient word related to a
Sanskrit term meaning 'safe dwelling'.

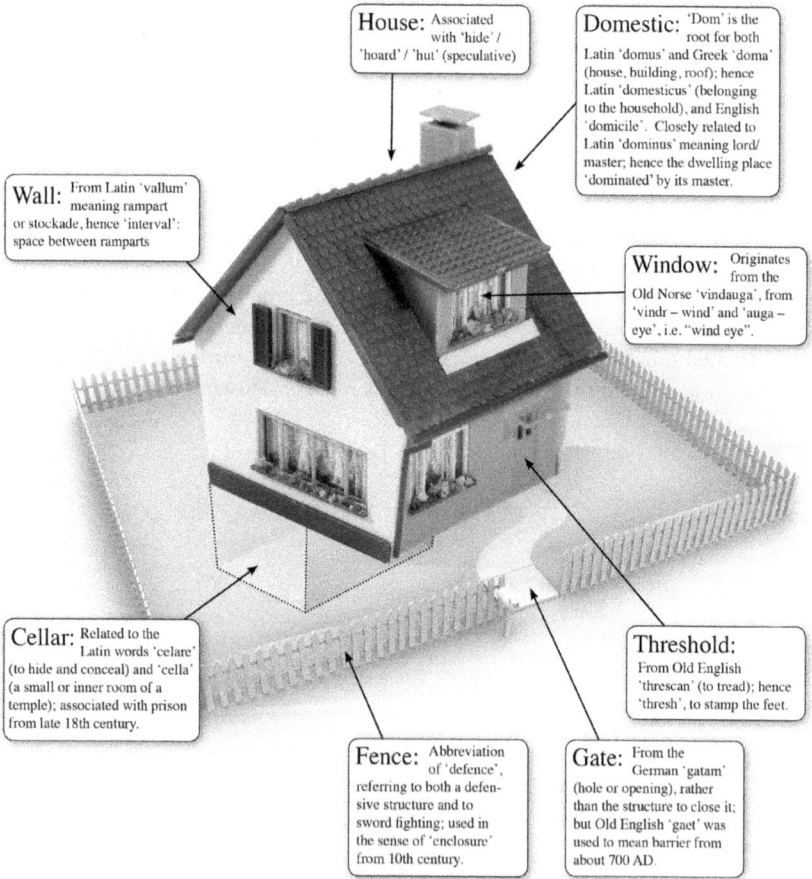

House: Associated with 'hide' / 'hoard' / 'hut' (speculative)

Domestic: 'Dom' is the root for both Latin 'domus' and Greek 'doma' (house, building, roof); hence Latin 'domesticus' (belonging to the household), and English 'domicile'. Closely related to Latin 'dominus' meaning lord/master; hence the dwelling place 'dominated' by its master.

Wall: From Latin 'vallum' meaning rampart or stockade, hence 'interval': space between ramparts

Window: Originates from the Old Norse 'vindauga', from 'vindr – wind' and 'auga – eye', i.e. "wind eye".

Cellar: Related to the Latin words 'celare' (to hide and conceal) and 'cella' (a small or inner room of a temple); associated with prison from late 18th century.

Threshold: From Old English 'threscan' (to tread); hence 'thresh', to stamp the feet.

Fence: Abbreviation of 'defence', referring to both a defensive structure and to sword fighting; used in the sense of 'enclosure' from 10th century.

Gate: From the German 'gatam' (hole or opening), rather than the structure to close it; but Old English 'gaet' was used to mean barrier from about 700 AD.

Components of the defended home, history of key terms (source: Julia Cresswell, *Oxford Dictionary of Word Origins*, Oxford Reference Online, Oxford University Press)

1

Introduction

> Why have fear and anger become such a prominent feature of social life, evidenced by violent responses to home invasion? Why is it that, contrary to the objective evidence, it is the people who live in the greatest comfort on record, more cosseted and pampered than any other people in history, who feel more threatened, insecure and frightened, more inclined to panic, and more passionate about everything related to security and safety than people in most other societies past and present? (Bauman, 2006: 130)

A walk around many of the world's leafiest and most prestigious neighbourhoods and new mansions reveals a world of relative secrecy, high security and what can only be described as a kind of fortification – of the private home. Were we able to leap the gates of many of the proliferating gated communities across the global north we would find similar products, increasingly tailored to those on middle incomes as well as the global rich. Whether it be the bomb-proof windows of ultra-prime properties like One Hyde Park in London, the gated mansions of footballers in Manchester's rural hinterland, the island retreats of celebrities and the super-rich, the palatial excess of Los Angeles' suburbs or the efforts of homeowners in risky areas to prevent burglary the trend is increasingly apparent, the feel of these neighbourhoods increasingly hostile and anxiety-ridden. Fear has been democratised and, where resource exists to do so, the sense of concealment, protection and defence is ever more apparent in the designs and adaptations now being deployed. So it is that our use of Zygmunt Bauman's pithy observation as an opening to this volume helps to reveal much about one of the social paradoxes of our time – why do we witness the presence of anxiety and fear among many of the globe's most affluent people, and how does this translate into a kind of urban life that offers both continuities and definite breaks with the built landscapes of even the recent past?

Many commentators on our social condition have emphasized that fear has become a defining component or index of contemporary life and our project in this book builds upon these concerns to offer a consideration of how it is that unease is increasingly linked to the private territories of home life. Domestic routines position us in a paradoxical relation to our fear since the home is both the site around which much apprehension is experienced (of invasion from outside, or of violence within the home), yet it is also a defensible space which can protect us from gnawing concerns about a more unpredictable world outside. As security has become a central aspect of the life of nations and urban centres it thus seems important to consider where the domestic home is positioned against a range of potential threats, and its place within these concerns. This is a new kind of home front that can be deployed as a crucial resource in a wider battle against a range of sources of anxiety that press upon us, as well as being bound up with the political projects of market freedoms and orientations that characterize so many aspects of social life more broadly. What has for some time been described as a culture of fear (Bauman, 2006; Glassner, 1999) has thus been met with an increasingly emphatic retreat by homeowners into fortified dwellings, extravagant houses, concealed bunkers and countless gated developments globally.

Many homes now feature numerous defensive security measures: alarms, CCTV, motion-sensing lights and some even include impregnable panic rooms. Yet the disquiet driving these physical and geographical responses is neither socially or historically novel, nor restricted to the rich and famous. Rising real household incomes and home ownership rates have enabled many households to adopt similar technologies, producing a type of home, the domestic fortress, that displays our fear in the solidity of the built environments around us, with homes and suburbs taking on the look and feel of increasingly secured terrains. As Bauman notes:

> The war against insecurity, dangers and risks is now waged inside the city [and home], and inside the city battlefields are marked out and front lines are drawn. Heavily armoured trenches and bunkers intended to separate out strangers, keep them away and bar their entry are fast becoming one

1.1 Safe house (night-time mode, shutters and doors closed), Poland

of the most visible aspects of contemporary cities ... in which the safety-addicted urban residents dwell (Bauman, 2005: 82)

While our homes provide us with a means of locking out the daily hardships and risks of everyday life, from them we witness and anticipate a range of troubling phenomena: internationalised and potentially unending forms of terror, regional warfare, the anxieties generated by global ecological change, the rise of ethnic and nationalist extremism, global flows of the dispossessed, feelings of loss and uncertainty around social identity, new-found insecurities of the workplace and our future welfare, to say nothing of the growing risks of flood, fire and other incalculable catastrophes. To go a little beyond Bauman's paradox we need to note that today's home is unevenly positioned – between offering a site that protects us, more or less, and yet which is also a fore-grounded space upon which we project many of our worst fears of potential invasion, violation or even destruction. In the context of a risk-based view of the world that emphasises the central role of indi-viduals in managing such possibilities (Beck, 1992) many industries now profit from these pervasive fears and have thus sought to sell a war against intruders, dirt and disaster and include insurance and security companies offering defensive home technologies (see Chapter 6). Thus fear combines with an individualised project of the self within homes hidden from view or fortified using diverse security technologies and in many ways absent of state safeguards or community supports. While defence has been a primary function of the home from the earliest times (Gardiner, 1976), and security measures have been variably emphasised within particular historical epochs according to prevailing social arrangements, the presence of new plans, designs and constructions suggests something novel is occurring across much of the global north and west. While these formations have connections with those of the past, a major aim of this volume is to discuss how and why what we see is new and distinctive.

Pervasive worry can be linked to the home in diverse ways – we are fearful when people knock at the door, irritated when salespeople or even friends call us unannounced, worried when we are not there to protect our property. Similarly we have nightmares about our house being broken into as we sleep, are furious and confused about media stories of elderly women raped in their homes, anxious about subsidence, ponder the risk of repossession and the risk of being 'under water' (in negative equity), or behind in our repayments, while at other times, we worry about being literally underwater from floods and other incalculable risks to the physical fabric and social life of the home. Such fears are by no means baseless, even if we may mis-estimate their occurrence, yet they not only tell us much about our own psychological states, but also about our fear of other people, the fragmentation of society into rich and poor enclaves, and the consequences of the state withdrawing previous assurances that it would protect citizens. Elliott and Lemert (2006: 8) argue that this social condition of pronounced individualism has generated:

> privatized worlds [which] propel individuals into shutting others and the wider world out of their emotional lives. Under the impact of privatism, the self is denied any wider relational connection at a deeply unconscious level, and on the level of day-to-day behaviour such 'new individualisms' set the stage for a unique cultural constellation of anguish, anxiety, fear, disappointment and dread.

These are strong words, to be sure, and ones that perhaps compel us to confront the pressures on us as individuals within less social and increasingly unequal societies. Yet the more important point we might take from such observations concerns how these social forces combine and propel forms of privatised responsibility and fear and the way that the private home has been situated as a potential safe/danger zone within this context.

Withdrawal and defence

Political ideologies of economic freedom combined with messages about social disorderliness form the worrisome backdrop of much of everyday life, implying competition with, and perhaps also fear of, our neighbours. Thus we see more and more lockable front gates, fences, external post-boxes, internal and external iron grilles, shades and shutters put in place to avoid the observation and social contact of those known and unknown to us. The fortress mentality and physicality of the modern home goes beyond achieving basic security through design, marking an even deeper commitment to the pursuit of status, loneliness and privacy as the bonds of community and state assurances have been loosened over time (Putnam, 2000). Looking 'through the keyhole', as the popular television series had it, or more appositely, through the fisheye viewer in many front doors, we see an extensive array of mechanisms through which the privacy and sanctity of domestic life is now managed and ensured: metal-reinforced doors, burglar alarms, bedside panic alarms, toughened glass windows, pressure pad and laser sensor intruder systems and even elaborate panic rooms, echoing past anxieties about incendiary or nuclear attacks. These are now the taken-for-granted measures of security in many homes, but they are supplemented by other strategies that extend beyond the home, such as gated communities, curfews, legal ordinances and other mechanisms to ensure 'civilised' behaviour in public space.

As an example, gated communities often represent a withdrawal into the perceived safety of more secure neighbourhood spaces, despite the fact that no guarantee exists that the dangerous outside world is fully excluded or that neighbours will not present a threat (see Chapter 4) (Atkinson and Smith, 2012). Data on the extent of gated communities suggests that around 6 per cent of all households in the USA live in gated communities (Sanchez et al., 2005); in Australia, just under 6 per cent (5.9 per cent) of households live in homes with secure entry systems (in gated communities and apartment blocks using pin code entry systems, and so on) (Atkinson and Tranter, 2011), while in the

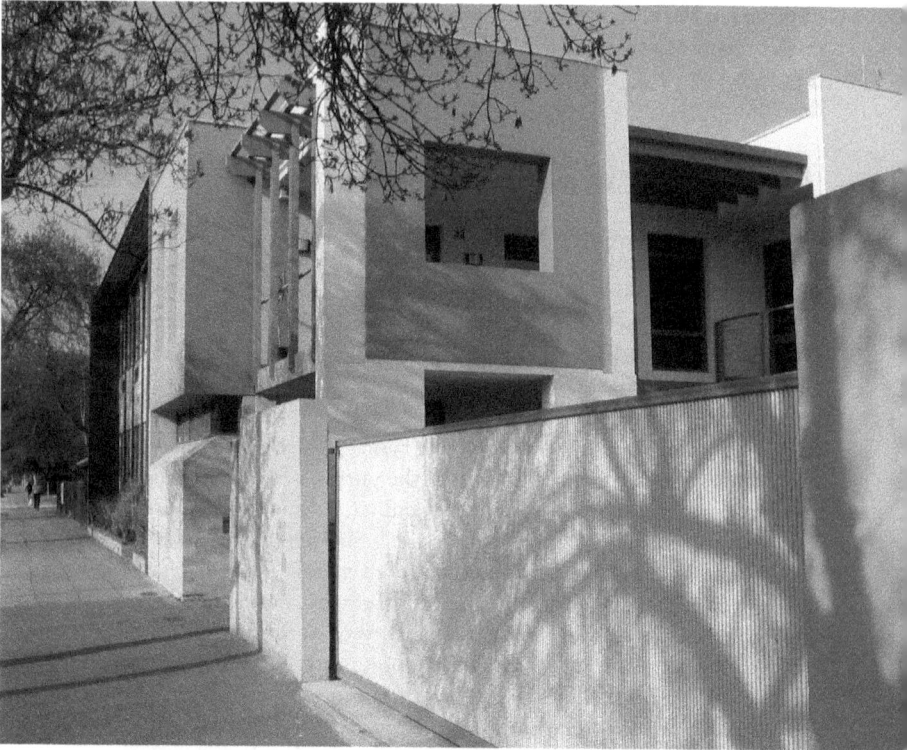

1.2 House with side-scrolling electronic gates, Adelaide, Australia

UK, there are now more than a thousand gated communities (Atkinson *et al.*, 2002). Current figures for each country are now likely much higher.

Both within and outside gated enclaves, we find diminishing levels of sociability and anxieties about contact with others that are reflected in the design of houses, many of which are large enough to accommodate a wide range of home entertainments making the home the centre of daily life. New detached homes are being built to a higher density and have become larger, swallowing up garden space with their expanded floor plans and double or triple garages (Australian Bureau of Statistics, 2007). Such air-conditioned 'McMansions' provide a dramatic contrast with their harsh external environment and are often equipped with the latest technologies of private consumption, such as home cinema systems and games rooms that substitute for public alternatives. The desire for more privacy and for social withdrawal by homeowners is both manipulated and met by the housebuilding industry.

Tenure and jurisdiction

Our primary focus in this book is on home ownership, particularly in England, Australia and the USA. We are interested in the ideological, economic and legal status associated with ownership, themes running throughout the book that we use to explain the connection between the private home, an increasingly individualised society, and the primacy of the economy to political life and social fear, more broadly. Certainly these are themes shared in the conditions of the global south and poorer nations characterised by higher levels of urban violence, inequality and forms of criminality that have generated a firmer basis and entrenched position of gating and domestic security. While touching on these issues our focus remains broadly on the affluent within affluent countries, searching for answers as to why patterns of fortification and exclusion should be so pronounced in locations where crime has been falling for some years.

While all three of the countries we focus on here exert significant economic power, this wealth is unequally distributed amongst their citizens in comparison with most other nations (Wilkinson and Pickett, 2009) and, as former English colonies, the USA and Australia have the same common law system. Further, each of the three countries has high rates of home ownership compared with other leading economies, albeit not the highest rates in the world. There are a number of 'ideologically convergent features', despite some differences, in how the UK, the USA and Australia have respectively achieved mass home ownership (Ronald, 2008: 162). In England, the USA and Australia, rates of home ownership peaked at over 70 per cent between 1996 and 2008, before gradually decreasing as a result of declining affordability and the global economic recession. Each country has also seen a significant rise in housing prices over the decades since the 1990s, albeit interrupted by the 2008 financial crash. We turn to an analysis of these countries, then, for linguistic, legal, data availability and research reasons, yet also intend to offer a diagnosis that has wider applicability to the wider global north and beyond.

Changes in housing tenure are not merely residual features of the economies we highlight in our analysis here; the increase in ownership and wealth has been viewed as fundamental to the economic base of these societies, apparently freeing many households from the 'waste' of rent payments and landlord servitude that make this tenure incredibly important in ideological and cultural terms. The financial crisis that began in 2008, however, highlighted the consequences of over-extending these dreams and the catastrophic impact of mortgage loan default, super-light financial and political regulation and the push by governments to ensure political popularity by offering low interest rates and economic conditions favourable to ownership. The private home is also deeply and ideologically implicated within the need for financial security in the contemporary homeowner's consciousness and those that aspire to be homeowners. The home is now a key part of what has come to be known as equity-based welfare, in which the store of value in the home becomes a substitutive resource, drawn from at times of ill health or in retirement, to top up the decreasing entitlements available to private individuals from western governments (Kluyev and Mills, 2010). Home ownership has thereby come to be seen as essential for the maintenance of personal income and 'welfare' in societies such as the USA and Australia, and this is important to understand the vital social position of ownership as a perceived bulwark against potential insecurities that may present themselves to the individual and household.

There has also been a fundamental change over time in popular understandings of the home, from providing a safe habitation to a tradeable, wealth-generating asset. The recent financial shake-down was linked not only to the role of financial institutions' lending practices in the pursuit of home ownership, but also the complicity of governments in allowing the unfettered rise in value of housing assets because of the intense feel-good factor such economic growth generated. For example, Alan Greenspan (then Chair of the US Federal Reserve Bank) felt it was his duty to assist in a low interest environment to help promote home ownership as the cornerstone of a property-owning society, even while acknowledging that the sub-prime mortgage market was risky (Greenspan, 2007). So deep-seated are these connections between affluence, liberty and property, that the effects of deregulation and the profound and embedded concurrent social inequalities were ignored until it was too late.

Tessellated neoliberalism

Throughout the book we consider what we see as an important relationship between the private home, political life and the economy that we seek to capture in the term *tessellated neoliberalism*. By this we mean the ways in which we can understand the wider order and values of exchange and economic life that expand outwards from the micro-scale of a multitude of owned homes and into the fabric of the macro-economy, guided by prevailing ideologies and decisions by ruling parties and financial institutions. Thus the architecture of ideologies prescribing homeownership is constructed to a significant degree by this pattern of individual interests and physical structures within everyday, lived realities. The alignment of interest has helped to generate deeper social inequalities, amplified through the housing market (Dorling, 2014), fear of crime, the securitisation of the home (as a financial and physical asset), competitive home ownership, and unsustainable property price rises.

In the uncertain times following the global financial crisis of 2008, homes have become perhaps an even more precious asset that needs defending – rising repossession rates and concerns over national economic futures have exacerbated these concerns. The ability to secure the home is predicated on particular material and legal relationships and conditions such as our relative wealth and housing tenure. Whether we own a property or not affects the stakes we have in our home and determines the extent to which we can make modifications without permission from a landlord. Home, or rather home ownership specifically as a particular kind of legal relationship to it, has become an obsession across the Western world. Governments have responded to and manipulated the deep, psychological need by humans for security by using interventions such as subsidies toward mortgages and maintaining low interest rates while also overseeing the relative insecurity and low regulation of the private rented sector and planning system as well as the continued withering of the welfare functions of the state. The rhetoric underpinning state encouragement of homeownership has long been evident in all three countries we examine here and is very clear in this example, from a 1943 speech by Albert Dunstan, Premier of Victoria, Australia:

> Invariably, the man who owns his home is an exemplary citizen. His outlook on life is immediately changed from the moment when the first nail is driven into the structure that is eventually to become 'his castle' ... The homeowner feels that he has a stake in the country. (Dunstan, 1943, cited in Ronald, 2008: 155)

The metaphor of the home owner's 'castle' is of course a much-used trope. We utilise and interrogate it throughout this book, given its ability to conjure defensive ideas about personal jurisdiction, autonomy and control over access. The image derives from a law report by Edward Coke, then Attorney General for England, of *Semayne's case,* heard at court in 1604 and included by Coke in his later publication, *Institutes of the Laws of England*:

> The house of every one is to him as his castle and fortress, as well for his defence against injury and violence as for his repose. For a man's house is his castle, *et domus sua cuique est tutissimum refugium* [and each man's home his safest refuge]. (Coke, 1644: 192)

This original wording was 'cheapened' into the now familiar phrase 'an Englishman's home is his castle' by Freeman (1873), according to Joseph Rykwert (1991: 53). The essence of this usage lies in suggesting that the owner is able to exclude all others and should be supported in being able to actively defend their property from attack or intrusion. The law supports this by defining as trespass even the slightest and most harmless trespass of another's property. In the eighteenth century, property rights were described in another phrase that has had lasting power as exclusionary 'despotic dominion', what might be thought of as a kind of sovereignty expressed at the domestic scale (Blackstone, 1768: 2). Ownership thus enjoys firm support from the state that connects with the arguments of some commentators who have suggested that the desire to own one's home is driven by deep territorial and acquisitive instincts (see Saunders, 1990: 69). So we can suggest that the psychological and legal justifications of property ownership chime with suggestions that 'human territoriality' is best understood as a spatial strategy of control and as an expression of social power (Sacks, 1986) which plays itself out through our built environment and the homes we inhabit as expressions of these attempts at mastery and exclusion.

1.3 Small town defensive architecture, UK

Shared understandings of the home as a place of repose and refuge, to borrow Coke's words, suggest a space of socialisation, contentment and relaxation. The autonomy associated with ownership of the home implies a haven from interference in a wider unstable public realm, but the home also presents a burden of responsibility. While the state encourages homeowners to provide security for their family and household, the relative burden of ownership is at least partly responsible for creating the circumstances that require maintenance and defensive measures. In the USA, Australia and the UK, the state's withdrawal from provision of public services and the implications of this move have been well documented (see for example, Rose, 2000). Policing cuts have also widely been perceived to leave homes vulnerable, and any breach of the security of the home exposes the problematic relationship between the individual, the state and official agencies of law enforcement.

These initial observations lead us to a broader conclusion about the role of the home and of home ownership – that notions of territory, legal ownership and markets are core to how we understand our position within society more broadly. The idea of neoliberalism as an extending and deepening mode of government that presents and advances exactly these interests and values has been a regular theme of social science for some time (see for example Peck, 2010; Harvey, 2005). But perhaps we might go further. Something interesting and important is happening that exists in a figuration, or set of links, between property ownership, neoliberal governance and the home itself. Like a tessellated mosaic we can look down upon increasing sections of the urban system and see an interlocking patchwork of affluent housing, compounds and gated enclaves that are the very bedrock of the systemic architecture that favours ownership, exclusion and market autonomy. In the domestic fortress we find social values that are aligned with market rationalities, interest in the state of the macro economy, stock markets, interest rates and mortgage products, to say nothing of house values. Meanwhile the state, despite its mantra of rolling back to allow unfettered social and economic activity, firmly orchestrates and appeals to the interests of those living in the kinds of districts and homes that this volume discusses.

In many ways the project to promote home ownership, particularly in the past quarter century, is aligned with politically assisted market rule (Peck, 2010). Successive governments in many countries have helped to create favourable conditions for ownership and the political capital that stems from them. The championing of freedom viewed in terms of unhindered markets appears to be closely related to the property market and what it is seen to do for those who benefit from it. In this sense the home is protected by the state in legal terms as property, but is also held up and protected as a way of being that meshes with wider projects of financialisation and the privileging of the wealthy.

While home ownership offers a range of freedoms and advantages, not least the escape from a low quality and largely unregulated private rented sector, vast social and economic inequalities prevent such emancipation for many. The reality of the political drive to promote ownership and growing social divides are often starkly witnessed in the visible differences between the physical homes and neighbourhoods that put the winners and losers on show. Whereas in previous generations affluence could be seen in terms of the divide in terms of tenure, today we see the widening of material differences in the highly securitised and fearful landscapes of wealthy neighbourhoods, homes and suburbs. These have been built partly as displays of prestige but also to help exclude the risks from a less predictable and hierarchically ordered social world outside. Fortress homes and neighbourhoods help to manage and block out this risky world and impressions of risky 'others' who do not belong. In a sea of social precarity the gains of the very affluent can be deployed to shield their conspicuous gains from those least able to achieve them – behind gates, high walls and protected homes. If a shared public realm could be used to galvanise the motivation for common taxes and spending in decades gone by, the fortress home and gated community now enable spaces of uninterrupted enjoyment by social and economic elites who are catered for by private services and club goods. Whereas the risks of disinvesting in the public realm or insuring the poor were once well understood the new-found ability to live uninterrupted behind gates and walls facilitates a political logic of extending market provision; any social friction generated by inequality (Dorling, 2014) can be ignored as a distant sideshow.

This discussion leads us to an important conclusion about the relationship between space, the home and contemporary politics which is to suggest that physical form both follows and feeds the kind of prevailing market orthodoxies and ideologies that have fed the kinds of social divisions we see today. In this context the homes of the affluent and of homeowners form a tessellated system of almost interlocking spaces that build-up wider districts, but also form the basis for legitimating the projects of market excess and freedoms which must be protected alongside the rights to private enjoyment of property. We will return to these themes throughout the book as we examine the relationship between home, the wider built environment and the kinds of social politics in evidence today globally. In this context the changing urban landscape suggests to us a complex series of relationships between self, home and security that combine with the emergence of markets and inequalities as increasingly dividing and divisive processes today (Piketty, 2014).

Crime and fear of crime

Burglary is the most obvious form of transgression to which the home is vulnerable. We use this term to refer to all kinds of forced entry into the home with criminal intent. Legislation in some US states also criminalises 'home invasion'; definitions vary, but typically include forced entry into a residential building when the occupants are at home,

involving the use of weapons or physical intimidation. The annual rates
of actual or attempted burglary of households are consistently high
in England and Wales (7.9 per cent), the USA (7.5 per cent) and
in Australia (6.1 per cent), as compared with a global average of
4.4 per cent and with much lower rates in Scandinavian countries, for
example (Bernasco, 2014). However, in all three countries, the numbers
of burglaries have decreased since the mid-1990s, after a post-war pattern
of rising crime rates. In fact, there has also been a general decrease in
the fear of crime, though with variabilities by particular groups and
areas, despite a huge emphasis on crime and fear within the popular
media. The fear of burglary is, of course, linked to anxiety about an
invasion of privacy alongside worry for the loss of financially and personally valuable effects. Even if much fear is dysfunctional and arguably
unnecessary, it is essential that we respect the validity of these emotions,
the real impact and harms of burglary, and importantly, the wider social,
political and media influences on these states of agitation and anxiety.

Burglary is significant not only because of the financial cost resulting
from loss of property and the consequent (re)investment in home security measures. It is equally if not more important because of the unsettling prospect of its occurrence and its psychological impact, as our
homes and belongings are essential elements of our private and public
identities (Chapman, 1999). So, for example, we see Douglas Porteous
(1976) writing about the home as a 'territorial core', a psychic and
physical space, building on notions of personal space developed by
Erving Goffman (1971), who considered the home as a kind of fixed
territory or aspect of the self. According to environmental psychologists,
there are three ways of infringing on another's territory (Altman, 1975):
invasion (taking control), violation (vandalism), and contamination (for
example, defecating in the home during a burglary; Friedman, 1968).
These types of infringement remain at the core of defensive concerns
about the home, which Irving Altman (1975) considers to be the
primary and therefore the most potent, personalised and permanent
form of human territory. The complex result of burglary victimhood
includes both anger and fear.

Many of the understandable fears of homeowners are fanned by
media reports of global dangers: home invasion, shootings in quiet
neighbourhoods, stories of prisoners and domestic slaves as well as
terror, war and environmental catastrophe that stream into our homes
via proliferating media systems, from televisions and internet to social

1.4 Brooklyn, New York city

media more broadly. We are also subject to constant 'crime talk' (Sasson, 1995), through which stories of danger and harm are amplified by local papers and the gossip of peers and social networks. These influences further raise the value of the home as a calm defence against the exterior chaos; in this context, the home is an ontological anchor, a space which helps bind us to the reality and continuity of the world around us. Yet the home is often placed at the forefront of public debates about crime and disorder, which stokes fear in the collective imagination. There is an established public and media perception that violation of the domestic home is widespread and that the law does not sufficiently help householders to defend their own territory, which, we argue, has generated a deeper fortress mentality than a simple analysis of gated communities and fortress homes allows us to index.

The interlocking of fear, security and the home is further cemented 'by the commercial security industry, whose sales of security devices fuelled the public's fears and insecurities at the very moment that it claimed to allay them' (Garland, 2001: 161). The insurance industry has done well from these fears, and in turn, it ensures sales for purveyors of security by making the installation of security features a condition of providing home insurance. The house-building companies that construct and renovate homes and their sales agents hold out the promise to homeowners of release from their anxieties, marketing even ordinary homes as the realisation of a dream of total privacy and security. At the other extreme from this home market, the global security market was estimated to be worth £410 billion in 2012 and was forecast to rise to £571 billion by 2016 (UK Trade & Investment, 2014), extraordinary figures which encompass the commercial, military and residential security market sectors. Another projection forecasts the residential security market in the USA to grow at a *compound annual growth rate* of 32 per cent over the period 2014–19, and the European residential security market is slated to grow at 16 per cent over the same five years (Technavio, 2015a and 2015b). The huge profits generated by selling residential security connect the fears of owners with the power of media and industry narratives that focus on threats to the home itself.

Another marked impact of the profound wealth generated in recent decades has been both the ability and desire of the rich to take much greater precautions in home security. The use of bodyguards (also known as close protection personnel) is well known, but there has been an accompanying and much larger investment in strategies designed to keep their homes secure. Purchasers pay huge sums for extensively fortified homes, equipped with bulletproof windows, electronic alarm systems, motion-sensitive cameras, voice and fingerprint security entry systems, secure panic rooms and round-the-clock guards. A survey of the wealthy found that over 98 per cent of those with a net worth of over $25 million had paid for personal security services in the previous few years (Farrell, 2008). The security spending of Chief Executive Officers of the 'Fortune 100' companies (the largest by gross annual revenue public and privately held companies in the United States) is published annually in *Fortune* magazine. The figures for 2013 include two reports of expenditure over $1.5m, by Amazon's Jeff Bezos and Oracle's Larry Ellison (Zillman, 2015), though of course, this does not include the raw expenditure of many wealthy people on the home as a defendable asset, such as the 'bomb-proof' apartments of London's One Hyde Park development with prices as high as £140m.

As the wealth of the super-rich has increased, so have investments in assets like second and third homes, yachts and planes, that also need to be secured by domestic security systems, trained bodyguards and remotely accessible surveillance. In 2008, *Forbes* magazine reported on some of the most advanced security systems installed in the homes of the super-rich (Farrell, 2008). These included perimeter command centres inside custom-built homes, long-range infrared cameras, fence and other motion sensors. One particular hedge fund manager installed biometric access scanners and trap doors in a 'fortress' that cost $10 million. In some homes equipped with panic rooms, the whole house can be flooded with tear gas in the event of a break-in, no doubt also bringing to mind stories of raids on the homes of the super-rich in the French Riviera where the use of sleeping gas by a gang of jewel thieves was alleged.

The role played by the media in shaping our tastes, fears and aspirations, is another key theme of this book. Media empires profit from and boost the cult of the celebrity and the public's apparently limitless interest in the homes and interior designs of the rich and famous, extending to details of top-of-the-range security measures and hi-tech installations ordinary homeowners may only fantasise about. Take for example the Manchester United and England footballer Wayne Rooney. A newspaper article gives extensive details about his modern mansion, with its cinema, pool, indoor sports complex and tennis courts, as well as five-a-side football pitch (Wilkes, 2009). We would suggest that the ready availability of this so-called property porn featuring the homes of multimillionaires also fuels aspirations to upgrade our own homes by installing cheaper imitations of their hardwood floors, kitchens with stainless steel appliances, and defensive technologies. The necessary loans and refinancing secured on homes as collateral thereby locks homeowners further into debt; for example, Australia's 'renovation economy' was valued at A$28.1 million in 2006–07 (Allon, 2008: 26).

Technologies of domestic security and neighbourhood organisation present a form of domestic arms race, in which the major beneficiaries are an enlarged commercial sector from housing developers to car manufacturers, marketing products on the basis of their defensive properties. Many of the most extreme examples of such domestic fortressing lie outside the Anglo-Saxon societies which are the focus of this book, but which as time goes on, are marketed to and adopted by homeowners in Australia, the UK and the USA. In South Africa, for example, where some of the most extreme rates of violence occur, the process of fortification has been taken to its conclusion:

> They raise their low, picturesque garden walls by two, three or sometimes even four metres, and top them with spikes or glass chips; they unfurl razor wire ... along their perimeters; they add electric fencing, designed to shock when touched; they install automated driveway gates and intercom systems ... to pass from sleeping to living to kitchen areas may involve unlocking three security gates ... If one house on a street installs an electric fence, the others feel pressurized to follow suit, afraid of becoming the most vulnerable property on the block. (Bremner, 1998: 8)

As consumers, we feel obligated to install the latest security technology or find ways to prevent our comparatively less protected home from being the next target. Similarly, as more people move into gated developments, burglaries tend to be displaced on to people who are less well-protected. The growth of gated communities and the increase in defence of homes by security measures such as alarms, vigilantes or private police forces illustrate in material form these contemporary social pressures and responses.

Vengeful homeowners

Homeowners have adopted an increasingly strategic approach to the defence of the home and a progressively vengeful rhetoric, also amplified through the media, against those who might present a threat. These calls for the obliteration of risks and risky people echo the principles of criminal justice systems today and the use of probability estimates to locate and manage risky populations who threaten those within 'included' or respectable society. In this sense, there is now a clear connection between affluent groups seeking to protect property, the media's role in representing these feelings as the fears of respectable society and political systems which are aligned with these constituencies. The public conversation that stems from these alliances often expresses punitive sentiments and crude representations of the lived reality of the socially

1.5 Gated community, Hong Kong

excluded and poor, seen by many homeowners as those from whom they would like to escape. It is a short step from the lawful right to exclude to demanding the right to exclude by force, now legitimated in many US states – an indicator of the combination of fear and desire for action by many globally.

In some cases, fear is indicated in less visible ways than architecture, for example, the presence of guns in the home and a readiness to use them. Our understanding of the defence of the home must therefore be broadened beyond an analysis of the basic defence and physical security of the home to include broader indicators like the demands upon political and legal systems by the affluent for using maximised and potentially violent force against any threat to the home. Having engendered these perceived needs, the forces associated with financial and political capital have given birth to a constituency that seeks security at every scale, even those external to the home, as a non-negotiable necessity (Simon, 2007). Physical, social and legal measures in the pursuit of domestic safety are thus significant elements of the wider constitution and mood of society, while remaining centred on the home.

The meaning of home

Given that the home occupies such an important position in our lives, it is not surprising that there has been considerable discussion about

its meaning, from the viewpoints of many academic disciplines including sociology, anthropology, feminism, psychology, law, human geography, history, politics, economics, architecture and philosophy (Mallett,
2004). The symbolism of home and the fascinating varieties of meaning
attached to the concept of home have occupied the attention of many
writers on the subject. Environmental psychologists consider the home
to be essential for satisfying basic human needs for privacy and personal identity formation (Bell *et al.*, 1996: 303). Home has also been
defined in economic terms as a 'socio-spatial system' that incorporates
both the physical dwelling and the household residing in it (Saunders
and Williams, 1988: 82). It can be seen as an investment, as a physical
structure, as territory, as the founding block of identity, and as the
most basic social and cultural unit of any society. Functions and activities associated with the home include caring and upbringing, intimate and familial relationships, leisure, consumption, work, inheritance,
and it is a primary site of emotion, memory and nostalgia. Homes are
used to promote our public image (Goffman, 1971) and to express
our identities through décor and taste (Cooper, 1995). What clearly
emerges from the debate over the meaning of home is that, although
'white Western conceptions of home privilege a physical structure or
dwelling' (Mallett, 2004: 65), the idea of home can exist equally in
the imagination, and this concept has a shared cultural significance,
despite class, gender and ethnic differences, that lead to very different
experiences.

   Joanne Moore has pointed to the irony 'that while home is examined
largely because it has physical form, this feature of home has been left
relatively unexplored in comparison with the personal and psychological aspects' (Moore, 2000: 213). In this book, we attend closely to the
home as a physical and defended structure, but we also want to convey
the idea that home is a place and concept around which our dearest
ambitions and deepest fears find focus – the 'shell' that protects our
psychic development and wider sense of assuredness in the world. As
well as the ideal of a shelter providing for each individual's most fundamental psychological, social and physiological needs, home is therefore at the same time a lived reality, which can at times be disappointing,
frightening or oppressive. Such themes are explored in Michael Haneke's
2005 film *Caché* (*Hidden*), which takes us inside the domestic life of an
affluent family in an inner Parisian neighbourhood. It is not only the
past that is concealed from view in this multi-layered drama; the

comfortable residence that forms the centrepiece of the film is itself secluded from view, a place barely perceptible, unremarkable to the passer-by. The kind of everyday domestic bunker seen in *Hidden* shows us evidence of a deeper anxiety around social contact and disturbance more generally – who might be observing us, how might our own pasts come to haunt us and will the walls of our home protect us from these possibilities, even if it cannot ultimately allay those fears?

Hidden explores the private world of the home and the trauma that may lie concealed behind the doors in everyday family life. Freud's 1919 well-known essay on the *unheimlich*, translated as the 'uncanny', raises the related question of how seemingly familiar objects may create feelings of dread, even horror (Freud, 2003 [1919]). These are emotions that we may all relate to: the fear of particular recesses, familiar rooms viewed in twilight or darkness, the feeling of hauntings or other presences. The uncanny or *unheimlich* is also that which *ought* to have remained hidden, causing us to feel alarm or anxiety at its exposure. The trauma may take a real as well as psychological form in homes that conceal spaces in which lives are ruined or even ended. So it is that shocking statistics on domestic violence and revelations such as the Fritzl dungeon in Austria that came to light in 2008 (after his daughter had been imprisoned there for twenty-four years) and the 2009 Jaycee DuGard case in the USA, puncture our shared understandings of domesticity as being essentially a nurturing environment.

The argument of this book

The object of our enquiry is complex, and it is distinct from the idea of the home as a place of basic refuge. Few would argue against or deny the fundamental human needs for privacy and security. What is distinctive about our project is that it seeks to understand what we see as the over-development and layering of security arrangements, strategies and fears that have been generated particularly in the last quarter of the twentieth century. Our contention is that social anxiety, inequality and profound economic changes have connected with housing tenure to produce a defensive and physically bolstered form of home ownership, an archipelago of domestic fortresses in a social environment that celebrates private ownership, retreat and fortification (Minton, 2012). We argue that the market orientations of many governments has shaped the production of particular types of domestic and urban space – home

territories that form larger aggregations of affluent and vocal constituencies. This tessellated form of neoliberalism comprises householders
seeking economic conditions that satisfy their material desires and social
aspirations for privacy and security. Yet of course it also suggests a continued role for governments as stewards of economic systems generating
particular kinds of inequality that are firmly expressed around divisions
generated by housing tenure.

The preceding decades have witnessed the general triumph of neoliberal thinking that envisions markets as the very cornerstone of social
life, and this has also generated deep shifts in how we think about our
houses (Dorling, 2014). The home has been ideologically positioned
as a space of emancipation and as an asset, generating wealth and lever-
age for the advanced consumerism associated with affluent society.
The dividends of home ownership have come to be culturally associated with control, status and identity, but the safety and predictability

1.6 Underground access and defensive frontage, London

associated with western homes is eroded by the very systems that offer the patina of remarkable possibilities of freedom through private property ownership. Just as these dreams have materialised, so have the wider costs of social exclusion and inequality that induce nightmares about envy, destruction and the invasion of the home. Impressions of risk have been distorted by governments, the media and security interests to the extent that the privately owned home is enmeshed with concerns about crime, disorder and numerous sources of less tangible forms of social harm which even extend beyond national borders. Under these prevailing conditions, home ownership has become the site of what we see as a rather more defensive, and sometimes quite aggressive, social disposition.

This book is an attempt to understand the social, economic and political forces that have, in a sense, domesticated fear. That is to say, we can see social anxiety being played out at the levels of the national, urban and domestic scales, yet it is within and through the lens of the home that such fear is ultimately realised and made concrete. Reflecting on the transformation of the home into the domestic fortress can help us understand more clearly a number of wider social, economic and political transformations.

The book is structured as follows. Chapter 2, 'The myths and meanings of home security', sets out the processes and forces that have normalised the contemporary fortress-home. It deals with the social changes in the second half of the twentieth century that undermine collective responses to risk and insecurity and promote a much more individual perspective. We argue that neoliberal government policies have shifted responsibility for protecting households from crime and disorder away from the state onto homeowners, whose homes have come to be seen as commodified financial assets. The consequent retreat into the protective haven of the home is reinforced by the legal emphasis on control as the most important feature of property ownership. The need to defend this combined asset and refuge is further underlined by media accounts of the elaborate security measures employed to protect the homes of celebrities, which feed perceptions of home as a site of vulnerability, prestige and status.

The third chapter, 'A shell for the body and mind', continues the themes of individualism, privatism and withdrawal, but from a different perspective: their effect on the meaning and importance of the psychological aspects of the private home. It has been argued that home ownership provides us with ontological security in today's troubled times as trust in community has been lost. Psychoanalytic and sociological theories of consumption practices are used here to examine the role of home in psychic development, illustrated through fairy stories, fiction and films. The home acts as a bridge or mediator to the public world outside, but may also be a private place of dreadful secrets. Feminist analyses of the development of gender roles in the home and data on domestic violence show the darker side of the sanctified private home, not always a haven.

Chapter 4, 'Invasions of privacy', focuses on the risks that are perceived to threaten the home. Contemporary life presents us with new problems and terrors which may invade the home, such as identity theft, predatory paedophiles, telesales and so on. The chapter discusses the extent to which home ownership can ensure absolute control and protection, against the powers of the state as well as against neighbours and varied forms of privacy invasion. Chapter 5, 'Fear, crime and the home', addresses anxieties about crime and particularly burglary. It connects to how we are taught to fear in our childhood homes and the contemporary forces that amplify the perceived need for home defence. Data on burglary rates and fear of crime are deconstructed, and the inter-connected roles of the media and of government in feeding fear are analysed. We argue that the news media's reportage of rare and horrific events have cumulative and traumatic effects on our perception of the relative safety of the home. The chapter also looks at the treatment of the home, crime and fear in popular culture, through fiction, films and videogames highlighting terrorised occupants and invaded homes.

In Chapter 6, 'Technologies of the defended home', architectural features and defensive technologies are examined. The ebbs and flows of fortification are traced over time, exposing the origins of contemporary alternative home designs of stealth and spikiness. The recent increase in defensive technologies has turned homes into the architectural representation of our fears, from which we can never be truly free. We now fear to stop fearing, and the contemporary homeowner must forever be alert.

The central issue discussed in the seventh chapter, 'Withdraw, defend or destroy', explores the balance of responsibility between the state and the individual homeowner to protect the home and to punish the intruder. The focus of this chapter is the legal position of the homeowner who uses lethal force in defence of the home, foregrounding a lack of confidence in governmental ability to prevent crime and the rising status of victimhood in popular culture and criminal justice systems. The ultimate deterrent and defensive weapon is the personal firearm. We point to links between attitudes to gun ownership in the USA and recent legislation there that appears to prioritise property over human life. In contrast, the political and legal systems of Australia and the UK are lobbied by affluent constituencies and the populist media to eliminate perceived threats to the home, calling homeowners to arms and pressing the state to sanction lethal force.

Chapter 8, 'The fortress archipelago', examines the rising trend in organising homes and neighbourhoods around defensive principles. The rise of gated homes and the domestic fortress are architectural motifs that have become normalised in many suburbs and districts. Taken together, these shifts mean that a more prickly and defensive form of home ownership has arisen, the result of which is a neoliberal endgame, penetrating the innermost civic and domestic spheres of our lives. Scripts of domesticity emanate from the home, articulated in the way that public spaces, neighbourhoods and even national boundaries are controlled.

Our concluding chapter, 'Complexes of the domestic fortress', reflects on the difficulty of imagining a way out from the forces that have generated this more anti-social and defensive mode of home ownership and security landscapes. Here we suggest that a range of political and corporate entrepreneurs draw profits from fear – developers selling gated communities, politicians arguing for tough law enforcement and private security companies with an increasingly sophisticated array of technologies designed to seal the home. While these designs have helped secure the home, the dividend does not include any significant reduction in social fear. Instead, the evolution of the defended home suggests its presence as an increasingly anti-social and counter-civic moment in advanced capitalist society, one that may be highly difficult to unravel, even if the social and political will existed to try and achieve this. The generalised retreat into the private home exposes the individual owner's defensive capabilities, choosing or forced to abandon collective responses to disorder and taking responsibility for a shared, gentler and less fearful form of social life.

2

The myths and meanings
of home security

While we are not suggesting that every contemporary home is fortified in ways that recall medieval architecture, nor that every householder makes extensive use of new protective technologies, one of the aims of this book is to understand the reasons why attitudes to the home have been so significantly transformed over the past half-century or so. In this chapter, we consider the major social and economic forces that have combined to fuel the development of what can best be described as a more defensive form of home ownership. Subsequent chapters will explore the consequences of these changes for how people live in their homes, for how trusting or fearful they are of others, and therefore, what measures they feel are necessary to defend their homes from threats and various risks. Here, we also begin to focus further on the ways in which the home has become the foundational component of a tessellated form of neoliberalism.

The changes in our experiences and expectations of home, outlined in the last chapter, are in many ways the result of market-focused and neoliberal policies adopted by western governments from the last few decades of the twentieth century onwards. However, the encouragement of home ownership is also connected to the aspirations and ideals of many people who have come to see owning a home as being socially as well as economically advantageous (Saunders, 1990; Atkinson and Jacobs, 2016). We can suggest that social changes and deep-seated legal concepts of property ownership are closely aligned with territorial instincts and the desire for economic prosperity, both of which paved the way for the neoliberal economic and political privileging of a societal vision in which individual freedoms were celebrated, none less so than through the achievement of home ownership. Such visions were arguably first put into practice by Ronald Reagan in the USA and Margaret Thatcher in the UK, based on the understanding that the individual, the market (to which the state should be subservient) and property ownership were the three fundamental elements of a 'natural social order' to which governments should respond as enablers of aspiration and personal affluence (Harvey, 2005; Brenner and Theodore, 2002). Neoliberal arguments that the market should be inserted into every interstice of civic society and its operations also underpinned the idea of home ownership as a 'natural' tenure to be chosen by every responsible and rational individual, as President George W. Bush emphasised in 2003:

> Home ownership is more than just a symbol of the American Dream; it is an important part of our way of life. Core American values of individuality, thrift, responsibility, and self-reliance are embodied in home ownership. I am committed to helping more families know the security and sense of pride that comes with owning a home. (Cited in Basolo, 2007: 100)

Yet the deeper impact of these ideological projects and assertions about what was right or natural also had the effect of encouraging homeowners to retreat ever more into the private sanctuary of their homes as it came to be viewed as a primary social space, surrounded by an increasingly denuded and defunded public realm from which governments had withdrawn and which felt increasingly risky. Policies on taxation and public spending also led to unprecedented increases in property prices and a consequent shift in the perception of home, making it as much about investment as a place of shelter and social nurture. This repositioning of the home as the basic building block of tessellated neoliberalism also had dramatic future consequences as the housing market became a major element of the national economy and the reason for the 2008 global financial crisis. This latter crisis has, of course, come to destabilise or even remove the home from many owners while also generating perceptions of systemic risk and precariousness. If anything, these developments further emphasise the role of the home as a space of shelter and retreat from an uncertain world outside.

Legal underpinnings

Politicians have long understood and characterised property ownership as the foundation of a democratic, choice-based political economy and as the guarantee of a settled, law-abiding and responsible citizenry. Indeed, property ownership was once the qualification for enfranchisement; for nearly one hundred years after England's Great Reform Act of 1832, mere tenants could not vote. Property ownership is also seen as a fundamental civil right, necessary for individual freedom, enshrined in Article 17 of the Universal Declaration of Human Rights 1948 which states: 'Everyone has the right to own property.' These legal links between property ownership and political power date back to feudal times and although long vanished, they have 'left symbolic traces in the notion of "property as propriety"' (Davies, 2007: 59). The core of these ideas is that distinctions have been drawn around who is included and excluded from mainstream political and economic life, and that these notions have long been deeply connected to housing tenure.

As well as indicating propriety or respectability, the concept of property is linguistically linked to 'appropriation' of land and making 'proper' use of its resources. This is particularly clear in the work of the seventeenth-century English philosopher John Locke, who argued that property is a natural right and that land is appropriated through labour: therefore, the person who works the land should be entitled to claim ownership of it (Locke, 1978 [1689]). Locke's views on property were extremely influential in North America, leading to long-standing and disastrous implications for the nomadic indigenous peoples of the USA and subsequently in Australia, whose relationship with the land was enshrined in an almost fully inverted understanding of the community belonging to the land. The model of ownership as individual rather than collective became firmly entrenched in English colonies, with this core concept transplanted to produce the 'moral tales of yeoman farmers and wild west pioneers [that] lie at the heart of the American and Australian dreams of home ownership' (Gurney, 1999b: 178; Kemeny, 1983). The image of the responsible twenty-first-century homeowner echoes the self-sufficiency ethos of the sturdily independent seventeenth-century English farmer, adding weight and historical power to home ownership in political ideology and legal constructs of rights.

When contemporary homeowners in the USA, England and Australia are asked to describe their feelings about home, they almost invariably respond using these terms: 'control', 'permanence', 'security', 'refuge', 'status', 'self-fulfilment' and 'family life' (Rakoff, 1977; Richards, 1990; Saunders, 1990). Saunders suggested that the need for ontological security, an unconscious and emotive sense of confidence and trust in the world as it appears to be, could best be satisfied by the private realm of the owner-occupied home. He identified three aspects of satisfaction, namely, home as haven (a place of safety and security); home as a source of personal autonomy providing the roots of individual identity; and home as a source of status and pride. Control has now become associated and perhaps conflated with ownership as the tenure thought best to ensure household permanence and security. This theme has also been emphasised by politicians, such as the pronouncement by Herbert Hoover (US President 1929–33) that ownership was preferable to renting, as tenants must cede to landlords 'the control of the place that is the center of your whole personal and family life' (cited in Rohe and Watson, 2007: 26). The idea of home ownership as self-fulfilment, enhancing personal identity, can be traced back to philosopher Georg Hegel's view that property ownership is constitutive of self-identity (Hegel, 1821). Its vestiges can also be detected in many legal judgments that depart from their traditionally dry and unemotive language, for example defining the home as providing 'personal security and well-being' (*Gillow v UK*, 1986: 46) and as 'the place where [an individual] lives and to which he returns and which forms the centre of his existence' (*Utratemp Ventures Ltd v Collins*, 2001: 31).

Home ownership represents the respectable and legally sanctioned form of that apparently innate 'hidden nerve of irrational animism that binds the individual to the object he appropriates as his own' (Beaglehole, 1931). This expression of the territorial sense through which we see our homes, asserting control over them through exclusionary techniques, is foundational to much property law and has been influential in reinforcing social values with relation to the home itself. In the much-quoted words of the eighteenth-century English jurist William Blackstone:

> There is nothing which so generally strikes the imagination and engages the affections of mankind, as the right of property; or that sole and despotic dominion which one man claims and exercises over the external things of the world, in total exclusion of the right of any other individual in the universe. (Blackstone, 1768: 2)

Although Blackstone went on to make clear that he did not see this dominion as a natural state of affairs (Schorr, 2009), most legal philosophers up to the present conclude that control, implying the right to exclude all others, is the essence of property ownership (for example,

Munzer, 1990). However, property ownership is so privileged in law that when people must 'deal with territorial invasions, their defence is typically based on laws that defend territorial rights, rather than brute force' (Altman, 1975: 306–307). This 'defensive' use of the law is typical, though we later examine a series of legal cases involving homes protected through brute force. We should also note that the law can be used effectively as an offensive weapon by those with determination and the wealth to ensure access to the best lawyers in the defence of their home territories.

The territorial rights of the homeowner are protected in England, the USA and Australia by the common law doctrine of trespass which applies to any direct physical interference with property, even where there is no criminal intent and no actual damage is caused. There is a very different attitude to land ownership in northern Europe, where citizens may freely access privately owned fields and forests provided no harm is done. By contrast, the common law of trespass was summarised over two hundred years ago in the words of the contemporary English Lord Chief Justice: 'Any invasion of land, be it ever so minute, is a trespass. No man can set his foot upon my ground without my licence' (*Entick v Carrington*, 1795: 1066). Owners may therefore legally use reasonable force in removing anyone who entered their property without express permission, or who refused to leave when asked to do so (*Porter v Commissioner of Police for the Metropolis*, 1999).

The longstanding common law rules that enshrine the right to exclude all others from home and land in fact apply to all occupiers, whether owners or tenants. However, over the course of the last century, it has become taken for granted that ownership is essential or indeed the precondition by which we may define the home as an arena of privacy, 'a sanctuary needed for personhood' (Radin, 1993: 59). The privately owned home is therefore now equated with 'sovereign control over territorial space' at a domestic, personal scale, with obvious linguistic and conceptual links to sovereignty at the national scale (Gray and Gray, 2009: 105) that we discuss further in Chapter 8. These rights to control and to exclude, enshrined in law, enable the homeowner to withdraw into the privacy of an apparently invulnerable home. Privacy and security have become seen as increasingly important and desirable attributes, as social changes and neoliberal policies have affected the balance between individual and community over the course of the twentieth century.

2.1 No trespassing

Social changes and neoliberal policies

The first half of the twentieth century was experienced by many in the USA, Australia and the UK as an era when house doors were left open and neighbours were befriended and trusted (Putnam, 2000). Nowadays, the majority of urban residents know few other people in their neighbourhoods and live behind closed, sometimes steel-braced and fisheyed, doors. One reason for this change is the revolution in the conditions and expectations of employment; another is the role of women in western society, evolving since the 1950s. The nature and fabric of more traditional forms of community and social association have disappeared. More recently, communication technologies and globalisation have increased geographical mobility and generated new kinds of social networks that similarly affect the nature of local social relations and trust.

The impact of the social and economic changes that took place following the Second World War has been extensively explored in fiction. Quintessential novels of that time, such as *The Man in the Gray Flannel Suit* (Wilson, 2005 [1955]) and *Revolutionary Road* (Yates, 2001 [1961]) revealed new suburbs as places of ongoing anxiety around status and consumption, highlighting the insecurity of family lives subjected to the new regime of corporate office work. The phrase 'Keeping up with the Joneses' encapsulates the contemporaneous phenomenon of competitive home ownership and the acquisition of new consumer goods. The home, more than ever before, was used as a place to display status and prestige; one's home and possessions measured against those of the neighbours. Thus the neighbourhood, once the home's important social and community setting, became more emphatically the physical setting that enhanced or detracted from property values (Wellman, 1999) as well as being a site of psychological tensions rather than social cohesion. These social changes occurred in tandem with government strategies embracing the market and retreating from welfare provision, emphasising individual choice and personal responsibility and reinforcing the separation of private life from the public sphere. Such policies also had significant effects in decreasing both levels of trust in others and acceptance of social responsibility for those outside the home circle of family and close friends. Thus many people have been pushed back onto their own resources, which could mean literal self-reliance (closely allied with prevailing national value systems in the case of the USA and Australia) or at least reliance on family rather than on community.

At the start of the twentieth century Australia and the USA had comparable rates of home ownership: in the USA, 46 per cent in 1910 (US Census Bureau, 2011), while Allon (2008) cites the rate of 49 per cent home ownership from the 1911 Australian Census. The supposedly natural instinct to own one's own home was then incentivised through various government schemes in both countries. By 1961 home ownership rates had reached 70 per cent in Australia, and 61 per cent in the USA where the 'surge in home ownership was remarkable', following the Second World War (US Census Bureau, 2011). These rates mask considerable variation between different states and population sectors, with current home ownership rates amongst Americans of African origin and Aboriginal Australians far below the average.

Meanwhile home ownership rates in England and Wales languished at 23 per cent in 1918 (Office for National Statistics, 2013a) and lagged behind those of the USA and Australia for most of the twentieth century. The position here had resulted from the dominance of private landlordism in the growth of industrial cities in the nineteenth century (Stewart, 1981), and reflected the tenure pattern in continental Europe where renting is still popular today. While home ownership in both Australia and the USA had always been emotively allied to the collective dreams of those nations from the early twentieth century, in England the aspiration to own a home was encouraged by government policies and rhetoric, rising affluence in the post-war period and the desire to escape appalling housing conditions in the private rented sector.

The Conservative Government in the UK marked a step change with their early 1970s housing policy document that asserted 'Home owner-ship is the most rewarding form of house tenure. It satisfies a deep and natural desire on the part of the householder to have independent control of the house that shelters him and his family' (Department of the Environment, 1971: 4). The masterstroke of Margaret Thatcher's government in 1980 was to introduce a Right to Buy for tenants of social landlords, enabling them to buy the houses they were renting at discounts that increased with length of residence. This measure boosted home ownership while demoting the status of the social rented sector, arguably achieving two aims dear to the heart of this nascent neoliberal government. During the Second Reading of the Housing Bill in the House of Commons, Michael Heseltine (then Secretary of State for the Environment) used terms familiar from Australian and US political documents:

> There is in this country a deeply ingrained desire for home ownership. The Government believe that this spirit should be fostered. It reflects the wishes of the people, ensures the spread of wealth through society, encour-ages a personal desire to improve and modernize one's own home, enables parents to accrue wealth for their children and stimulates the attitudes of independence and self-reliance that are the bedrock of a free society.
> (Hansard, 1980)

Since 1980, both Conservative and Labour British governments have stressed the benefits of home ownership, the tenure now providing accommodation for two-thirds of English households, and have put forward the idea that renting from a social landlord is a tenure only for those unfortunates with social needs unable to provide for themselves. These discourses have had profound effects on the way English people see their own homes and on their aspirations about future homes.

For centuries, until the Industrial Revolution, the family home was also the workplace and the household was the basic economic unit. With the advent of tessellated neoliberalism, the earlier link between home and the household economy has been restated, albeit with a new twist: that homes, like other forms of property, should be treated as assets for trading on the market. 'Investing in property' used to mean owning houses and renting them out for others to live in as their homes, but the owner-occupied home has now become an investment, a fundamental unit in the architecture of the international financial market and the basic building block of the economic order. As a result, '"house and home" are often conflated in the popular media, typically as a means of selling real estate and promoting "home" ownership' (Mallett, 2004: 66).

These views have been fuelled by steadily rising house prices up to 1990, further boosted by nearly two decades when interest rates fell and appreciation in value accelerated. In the USA, house prices adjusted for inflation have nearly quadrupled over the 60-year period since the first housing census in 1940 (US Census Bureau, 2012). In the UK, the average house price rose from £23,500 in 1980 to £190,000 in 2015 (HousePriceCrash, 2015). At the peak growth period in Australia, 1996–2003, 'the average price for a detached house more than doubled in nominal terms and rose by around 80 per cent in real terms' (Allon, 2008: 51). Although house values were hit by the 2008 financial crash, in all three countries prices have since started to make a good recovery.

During property booms, not only homeowners and property investors benefit, but also the financial industries, housebuilders, interior designers, DIY stores and providers of furniture and furnishings. The dream that fuelled this bonanza started decades ago in ambitions to renovate houses with flair, enjoyment and a minimum of expenditure, possibly selling it for a profit. This dream was reflected and fostered in numerous popular TV shows and in the many magazines devoted to home renovation, which extolled the fun of expressing one's idiosyncratic taste through decoration – whether or not one intended to sell the home afterwards. However, by the early 2000s, more hard-edged 'property as investment' shows began to dominate the airways as house prices took off. The point of decorating and displaying our homes changed from expressing some sense of our authentic selves, to impressing would-be buyers. As the term 'property porn' (defined in the 2005 edition of the *Collins English Dictionary* as 'a genre of escapist TV programmes, magazine features, showing desirable properties for sale, especially those in idyllic locations, or in need of renovation, or both') entered popular discourse, the number of magazines and TV shows devoted to property as entertainment grew, and the property market expanded. A more recent swathe of property programmes based on the home as investment has achieved a standardised international taste in home décor. This has arguably led to a significant loss of authenticity in the private realm best placed to offer us self-expression and release from public scrutiny: the home. An internal monitor now tells us what colours, patterns, layouts and impressions are most acceptable, as more 'individual' displays of taste and discrimination open up the prospect of less than maximal returns on a sale. At the same time, an apparently insatiable desire to see the interior of celebrity homes is fed by programmes such as *Through the Keyhole*, taken off air in 2008 after twenty-one years, and reinstated in 2015 as property prices recovered.

While the home's importance as the single largest investment in most people's lives has increased, its role of providing a place of social development and utility seems to have diminished. We now apparently think more about what our house is worth than what that home is for: to live in, to rear children, to enjoy ourselves, to socialise with friends and neighbours, to ensure self-expression and the full realisation of our identities. The obsession with property and accumulation has turned many homes into bland and characterless public and private display pieces, seen as necessary to maximise their potential as wealth-generating tools. The neoliberal equation of home as a tradeable asset has other unforeseen consequences, which we now explore.

Although the promise was held out that profits from home ownership would lead to greater equality across populations in property-owning democracies, this has not been borne out at the local level, where neoliberal policies have increased social and economic inequality. The effect is that we now live in an era of social exclusion rather than inclusion, when almost anyone outside the immediate household can be defined as a dangerous 'other' to be feared and excluded (Young, 1999). Over the last third of the twentieth century, the decline of social capital, defined as formal and informal networks of sociability (Putnam, 2000), coincided with a growth in inequality and a rise in private capital and its accumulation, which was privileged by neoliberal governments. Data from the European and World Values Survey and from the US federal government's General Social Survey indicates that 'levels of trust between members of the public are lower in countries and [in US] states where income differences are larger' (Wilkinson and Pickett, 2009: 52–53).

Data from the Organization for Economic Cooperation and Development show that the Gini coefficients (a measure from 0–1 of income distribution in a country's population, with 0 representing complete equality and 1 representing absolute inequality) for the USA (0.4), the UK (0.35) and Australia (0.33) are all above the OECD average (OECD, annual). Research has demonstrated that inequality affects levels of trust, rather than the other way around (Uslaner, 2002). In other words, the inequality that results from neoliberal social and economic policies produces mistrust and fear. The material success enjoyed by some home-owners in the USA, the UK and Australia has therefore played a large part in creating the perceived need to defend those homes. There is also a growing trend to withdraw into the home from the public realm as conspicuous shows of wealth have become seen as too risky. We have reached a point where, for 'the ordinary individual citizen exclusionary strategies have become, for the first time, a viable general response to the challenge of social interaction' that appears to threaten 'the hard won fruits of individual endeavour' (Gray and Gray, 1999: 17).

Risk and the home

Over the second half of the twentieth century, a greater awareness of risks of all kinds has developed, affecting states and citizens alike (Beck, 1992; Giddens, 1991). This transformation of unpredictable threats into calculable risks was possibly a consequence of modernity in general, rather than of specific politics, yet dovetails with the primary aims of neoliberal government. In particular, the ideal of shrinking the state has proved an important factor in the development of more defensive forms of home ownership and social politics. From the 1960s onwards, the withdrawal of the state and failure by governments to address minor crimes and disorder led to increased public anxiety about these issues, which we discuss further in Chapter 5. Neoliberal ideological framings of the role of the state have moved it away from its role in relation to welfarism to an emphasis on 'personal responsibility, rather than collective risk spreading … with a harshly enforced, highly moralistic criminal law promising almost total protection against crime, while emphasising how dangerous the world is despite these much-needed measures' (Simon, 2007: 23). Techniques of responsibilisation include the provision of information about risk, advice in combating risks, and alignment of a range of government policies to support individual efforts. Risk thus became re-cast as an individual problem: 'protection against risk of crime through an investment in measures of security becomes part of the responsibilities of each active individual' rather than of society or government (Rose, 2000: 327). At the same time, as society became less predictable and its members appeared less trustworthy due to the social changes discussed above, the privately owned home became an increasingly important arena in which control could be exercised.

The emphasis on risk has engendered a culture of fear, even as crime rates began to fall from the mid-1990s in the USA, UK, Australia and other western nations, and continue to decrease year on year. It is obviously important to governments that disorder, crime and the fear of crime are reduced. Yet some respected commentators have argued, perhaps cynically, that national policy makers and local police benefit from the fear of crime. Jonathan Simon concludes that states now 'govern through crime', garnering support for expensive regimes of punishment by emphasising the need to control and exclude criminals, rather than taking on the more difficult task of addressing underlying social concerns (Simon, 2007). Fear of crime can also be seen as a tactic of governance, to encourage responsible homeowners to minimise the likelihood of their becoming victims of crime, thus reducing the burden on the state (Lee, 2007). It is also in governments' interests to manipulate or underline popular understandings about what and who should be feared and therefore blamed: 'flawed values and dysfunctional families, not economic disadvantage or racism' (Macek, 2006: 56). Responsibilised homeowners, rather than an active and patrolling state, are thus encouraged to defend themselves against these dysfunctional and threatening 'others'.

Most police forces in the USA, Australia and the UK issue detailed do-it-yourself home security guidance notes. These often imply that no one can be trusted and that one's home should be made into a fortress. The emphasis on the need for withdrawal into the secure home well away from the hostile world outside has, for some, merely served to heighten the 'sense of being on your own [and the] consciousness of isolation' (Furedi, 2005: 72–73). Governments also increasingly make technological informatics used in the fight against crime available to the public, arguably further fuelling rather than diminishing the existing public obsession with crime and fear. For example, citizens in the USA and the UK can now obtain crime data linked to local police districts at the click of a mouse. The Deputy Chief Executive of the UK

2.2 Home security: Police advice

National Policing Improvement Agency explained that 'Fear of crime is known to outstrip the reality. The crime map will give people the facts about local crime and what forces are doing about it' (Home Office, 2009b); it is the most-used of all available government websites. However, access to this information may actually confirm fears, providing little comfort to those living in high crime areas and potentially supplying valuable information to criminals.

Burglary (home invasion) is the crime that makes households, whether renters or owners, feel most unsafe. In fact, it makes people more fearful than any other common type of crime such as car theft, vandalism and assault (Ditton *et al.*, 1999a). This is testament to the central role of home in our lives, causing a general anxiety that 'something could happen' even in lower crime areas where the risk is lower (Farrall *et al.*, 2009). This generalised anxiety has been described as 'derivative fear', a feeling of insecurity and vulnerability, fear that guides behaviour even when there is no immediate threat (Bauman, 2006). Kenneth Ferraro describes it 'as an emotional response of dread or anxiety to crime or symbols that a person associates with crime' (Ferraro, 1995: 24). The understandable fear of home invasion is also socially and culturally recycled through television reportage and a perpetual flow of crime and police dramas in the cinema and on television. The print media prefigured this obsession for many years, for centuries, in fact, but when television emerged as a mass phenomenon, it conveyed the same information with far greater visual force (Garland, 2001: 156–158).

Generalised anxiety about crime, specifically about burglary, has ironically been further fuelled by the security industry's marketing of defensive technologies, which raises awareness about risks to the home. The insurance industry has done well from these fears; in turn, it ensures sales for purveyors of security by making the installation of security features a condition of providing home insurance. The house-building companies that construct and renovate homes and their sales agents hold out the promise to homeowners of release from their anxieties, marketing even very ordinary homes as realised dreams of privacy and security. The development of spatial techniques designed to prevent crime have been greatly influenced by Oscar Newman's concept of 'defensible space', based on behavioural principles of territoriality (Newman, 1972). Newman's particular concern to separate public space from clearly bounded, controllable private space underpins techniques of environmental criminology and its policy offshoot, situational crime prevention, which has been adopted by governments in the UK and the USA (Kitchen and Schneider, 2001; ACPO Crime Prevention Initiative, 2004). Vulnerable targets are identified by assessing the residential environment through the eyes of the criminal, and are then made secure by 'target hardening', such as fitting extra locks and fences. The alternative approach, crime prevention through environmental design was originally developed in Australia and is closely linked to psychological understandings of how residents (rather than criminals) experience their surroundings. Both methods emphasise the importance of territorial control and ownership.

Awareness of risk and taking steps to minimise it by no means ensures freedom from anxiety: 'For some, the crime problem has become a source of anxiety and frustration; an urgent daily reminder of the need to impose control, to take care, to secure oneself and one's family against the changes of the modern world' (Garland, 2001: 155–156). These everyday but significant fears can be exacerbated by the complex spiral in which celebrities and the media are currently entangled. The homes of the wealthy often appear to be displayed for ordinary homeowners to emulate. For celebrities, defensive home ownership is not just about protection from crime, burglary and stalkers, but may also be central to managing their exposure to the public and media. Wealthy people often choose to live as far from others as possible, but we can also track a more aggressive stance by affluent residents. Their responses to risks to the home influence the idealisation of more fortified or concealed home design, which will be explored further in Chapter 6. Media exposure of celebrity lifestyles offers details of top-of-the-range security measures and hi-tech installations to which ordinary homeowners might only aspire. A prime example is the penthouse at One Hyde Park, Knightsbridge, London, for which a Ukrainian millionaire reputedly paid £136m in 2011, making it then the most expensive home in the world. The building's security system was designed by former British SAS specialists and includes bulletproof glass windows and internal panic rooms; the windows are of bulletproof glass, and the property is guarded around the clock. Entry can be achieved only after electronic recognition of a vehicle's licence plate in the garage and of human eyes by iris scanners fitted in the lifts. This street has been associated with ostentatious displays of wealth since the days of George III when it became popular for aristocrats to build their town houses and mansions opposite Hyde Park (Walker, 2011).

Of course, only owners (not tenants) have the right to modify the physical fabric of the home by installing security devices, displacing their anxieties through exercising a 'residual form of mastery in a very insecure world' (Lupton and Tulloch, 1999: 517). Owners can transform their homes into fortresses. It may be necessary to obtain planning consent, but government planning policies are favourable to the installation of home security features. In contrast, tenants must seek permission from landlords before installing security devices, or they must make do with any existing defensive features. This important tenurial distinction is highlighted by the account of the experiences of a wealthy tenant, Rebecca Wang. Thieves gained entry to her exclusive London apartment and stole property worth more than £500,000 while Ms Wang's servant was in the basement; Ms Wang was so traumatised, she had to move into the Dorchester Hotel, one of London's most luxurious and expensive hotels. She then sued her landlord for failure to protect her and her property from burglars, on the grounds that the burglar alarm was faulty because the landlord's agent had not maintained or repaired it and an insufficiently large built-in safe had been provided for her (Savage, 2008).

The credit crunch and financial crash: 'as safe as houses'?

The sense of guaranteed security conveyed by the nineteenth-century expression 'as safe as houses' (Hotten, 1859) underpins many assumptions behind the growth in home ownership: that investing in your home is always a wise move and coincides with notions of security and privacy. After the UK railway investment collapse of 1845–47, shrewd investors and speculators put their money back into property where it would be literally 'as safe as houses'. This phrase now has a hollow ring against the background of the recession in 2008 with its foreclosures, repossessions and homeowners who simply walked away from their homes because they could no longer pay their mortgages. The importance of homeowner financing on a global scale was dramatically revealed by the domino effect, initiated by a relatively small problem with the US sub-prime mortgage market but which then culminated in governments around the world intervening to rescue stock exchanges and the banking industry. Rising house prices had led to further investment in property, facilitated by artificially low interest rates that made it very easy to get credit. In the years leading up to the financial crash, people took on more debt to achieve their ambition of becoming homeowners, believing that price growth would continue unchecked, even as it became clear that new owners were being locked out of the market due to these rising costs. The response of the financial lending institutions was, disastrously, to offer more money to more people to keep the wealth machine rolling.

Alan Greenspan, then Chairman of the US Federal Reserve Board, argued that widening home ownership was worth such risks and that home-equity loans were beneficial to the economy as a whole (Greenspan, 2003). Deferred interest loans (mortgages with negative amortization, or 'neg-am' mortgages) in the USA and Buy to Let loans in the UK 'were based on the assumption that houses were primarily investments' (*The Economist*, 2009: 78). In the 1980s, Australian Labor governments pursued policies in which people were not only offered significantly low interest rates to buy their own homes, but were also guided to invest in additional properties that could then be let out, benefiting from enormously advantageous tax exemptions on the purchase cost (Brett, 2003). The result is that around 17 per cent of Australian households currently own one or more houses in addition to their primary home, far exceeding the rate in the USA or UK (Allon, 2008: 5).

We have become so used to homes increasing in value that many homeowners still find it hard to believe that their homes could ever be at risk, failing to understand the underlying paradox that when borrowing money to buy a dream home, one also gives the lender the power to take it away. Certainly, the promise held out by governments over many decades built on earlier notions that 'if the householder buys his [*sic*] house on a mortgage, he builds up by steady saving a capital asset for him and his dependents' (Department of the Environment, 1971: 4). Governments began to see owner-occupied housing assets as a means to build up individual welfare security and to offset pension shortfalls in retirement, thus reducing the burden on the state and by extension, upon tax-averse affluent households. In societies like the USA, UK and Australia, owning a home became not only a primary vehicle for personal wealth accumulation, but also an important element in assuring welfare in retirement and providing a financial cushion against unforeseen events. Relying on ever increasing property prices, a high proportion of homeowners began to use the equity in their home 'as an ATM', more often to meet uninsurable needs than to fund conspicuous consumption (Kluyev and Mills, 2010). Over one-third of UK homeowners and more than two-fifths of Australian homeowners used their homes as collateral in at least one of the years between 2001 and 2005, increasing their net mortgage borrowing by an average of

£5,000 to £7,500 in the UK and $20,000 to $26,000 in Australia (Parkinson *et al.*, 2009: 370–371). In the USA, the picture was the same, with total mortgage equity withdrawals reaching $9 trillion between 1997 and 2006, amounting in that last year to more than 90 per cent of disposable income (*The Economist*, 2009: 76–78). Household mortgage debt as a percentage of disposable income was highest in Australia (at 130 per cent), Britain (120 per cent) and the USA (101 per cent). This compares with 76 per cent for Canada and 64 per cent for Japan (*The Economist*, 2009: 78). These differences illustrate clearly the effect of government policies.

When the sub-prime mortgage market collapsed in 2007, the desperation with which governments pursued policies aimed at freeing credit arrangements for home purchase became even more marked. The US government injected huge amounts of money into the two government-backed mortgage corporations, Fannie Mae and Freddie Mac. This intervention, together with legislation designed to protect homeowners and advice directed at helping defaulters to remain in their homes, the Homeowner Affordability and Stability Plan, cushioned homeowners against the worst effects of the recession. However, in 2008, 2.3 million families in the USA lost their homes or faced foreclosure; there were 2.8 million in 2009, double the average before the crisis (RealtyTrac, 2009; 2010). Cleveland, Ohio, was described as 'the sub-prime capital of the United States'; one-tenth of homes in the city were 'vacant, and whole neighbourhoods have been blighted by foreclosed, vandalized and boarded-up homes' (Schifferes, 2007). In the USA the annual number of foreclosures reduced to 1.1 million in 2014 (Realtytrac, 2015). The UK government was quick to establish measures to minimise the number of homes lost in the recession (Department for Communities and Local Government, 2009). These seem to have been successful in avoiding a repeat of the previous recession when mortgage repossessions (foreclosures) peaked at 75,500 in 1991; in 2008, there were 40,000 homes repossessed through court action, and 21,000 in 2014 (UK Government, 2016). These figures are based on court records and do not take into account the many homeowners who give up their keys to the lender and walk away from their property. The swift state action to shore up home ownership under threat is a powerful indication of its fundamental importance in the current macro-economy (Dorling, 2014). Perhaps it is not so foolhardy to imagine that one's home is 'as safe as houses' when governments so readily step in to avert repossessions while more generally creating a favourable economic environment, notably the maintenance of low interest rates.

The deep impact of the loss of the home through repossession or foreclosure has proved overwhelming for many. Aside from new forms of homelessness and household break-up there have been tragic cases of suicide resulting from these financial and personal pressures. In the post-crash recession, there were also many instances of suicides who killed other family members (for example, Adams, 2009; Telegraph, 2009). A UK businessman shot his wife and daughter before killing himself and burning their luxury Shropshire mansion. Ironically, it was only by later examining the footage from the surveillance technology installed to protect the home and family that this tragic course of events could be established (Barranger, 2008). This human cost of broken middle-class dreams is memorably captured in the film *99 Homes* (Bahrani, 2015). For most ordinary people, it proves impossible to follow the mantra of the property developer in the film: 'Don't get emotional about real estate' when it is your home that you are about to lose.

Conclusion

The home has come to be seen as a floating and realisable asset that must be traded on the market in order for the owner to ascend a property ladder of increasing wealth and scale, and in this chapter we have discussed some of the forces which have driven these ideas. Protection and defence of that home are fully realisable only when that home is owned rather than rented. Thus security measures (including home insurance, voting for political parties espousing the values of ownership, investing in value-inflating rather than personal aesthetics, and adaptations and the installation of security features) are seen as necessary to protect the owner's investment and insure an upward lifetime trajectory. The heightened awareness of risk that characterises the current era and the withdrawal of the state from its traditional everyday policing role serve to reinforce the individual homeowner's perceived need for defence and withdrawal. These shifts have been further emphasised by the focus on issues of crime and disorder by politicians and the media (a point we will discuss further, particularly in Chapters 5 and 7). The home is therefore increasingly valued as a refuge, and the less secure we feel, the more likely we are to buy into the ideology of home ownership that promises territorial control and appreciating wealth.

3

A shell for the body and mind

Almost all of our life was lived toward the back of the house … where no one else ever came. We left the front of the house turned toward the highway and the village, and went our own ways behind its stern, unwelcoming face. … When we sat on the back lawn no one could see us from anywhere. (Jackson, 1962: 21)

The home is a varying structure that envelopes a variety of social configurations as well as offering protection for us as individuals. The home can be seen as a nest that keeps us safe from threats and the elements, but that also enables us to thrive as individuals with inner, subjective lives. This chapter continues our exploration of individualism and social withdrawal by extending the meaning of home to include the way it may provide a shield for both our mental and physical selves. We seek to make two points in this chapter. First, that it is important to consider the home in relation to us as developing and thinking individuals who possess personal biographies, entwined with the physicality of the structures we inhabit. In this sense we need the sense of safety and nurture that a predictable and secure home offers, yet may be unable to find places of refuge because of our own inner turmoil, within our families and households, or because the home itself is threatened (perhaps by family breakdown, repossession, homelessness and so on). The second main point is that the home is a place of sanctuary to which we attach ourselves and which contrasts strongly with a world outside often deemed to be out of control, dangerous and threatening. Such themes resonate in the idea that the home is a safe haven or territory, both as a space and a core element of our self-identity. Yet this possibility may also be unsettled by the realisation that anxiety and trauma can be generated from within the home itself (through domestic abuse, family violence, and so on) and such experiences are not at all rare. So this chapter considers the complex relationships between the hard, physical shell of our dwellings, the softness of its residing human tissue and the even more damage-prone nature of the psyches within us as accommodated individuals.

Our shell

Many commentators have argued that owning a home enables a greater sense of predictability, continuity and thus safety in the world around us. This connection is built on the work of writers like Giddens (1991) who use the concept of ontological security to encapsulate the kinds of meaning-making and need for social stability required to flourish in our personal lives. Giddens describes such security as a deep faith in the independent existence of persons and objects around us and the continued existence of these arrangements and supports in our lives. For Giddens, lurking behind mundane social interactions and encounters, there is always the possibility of chaos; we respond with attempts at building routines and stability in the world around us. Such ideas form the basis of arguments from housing theorists like Saunders (1990) who connect social projects for personal security with the social and legal foundations of home ownership – seen as a preferable tenure because of the ability of owners to adapt and control this environment. Here again we find the idea of tessellated neoliberalism in evidence, as the very core values and spaces of the home appear aligned with the wider ideological wrappings of home and ownership, as well as the grounded reality of such arrangements – the home can be seen as the key site of social reproduction, wherein values and ideas about how the world operates are inculcated within the family or household unit.

Many observers see a deep need for safety that may be expressed through owning our own home in order to achieve some form of autonomy and control in our lives that is, if not absent, diminished where we are placed in the subservient position of renting from another person or institution (despite the fact that repaying a mortgage for twenty-five or more years to a bank places homeowners in a not dissimilar position). In a similar way the privacy associated with the private home allows us to escape the pressures and controls we sometimes find in our social relationships or the surveillance and strict time-keeping of

3.1 A blank face towards an uncertain world outside; inner suburban home, UK

the workplace. These influences can be identified in social mythologies that have evolved in particular national contexts where home ownership has become particularly developed. For example, Dupuis and Thorns (1998) highlight the manner in which the 1930s depression powerfully influenced the extent home ownership was considered as a bulwark against economic insecurity in countries like Australia and New Zealand. They argue that past memory haunts the social values of today and remains an identifiable pursuit through which greater personal welfare and thereby security can be achieved through ownership, in lieu of assurances from the nation state.

At a time when our trust in community and feelings of mutual support have become more fractured (Uslaner, 2012), the need for security has become increasingly emphasised in public discourse. It is not difficult to identify the kinds of chaos within everyday life that Giddens suggests lurks behind our everyday world and which stands in stark contrast to the relative sanctuary, control and order that we want our homes to provide. Nevertheless, the home occupies an ambivalent position in contemporary culture. For example, some analyses of our contemporary social condition, such as Bauman's (2006), see fear increasingly permeating our lives and link this to the ephemeral nature of consumer society and the decline of religiosity and transcendent belief systems. Feelings of competitive and precarious social being (Standing, 2011), characteristic of many Western societies, foster the sense that we are the emancipated authors of our own lives, but the cost of this is the realisation that success or failure has come to be our own responsibility. A declining sense of social support from the state and community form important background concerns within discussions about the role of the home and of home ownership, shaping the kinds of strategies many employ to manage these anxieties.

Building on these themes we can suggest that the physical home offers a kind of psychic armour, a carapace that protects both our bodies and our subjective position within the broader world around us. These are of course important themes within psychoanalysis and appear in the more psychological readings of the domestic realm that view the home as the primary location in which we develop in relation to the primary relationships of parents and children; it is in this context that various forms of anxiety and trauma may occur (Phillips, 1998). When our position in the world is challenged or subjected to sudden shifts, the assurances we require to measure and regulate our own lives are transformed and potentially threatened. Even within the same society, personal life-courses are subject to extreme variation. Within our homes, our psychic lives (in the analytic sense of the inner life of the mind and our subjective outlook) develop, but we are also subject to subtle forms of damage and loss. The setting of the family is fraught with difficulties and challenges that place the home in a Janus role for many, split between a public position of goodness, civility and domesticity and a range of private experiences that may include anxiety and other forms of psychological damage (Lasch, 1995). For psychoanalysts, the process of personal development and socialisation is fraught with difficulties, tensions and loss in its various forms.

The deeper meaning of home has also long interested philosophers of mind and place. As Yi-Fu Tuan (1975) suggests, it is from the hearth of the home that we view and understand the broader cosmos around us. The home provides us with deep feelings of protection; it is our sheltered vantage for the social and wider universe. This primitive association of home and its role in offering a space of companionship, a refuge from elemental forces and a protective device placed around our subjective 'selves', is critical for analysing the psychological underpinnings of the social project of ownership, security and predictability. It is to home that we return daily, and it is this space that above all others we imbue with an emotionally rich vocabulary of attachment, protection, nurture, primary social relationships and a sense of the broad direction and goals for life. As Tuan remarks, 'We go to all kinds of places but return home, or to homelike places. Home is where life begins and ends' (Tuan, 1975: 155). In his 1958 book *Poetics of Space,* the French philosopher Guy Bachelard observed the particular pleasure we feel at discovering a bird's nest, noting that there is something comforting in an object which appears to respond to our own wishes to find somewhere secure and safe. The point here is also that we project onto particular spatial forms our desires and need for a home that responds to our many and varied requirements for security and freedom. Certainly notions of fear and hope are regularly laid at the door of the private dwelling, as Wright suggests:

> … one must again speak of separate psyches, longing for stability in a world that is often alienating, eager for the comforts and pleasures of home – sensual, familial, or merely private – yet fearful that these joys will prove ephemeral. And so we seek stronger evocations of the self or the family we want in our homes; gestures to buttress what we want to be. (Wright, 1991: 223)

Such reflections place us in a kind of limbo – caught between a worrisome world outside and the possible fear of life within the household and home – feelings of agoraphobia that operate in tension with domophobia (fear of the home). This may seem an overstatement, so let us turn for a moment to Freud's essay on the *unheimlich* (or unhomely/ uncanny) and its deeper associations. For Freud, the homely (*heimlich*) is connected to ideas of homeliness, stemming from notions of *heimat* or the homeland, from which we derive stability, contentment and

feelings of ease. In clear contrast, the uncanny highlights not only feelings of being *un*settled, but also a sense that the observer is uncovering
something that should remain hidden. We can see how these two ideas,
the homely and unhomely, revolve around that which is ours versus
that which is not ours, and related feelings of security and anxiety. Such
distinctions can be seen at work in particular treatments of the home
by psychoanalysts:

> the home is no place of harmony ... [it] is irredeemably driven by the
> presence of ghosts, its comforting appearance of womblike unity, doubled
> from the start by intruding forces ... untimely and dislocated hauntings
> of other times and places and other presences. (Bowlby, 1995: 77)

The nature of home as a place of comfort and safety is often emphasised
in children's books and stories that deconstruct its affective dimensions,
thus establishing a spatial and cultural order throughout our lives. The
Ladybird books *Key Word Reading Scheme* series published in the 1960s
showed Peter and Jane in an idealised suburbia, complete with cheery
milkmen, kindly policemen, and stay-at-home, smartly dressed young
mother, father always home from the office by six o'clock. These idealised versions of the child's home can be contrasted with other much-
loved children's stories in which ambivalence is expressed about the
sanctity or stability of the home (*Hansel and Gretel, Goldilocks and the
Three Bears, The Wind in the Willows*) and the disturbances generated by
invading or uninvited guests.

The historical telling of fairy tales builds on a sense of the home as
a preparatory space that enables us to adjust to the vicissitudes and
hardships of life. Bruno Bettelheim (1976) offers a fascinating analysis
of the role and meaning of such stories in his book *The Uses of Enchantment*. Here, he argues that the interpretation of life's meaning and our
self-understanding is promoted through these stories in much the same
way as Freud intended his psychoanalytic science as a means of self-
awareness. Such stories often offer moral messages and many of the
essential lessons of life, including its cruelty, unfairness and violence.
Readings of the wider canon of folk tales collated by the Grimm brothers, for example, reveal much harsher stories than those more often
repeated within our popular culture. Bettelheim's analysis of *The Three
Little Pigs* resonates with ideas of the defended home. Bettelheim argues
that the story of the wolf gobbling up the two pigs who build insufficiently robust homes (of straw and wood) highlight that planning,

resourcefulness and hard work are the ingredients of success, and ultimately in this case, bodily security. It is only the hard work of the older
pig and the time-consuming use of brick construction methods that
bring safety. Meanwhile, the pleasure-seeking immaturity of the younger
pigs allows them to deny the possibility that their efforts will be insufficient. This overtly Freudian reading also reveals that hearing such
stories instilled fear around the impulses towards pleasure in children,
while also preparing them for the world of work.

The deep-seated need to find a place of retreat and safety often
generates a tendency among children to find small hiding places that
mirror the relationship of the private dwelling in relation to the world
outside – a place under the covers, under the bed or dining table, playing

3.2 Gustave Doré, *Hansel and Gretel*

in the den in the garden or in Wendy houses (named after the protective house built by the Lost Boys after Wendy is injured in *Peter Pan*) – often imitating adult routines that anticipate future household duties. These early needs and fears of children appear to be played upon and reinforced by folk and fairy tales.

The mythologies of fairy tales reveal long social histories of storytelling that provide a means for children to identify safe or dangerous others and spaces. One example of this kind of storytelling can be found in *Bluebeard*. Written by Charles Perrault in 1697, the story deals with a wealthy aristocrat, feared because of his blue beard and allusions to his sexual violence, connected to knowledge that he has already been married three times, yet no one appears to know what has become of his former wives. His amorous approaches end with a local woman agreeing to marry him, after which she lives with him in his castle. Bluebeard leaves the marital home for a time and gives the keys to his wife, including those to a room he demands she should never enter. The wife becomes curious, and with her visiting sister, they enter the final room to find it covered with blood and the dead bodies of the former wives hanging on the walls. After this terrible discovery, the wife finds that the blood from the room will not wash off the key. The messages and morals of the story are not well hidden and it appears to be a parable relating an idea of the ubiquity of male knowledge of transgression and resonating with Catholic notions of original sin that cannot be removed. Bluebeard returns, and realising what she has done, flies into a rage as she escapes and locks herself in one of the towers. As with many gruesome fairy tales, a happy ending is offered when the wife's brothers arrive and kill Bluebeard before he can murder her. Bettelheim suggests that this story reproduces the sexual injunction that women should not enquire into the secrets of the male partners, lest their monstrous core be revealed; Bluebeard's long departures further suggesting tests of sexual fidelity.

For Melanie Klein (1975), the home life of the child could be identified as a time split into impressions of affirmation, wish fulfilment and reassurance and from forms of harm, rejection and embarrassment. Our deeper sense of self and identity, and metaphorically, the identification of the particular doors and keys through which we might understand our anxieties and worries later in life, are developed in this space. The idea that we do not fully know ourselves is one of the major contributions of the psychoanalytical framework; that the bulk of our psyche, which may be described as the subconscious, is tucked away because of the many psychic injuries and personal losses we have experienced and which would otherwise become overwhelming. Of course, the very idea of neurotic behaviour suggests that compressing and hiding away these forms of damage will almost always come back to haunt us as anxieties, behavioural oddities and destructive routines that must be confronted through dialogue in order to recover from those experiences. Psychoanalytic theory places the home and the family as the central focus of human development. Key to such theories is the notion that growing up and our relationships to primary caregivers are inherently traumatic processes. We are compelled to face complex sexual and emotional feelings in relation to those that nurture us; yet in the end, we must leave the parental home and become responsible adults in charge of ourselves and perhaps others in due course.

As a vast therapeutic literature suggests, many of us are the subject of traumas, humiliations and petty tribulations during our formative years. The child analyst Adam Phillips (1998: 81) succinctly expressed this difficult position arguing: 'we are all in the process of recovering from childhood', whether that childhood was apparently happy or deeply troubled. As the British psychoanalyst Donald Winnicott observed, 'Home is where we start from' (1990). However different our homes, most childhoods come bundled together with a common set of social and physical relationships – a mother and some kind of family, but also some kind of dwelling that houses these co-dependent relationships. From these processes, we emerge as adults with our own dreams, memories and sense of ourselves developed through inhabiting this space. Alain de Botton hints at this role of home in his discussion of the notion of an architecture of happiness, as he writes, 'We need a home in the psychological sense as much as we need one in the physical: to compensate for vulnerability. We need a refuge to shore up our states of mind' (de Botton, 2006: 107).

This point goes to the heart of the argument that the physical space of private dwellings offers a protection to us as subjective beings as well as to our physical bodies. The sense of an unordered and potentially threatening or disordering world outside the limits of the physical home is responded to by the sense of potential refuge and nesting (this rich metaphor is of course rife in accounts of building and maintaining the home) that we seek in our homes.

The social life of the home can be a peculiar thing, partly divorced from wider social conventions and norms. In contrast with the inter-subjectivity of social life (literally the sharing of thoughts and ideas by people that comes through the common ideas, symbols and linguistic conventions of everyday social life), the shared life of households and families often generates peculiar and private languages: pet names, curious habits and familial routines that deviate from what would be considered normal beyond the front door. These patterns of behaviour suggest that our homes provide a space that prepares us for our life as social actors, but also emancipates us by allowing us to perform in ways that are relatively free from observation or community censure. This is perhaps both a delight to those who are part of the household, but also a source of much potential danger because of the way that what happens behind closed doors can be understood as something private and unmonitored, and potentially monstrous, even as the outward veneer and routines of domestic life are maintained outside.

While we may appear to be able to do whatever we like in our homes we often find that social pressures and conventions may continue to constrain our behaviour. As Chapman and Hockey suggest:

> However determinedly we police the boundaries of our 'private' space, it is difficult to ignore or exclude the possibility of incursions into that space. The visit of outsiders, whether they are members of our family, friends and colleagues, plumbers and electricians, doctors and midwives, brings into sharp relief the fragility of the boundary between the public world and the private domain. (Chapman and Hockey, 1999: 10)

This sense, of intrusion and permeation, can be linked back to Freud's model of human nature in his later work, where he suggested more darkly that:

> Men are not gentle creatures, who want to be loved, who at the most can defend themselves if they are attacked; they are, on the contrary, creatures among whose instinctual endowments is to be reckoned a powerful share of aggressiveness. As a result, their neighbour is for them not only a potential helper or sexual object, but also someone who tempts them to satisfy their aggressiveness on him, to exploit his capacity for work without compensation, to use him sexually without his consent, to seize his possessions, to humiliate him, to cause him pain, to torture and to kill him. (Freud, 1961: 58)

The reference here to the neighbour is powerful. Given that this was written immediately prior to the Second World War, Freud's pessimism was at the very least prescient, writing in London where, as a Jew, he was exiled from his own home in Vienna. But there are also good reasons to adopt this impression of a veneer of social civility that may be stripped back to reveal the snarling core of our desires and destructive impulses. This extended vision of a 'war of all against all', as Hobbes described a state of nature in the absence of authority, is translated into a broader model of human conduct that gives good reason to maintain the home as a fortress against the risks of social breakdown or the antisocial conduct of even our own neighbours (such as in the case of civil wars like those of Congo, Bosnia, Israel–Palestine). These notions are also foregrounded as a meta-narrative of the home in which the lessons of childhood are based on the supposed existence of rules of the jungle. For parents, many of the lessons we teach our offspring, to beware of stranger danger, bogeymen and disorderly youths, are founded on a comparable conception of social life we need to convey in order to prevent a naivety that might expose our children to greater harms.

In his search for a human-centred approach to heal and understand the mental wounds and unstated anxieties of the self, Freud drew on the Greek word *psyche* or 'soul' (Bettelheim, 1983). These souls and their unconscious processes are nested within the shell of the home. The home places us all at this fundamental juncture, between the exterior universe and the universe of our interior nests and shells. The threshold of the front door bridges the gulf between the internal psyche and protective spaces and the outside world, both offering distinctive opportunities and risks. Jung made particularly interesting use of the home as a metaphor for the psyche, mirroring the spatial partitions of the home, as related by Bachelard. Here the sense being conveyed is that we choose in fact to deny the roots of that which troubles us by looking elsewhere:

> Here the conscious acts like a man who, hearing a suspicious noise in the cellar, hurries to the attic and, finding no burglars there decides, consequently, that the noise was pure imagination. In reality, this prudent man did not dare venture into the cellar. (Bachelard, 1958: 19)

Prior to venturing into the outside world, the home provides an uneven influence in our lives, a place capable of inspiring memories of this love and tenderness alongside those of violence, aggressive thoughts or

3.3 A hard shell to protect soft bodies inside, Australia

humiliation. These aspects of the home led Krishan Kumar to suggest that the surveillance, control and order of the home, as well as these darker aspects, should help us to understand those later urges to leave the parental home:

> [The home] offers privacy and security, or seems to, in an urban environment that appears increasingly dirty and dangerous. It is constantly referred to as a haven, though a more accurate image might be an embattled fortress around which a protective moat has been thrown. These images suggest a certain ambivalence, an uneasy mix of security and danger, fear and desire. (Kumar, 1997: 220)

As a material resource and fundamental platform for daily social life, the home connects the individual to the social structures, rules and shared culture of society outside. Yet, as Daniel Miller (2008) suggested, social science often mistakenly begins by assuming that people see themselves as directly part of wider society. Rather, Miller argues, people do not believe in society as such; they construct their own narratives in relation to what he calls the 'very very small societies' (2008: 295) of the micro-territories of the home. This observation illuminates highly personal and active engagements with a material culture that begins with domestic objects and spaces. Increasing consumption and individualism have if anything given us greater opportunity to express ourselves, and we tend to do this as culturally influenced individuals under the illusion that we have freedom of choice. Miller's discussions suggest that people derive significant comfort and a sense of life narrative from the objects in their home. While society may appear fragmented, individuals often remain connected to a sense of a broader, stable culture and to their social relationships through the way they order and fill their homes with material objects.

Dangers and horrors within

We have suggested that a range of forces have generated physical and psychological fortress mentalities, raising questions about how we as individuals in the micro-collectivities of households organise forms of psychic and physical defence. However, as we have already acknowledged, defence from a hostile world outside may belie the possibility of dangers within the home. The home is also a site of profound anxiety in its own right. Its solid walls and our preventive measures cannot prevent the entry of fear, despite our best intentions or actions. The fact of ownership brings along its own worries rather than simply offering some sense of security: how to ensure we make mortgage repayments, maintain the fabric of the building and so on. The extent of private violence taking place inside the home is dramatic – as Rykwert observed, feminist work in the 1970s on domestic violence and abuse had already:

> rendered problematic the notion of the home as a safe haven. Research into rape in marriage, domestic violence and sexual harassment unhinged the view that women need not fear men that they know: work colleagues,

boyfriends, partners and relatives. The recognition of the familiar and the
familial as no more trustworthy than the stranger put a very different
complexion on who is and who is not to be trusted and, by implication,
what places, times and people were risky. (Rykwert, 1991: 54)

Official statistics confirm that the home is more likely to be a locus of
peril for one or more of its occupants at the hands of another resident
than those of an outsider. Many of the most significant harms in daily
life occur within the home itself: intra-familial harassment, physical and
sexual abuse and violence. It is now well-known that that most accidents
happen in the home, but most homicides and cases of violence and
abuse also occur there, not least perhaps because of the invisibility and
ease of avoiding detection. Domestic abuse occurs in what we habitually
think of as the privacy of our own homes. This has led researchers like
Stanko (2000) to suggest that distinctions in relation to violence can be
made between the generally private, domestic clustering of female victimisation and the generally more public forms of male victimisation
that take place outside the home, and to make the point that what
occurs behind closed doors is not amenable to the usual forms of social
regulation and policing.

While the home may feel like a space of relative freedom, this quality
also facilitates the maintenance of homes in which the fiercer aspects
of human nature can find relatively unchecked expression. The balance
between the privacy of the home and the right of the state to intrude
to prevent harm has long proved contentious, not least because freedom
from any form of intrusion is seen as a cornerstone of liberal democracies and enshrined in legal statutes. Yet the patrolling of family life
through social work systems regularly generates anxiety because of the
need to find effective ways of combating violence and abuse in domestic
contexts. Given deep social taboos about family violence and child
abuse and public fury over infamous cases the role of the state, in terms
of its social work and policing functions, continues to raise questions
about approaches to such problems that occur in private spaces. The
idea that the home is a private and morally incorruptible space arguably
remained deeply entrenched until the late twentieth century, when the
'problem' of domestic abuse was more fully acknowledged following
the work of feminist researchers who began to reveal the scale and
nature of such violence and abuse. For example, in the UK around a

third (31 per cent) of women and one in five men (18 per cent) have experienced domestic violence since the age of sixteen (there are around 800,000 police recorded incidents of domestic violence each year according to the Crime Survey of England and Wales, 2012). Work by Syvia Walby and her colleagues suggested that the wider figure of such violence was around 13 million incidents of domestic violence estimated per year, claiming the lives of around two people per week, and that more than a third (36 per cent) of the population, predominantly women, experience domestic violence during their lifetimes (Walby *et al.*, 2004).

The problem of domestic violence has become recognised as a global health problem. In Europe, for example, an analysis of domestic violence studies found that around 1 in 4 women experienced domestic violence over their lifetimes, and between 6 to 10 per cent of women suffer domestic violence in a given year (Hagemann-White and Bohn, 2007). The same goes for the USA, where around 750,000 cases of intimate partner violence are recorded (this is proportionately much lower than in the UK, raising serious questions about the quality of such data and willingness of victims to come forward). In the USA many more women are killed by their partner each year than are murdered in total in the UK, around a thousand.

Domestic violence generates internalised distress where victims remain rooted to family homes, but also a steady and significant flow of vulnerable people, predominantly female, seeking new sites of shelter. For example, in the UK in 2014–15 roughly 6,000 households were accepted as homeless by local housing authorities in England as a consequence of fleeing domestic violence, and a further 6,500 received support in the form of sanctuary schemes which are used to reduce the vulnerability of victims by increasing the defensive capability of their homes (Department for Communities and Local Government, 2015).

Occasional media revelations have continued to expose previously concealed forms of violence and harm within the home, with documented cases of abduction, long-term kidnapping and contemporary domestic slavery being raised. Modern slavery exists in a range of forms, with trafficking into the UK for sexual or domestic labour that is bonded (a debt that needs to be paid to obtain freedom) involving thousands of women and children each year (Geddes *et al.*, 2013). Some children, in particular those from African countries, are trafficked through the UK to other countries, and most of these come mainly from Eastern and Central Europe, where poverty and aggressive paternalism make women more vulnerable in the face of local economic collapse and new global mobilities. The roughly 5,000 child sex workers in the UK, most trafficked into the country, find themselves compelled to work as sexual or domestic slaves (Craig *et al.*, 2007).

Notable cases of domestic slavery and violence further highlight the possibility of the domestic sphere as a sight of predatory relations and pure horror. A key example here is the case of Fred and Rosemary West, who were convicted of imprisoning, torturing and killing twelve women at their home in Gloucestershire during the 1970s and 1980s. The first victim was the daughter of Fred's first wife, murdered by Rosemary West. Another daughter was killed by them in 1979, but it was the rape of yet another daughter that started rumours that were picked up by the police who began to unpick the crimes of the couple in 1992. In 1994, the Wests were finally sentenced on the basis of these discoveries. In total, twelve bodies were discovered at their home, though they may have killed more. After Fred West hanged himself in 1996, their home was destroyed along with the adjoining house and made into a public footpath. All timber was burned and every brick crushed to prevent any form of souvenir-hunting. This process of destruction of apparently evil homes has been conducted in a number of cases linked to serial murderers and notable cases of homicide, such as the case of Anthony Sowell in the USA who had hidden the bodies of eleven female victims in his home, later demolished in 2011.

A horrific case of concealed abuse emerged in 2008 in what many media commentators considered to be the unlikely example of a small suburb in an Austrian town. To stunned social reaction, a 42-year-old Austrian woman named Elisabeth Fritzl was revealed to have been physically abused and raped by her father Josef since 1977 and imprisoned in the cellar of their house since 1984. The cellar was soundproofed, while the father claimed that she ran away to join a cult, even sending letters signed by her from this location. One of the most horrifying aspects of Elizabeth's lengthy internment was that she had given birth to seven children, all by her own father. One of these children died soon after birth, three were also imprisoned in the cellar and three were brought up in the family home with Josef's wife, who almost implausibly had no knowledge of these events. The unlikeliness of this situation was compounded by Josef Fritzl's claim that these three children (both to the police and his wife) were foundlings, left outside the home.

The discovery of the Fritzl home was spotlighted by interviews with unwitting and astounded neighbours, and newspaper articles featured cut-away views of the home. This occurred after the eldest daughter became seriously ill in spring 2008, so that her father allowed her to be taken to a hospital. Fritzl explained that he was driven to perform these appalling acts by a need to rape; over the twenty-four years, he visited his daughter once every three days to bring food and abuse her and would withdraw food and lighting to punish her, but even when the regime was less severe, his daughter was never allowed to see natural light. These terrible events continued despite local social services inspections that failed to uncover the concealed dungeon below. Even a tenant who rented a ground floor room in the Fritzl house for twelve years was not able to detect the arrangements put in place by Josef in the cellar.

Fritzl admitted that his plans to lock up his daughter developed while in prison for an earlier rape conviction, stating: 'I was born to rape, and I held myself back for a relatively long time. I could have behaved a lot worse than locking up my daughter.' Pictures of apparently happy family holidays fuelled incredulity at the events. It is possible to suggest the idea of the domestic dungeon as a perverse inversion of the idea of a dream home in which Fritzl was able to give free rein to his fantasies without social sanction. Via his lawyer, Fritzl admitted that: 'The cellar in my building belonged to me and me alone – it was my kingdom, that only I had access to' – a twisted variation on one of the common features ascribed to ownership of the home.

The public reaction to the Fritzl case was understandably one of horror, but in the search for blame, some commentators made links with a culture of privatism in Austria associated with an apparent tendency to look away from atrocities. On top of this was the realisation that the Fritzl case was the third in recent years in the same country alone; memorably, another case exists in which a young woman escaped from a cellar after eight years of captivity, following her abduction as a ten-year-old. A similarly incredible story emerged in the USA of Jaycee Lee Dugard who had been held captive for eighteen years following her abduction and who remained undetected by the neighbours of her captor. Such cases puncture widespread assumptions about the essentially nurturing character of domestic life, generating unsettling impressions of captivity and intense distress that may be mirrored in other, as yet undiscovered, cases. The sharp disjuncture between these horrors and the assumed respectability of suburban lifestyles echoes within many popular film representations (such as *Blue Velvet, Single White Female* or *Domestic Disturbance*). Representations of hidden violence now frequently characterise suburbia with violence as with notions of civility and calm; we have come to half-suspect the worst within the 'best' areas, as Wallace suggests:

> Crime in the suburbs is constructed as random, unpredictable and isolated, in contradistinction to the common, dangerous and racially inflected crime patterns of the city. At their root, crime stories support a belief in wealth as an inoculation against criminal acts, and construct affluent, suburban areas as less deserving of crime than urban areas. (Wallace, 2008: 407)

A central feature of these cases is the difficulty of reconciling their existence within a framework of human values; it is hard to comprehend the cruelty and nature of these crimes. True comprehension might threaten to fundamentally destabilise our own worldviews and conception of our own home environments. Nevertheless, both real and fictitious cases continue to shake our sense of social reality: to know even a little about such cases reveals fundamental gaps between external presentations of a civil domestic life and the possible realities behind closed doors. Our maintenance of ideals of domesticity and security requires continued and painstaking maintenance, sometimes by ignoring such crimes and other traumatic examples that would otherwise impinge on the stability of our everyday lives. Yet to shun such harrowing visions may of course also facilitate their concealment. Certainly, the infrequent discovery of cleverly designed dungeons and places of suburban captivity in Belgium, Austria and the USA in recent years suggests the possibility that similar cases in other countries around the world have not and may never be discovered. The common public emphasis on external risks to the home, such as burglary, is ultimately misaligned with the extent and profound damage of ongoing domestic abuse and cases of violence. The examples we have offered here present the home as a site of containment and hidden horrors, with the world kept from viewing such atrocities and their perpetrators often hiding in plain sight of ordinary neighbourhoods and communities.

The home plays a major part in popular culture. It is part of human nature to enjoy being scared, so we seek out that frisson of enjoyable terror found in tales about *unheimlich* homes, homes under siege, and homes where occupants are not all they seem. The home has provided a staple theme for myths, legends, fairy stories and novels (in diverse treatments like *Jane Eyre, The Turn of the Screw, Rebecca, Straw Dogs*) through the ages. In many horror films, the haunted house trope plays on such deep-seated fears. Variants on these themes can be found in many examples from modern fiction and film. A key example that plays with such themes is the film *Funny Games* (France, 1997; remade in the USA in 2007) in which a family are tortured, ostensibly for the amusement of two men, but with a wider cautionary critique of the kind of voyeurism implicit in much sadistic contemporary film. In the film the potential weakness of the home is revealed by a simple appeal to social conventions and expectations. The protagonists arrive at the door and ask to borrow eggs, thus gaining access despite the gates and other protections that the home might otherwise afford its residents. Here it is the everyday etiquette of home life that serves to weaken the home to the risk of intrusion and violence; the message appears to be that courtesy and hospitality are also potential chinks in the armour of the home.

Perhaps our worldviews have become bleaker as we operate in a context containing significant and cumulative portrayals of harm of so many kinds. The home is a shell that appears to offer sustenance and a response to our critical needs for security, yet it is also a space of bleak violence, neglect and everyday transgression. It is not only our own homes that fuel fantasies of persecution and worry; films like *Psycho* or *Friday the 13th* and latter day variants like *Funny Games* and *Hostel* have overwritten home-like spaces with unsettling associations. In *Panic Room*, a shiver of fear comes not only because we are able to identify with the plight of the character played by Jodie Foster as she tries to escape the invaders in her home, but also because the underlying message is that no matter what physical barriers and mechanisms we deploy, there will never be a failsafe means of immunising ourselves from the possible harms of the outside world. In films like *Sliver*, such messages are much more overt as the plot revolves around the security system of a new towerblock turned inward upon its residents, offering surveillance and paranoia in lieu of assurance. Cronenberg's *Shivers* takes such anxieties further as a futuristic apartment block is invaded by a genetically created venereal disease that turns the affluent residents into violent and sexually disinhibited zombies. These often ugly reversals of commonly shared understandings of home are the stuff of Hollywood logic; the selling of fear as entertainment presents us as vulnerable and ill-prepared for the moment when our own domestic space is challenged; who knows when that might be or what form it might take?

As official data and cultural sources might suggest, domestic life is a space of chronic violence and worry that shapes and damages our psyches. Certainly, the resulting impression of danger both without and inside the home leaves little room for manoeuvre into a space that might offer a real sense of deep security. Such themes were the mainstay of J. G. Ballard who, in books like *Super Cannes* and *Cocaine Nights*, suggested that the retreat of the affluent into compounds and palatial homes would see their ensuing boredom generate new forms of excitement through casual violence and sexual excess. Predicated on a Freudian conception of human nature, the violent forays of Ballard's characters, their home-made rape movies, gang violence, drug use and murder, suggest that the result of affluence meshed with profound security systems may well end in a return to base incivility fuelled by the sterility of these spaces.

Conclusion

Memories of the childhood home contain aspects, atmospheres and associations that we carry with us and often project onto new domestic spaces. A particular sound may evoke memories of either pleasant or unsettling events: the tone of a creaking door, a baby crying, a plate smashing on the floor or a harsh word. Specific smells (perhaps cork tiling, perfume, an 'alpine' air freshener) also have strong connotative powers and may generate particular sets of feelings, so it is not surprising that passageways, stairs, cellars, lofts and attics come to be associated with spaces of punishment or a feared unknown. As Ellin suggests:

> Even while seeking to harden the shells of our homes numerous anxieties and worries pass unchecked. There is something particularly futile about the way in which we shore up our defences, as we fail to recognize how it is that many of our personal fears will never be capable of being assuaged by such efforts. (Ellin, 1997: 43)

Hence, the home can be seen as a source of protection, a place that is widely linked to notions of self-reliance and individual development, but also a confined and potentially confining space where our own worst nightmares might be realised. These deep contradictions of the home are barely recognised in the habitual discourses that surround domestic life because as many have suggested, such horrors are better submerged than acknowledged.

4

Invasions of privacy

In the previous chapter, we examined the Janus-faced nature of the home as a source of anxieties, bound up with the fabric of domestic life as a site of everyday refuge. Here we turn to the wide range of external threats that challenge and undermine the attributes connected with home ownership in terms of its offer of relative security, control, privacy, status and wealth. This chapter explores perceived threats to the home ranging from the powers of the state to problematic neighbours and other invasions of privacy. We look at these risks through stories focusing on celebrities and the law, as well as the fears and experiences of less affluent homeowners aspiring to celebrity homes and lifestyles. Here we continue to develop the idea of the home and its micro-territories as spaces that contain and reproduce ideas about markets, autonomy and security.

One consequence of living in what has been termed a risk society (Beck, 1992; Giddens, 1990; 1991) is that we have become increasingly sensitised to potential danger. Awareness of risk, and awareness of the home as an asset to protect, in particular, drive fear and expenditure in equal measure. Contemporary life presents ever new problems and terrors to render the home insecure, including identity theft, cyber-stalking and predatory paedophiles, as well as nuisances like neighbourhood noise and unwanted telesales penetrating the home's boundaries, the letterbox invasion of junkmail, cold callers and proselytizers for various political parties or religions who disturb us at our doors. The sense of diffuse threat which permeates this social condition, which Bauman (2006) terms 'liquid fear', produces feelings of anxiety and helplessness in the face of apparently all-encompassing risks that erode our ontological security. Yet our perceptions of the actual degree of risk, the probability that such a disaster might happen to us, are often distorted if not irrational. Bauman suggests that in a world that seems unbearably complex and dangerous, one way of dealing with 'surplus fear' is to find comfort in controlling the smaller and more concrete aspects of our lives, primarily our homes.

Policing the boundaries of home

Attempts at controlling domestic territory highlight the importance of boundaries, designed to demarcate and protect the home as a place of security, privacy and refuge. Property boundaries give often physical but surely symbolic effect to one of the essential characteristics of property ownership: the ability to exclude outsiders, which is the basis of the law of trespass. Establishing a home distanced from neighbouring properties removes the possibility of direct disruption, and is at the same time a potent indicator of wealth and prestige because privacy and seclusion have become inextricably bound up with the status of the home. It is expensive buying a home surrounded by grounds, but the benefits are well explained by Joanne Harris, author of *Chocolat* and other bestsellers, talking about her home: 'I first fell in love with the house for its outdoor space; it's surrounded by grounds of five acres ... For someone who was used to living so close to the street, it's nice to finally have a barrier from the rest of the world.' This exclusive spaciousness and privacy even extends inside the home; Harris confided that her six-year-old daughter 'has a suite to herself' within the house (*Independent*, 2009). However, celebrity mansion owners with extensive grounds have lengthy and distant property boundaries to police and defend. Ensuring that a large and valuable property is secure at all times involves anxiety, time and effort – or alternatively it involves the cost of employing someone else to worry about securing doors, windows and the other layers of boundaries.

It is not difficult to understand why wealthy privacy-seekers become embroiled in legal disputes over access routes across their land. Footpaths and other legitimate rights of way are experienced as incursions into their privacy, which is an expensive commodity. In the UK, these issues have been highlighted by the Countryside Rights of Way Act 2000 which gives members of the public access rights to moorland and parkland. In the USA this legislation was viewed as 'a remarkable limitation on the right to exclude' (Anderson, 2009: 246). A similar struggle was being played out at Billionaire's Beach in Malibu, California. The law states that beaches are public property between the water and the high tide line, but the problem was gaining access to the beach. A landowner named Lisette Ackerberg had been granted permits in the 1980s to build a house with a pool and tennis court, on condition she provide an access way to the beach. Instead, she blocked access with a high wall and trees. Campaigners for beach access are now celebrating after Ackerberg lost in two court hearings and finally provided a path next to her house down to the beach (O'Neill, 2015). The UK legislation led to appeals by more than three and a half thousand landowners, most of whom were successful (Mitchell, 2008). The singer Madonna was among the celebrities taking legal action to protect their privacy, concerned that 'sightseers could approach within less than 100 yards of their home', a grade 2-listed Georgian mansion surrounded by a 548-hectare (1,370-acre) estate. However, Madonna's argument that this violated her human rights failed, and ramblers now have the right to roam over half of the estate, although not within sight of the house itself (de Bruxelles and Elliott, 2004).

Nicholas van Hoogstraten, another wealthy English landowner, adopted the legal strategy of buying up neighbouring land to achieve a greater degree of protective privacy. In the USA Mark Zuckerberg did the same in 2013, buying four properties adjacent to his Palo Alto home for over $30 million (Bailey, 2013). But Hoogstraten also unlawfully blocked up a 100-year-old right of way over his land, dismissing protests from the Ramblers Association as 'just nosy' and referring to walkers as 'scum' (*Guardian*, 2000). The local council meekly agreed to re-route the footpath away from Hoogstraten's land. Yet the Ramblers Association won their case at the Court of Appeal (*R (On the Application of Ashbrook) v East Sussex CC*, 2002). Hoogstraten then transferred ownership of his land to a nominally registered company under his control, exempted from fines and compliance with court orders to remove obstructions. The impasse was solved only by legislation to remove the loophole Hoogstraten exploited, the extremely short Highways (Obstruction by Body Corporate) Act 2004 (Ramblers Organisation, 2002; 2005). Although the law finally triumphed, Hoogstraten had resources that allowed him to challenge each and every threat to his beliefs about home ownership, which perhaps differ from the norm only in the extremity of his views.

4.1 Brecqhou Island, Channel Islands

Making your home on an island, as for example Richard Branson has done on Necker Island, would seem to ensure both privacy and defensible boundaries. The writer Adam Nicolson, who is an island owner himself, concludes that the love of islands 'is a neurotic condition. They are not so much islands as I-lands, where the inflated self smothers and obliterates all other forms of life' (Nicolson, 2001: 344). Sir David and Sir Frederick Barclay own Brecqhou, a Channel Island situated between the French and English coasts, where they built a replica Gothic castle. The Barclay twins, whose estimated wealth in 2007 was £1.8 billion, regularly feature in the *Sunday Times Rich List*. They use their weapon of choice: the law, to intimidate and financially punish those who attempt to breach the 'walls' of their island castle or threaten their privacy (Willman, 2007). The Barclays assert that their desire for privacy, which some would say verges on obsession, stems from the need to protect their families from kidnapping and harassment. Apparently the need for defensive territorialisation can never fully be satisfied, even on an island.

The home owner against the state

We should not forget that the saying 'An Englishman's home is his castle' derives from the seventeenth-century *Semayne's case* that established the rights of the homeowner against state forces (Coke, 1644: 192). The power of the state to breach home boundaries has arguably accelerated in the second half of the last century to the present, towards bureaucracy and officialdom and away from individual homeowners. This holds true in the UK, Australia and even in the USA, where the constitution protects the home against government intrusion. There are now many instances of legislation that enable local or national government to challenge the homeowner's property interests or that give state agents the right to enter private homes. The most obvious example of these powers is the right of the state to expropriate private property without the owner's consent, known as the doctrine of 'eminent domain' in the USA, 'compulsory purchase' in the UK and as 'resumption' (of the state's underlying land ownership) or 'compulsory acquisition' in Australia (for details of the different legal regimes see, respectively, Ross, 2007; Roots *et al.*, 2008; Jacobs, 2009). Although applying to wealthy and poor homeowners alike, there is a widespread perception that these state powers are less likely to interfere with the affluent.

The popular 1997 Australian film by Eric Bana, *The Castle*, concerns a Melbourne family's legal struggle to save their home from compulsory purchase and demolition to build an airport (Wills, undated; Allon, 2008: 168–169). It plays on the well-worn tropes of the little man against the state, and the home as castle. The Fifth Amendment of the United States Constitution establishes that 'private property [shall not] be taken for public use, without just compensation'. However, 'takings law' is often cited as an example of the state riding roughshod over the homeowner. The case of *Kelo v. City of New London*, 2005 provoked much comment along these lines, as it concerned private property expropriated by the local state for part of a comprehensive redevelopment plan. A 5–4 majority decision by the Supreme Court held that this was 'public use' and therefore permissible. At least the state offers compensation for the home lost to a road-widening scheme or to redevelopment plans. Tellingly, in the 1950s novel *The Man in the Gray Flannel Suit* (Wilson, 1955), the central character is unable to capitalise on his inheritance because of zoning laws. These present a fundamental challenge to the homeowner (or would-be), specifying the location, design or size of a home being refurbished or yet to be built. In the USA and in Australia, zoning may dictate what size property can or should be built, and even the number of floors and bedrooms.

The UK's planning system lays less emphasis on zoning, but more on the strict control of individual development. This extends to the style and look of property. A homeowner ordered to paint his house by the planning enforcement team at Torbay Council fell back on the usual clichés about ownership rights when expressing his indignation: 'I always thought an Englishman's home was his castle. It's my private property' (Telegraph, 2008). Planning authorities can exercise control over security features, giving rise to another concern about risk. Wealthy individuals planning a secure home or upgrading security features are now advised by experts that they should anonymise any document submitted to municipal planning authorities and that 'the security overlay should be filed separately from the architectural drawings so it doesn't become available to the public. Once privacy has been established the space can be properly secured' (Brennan, 2013). The more obvious risk is that the planning authority will reject the security proposals. In the Cotswolds, a UK homeowner who installed high-tech security including seven CCTV cameras and six floodlights was told to remove the 'ridiculous' level of security at his listed home (Macintyre, 2007) and similar requests regularly generate conflict in communities elsewhere. Film star Kate Winslet's application to install 2 m high gates at her fifteenth-century rural property to protect her family's privacy was refused on the grounds that the proposed gates were 'more suited to a suburban or urban area' (Cable, 2012). However, the combined wealth of multi-millionaire residents, who were determined to turn their street into a gated community by retrofitting steel gates without permission on a public road, forced one local council to back down because of the spiralling costs of the legal dispute (Buchanan and George, 2011).

The balance between rights of the state and the rights of homeowners came into sharp relief during the 2012 London Olympics. Security measures against potential terrorist attack included locating a Ground Based Air Defence system and military personnel on the roof of a residential tower block in east London. The residents claimed their human rights (in particular to 'respect for the home' and to 'the peaceful enjoyment of property') were breached. The High Court gave this argument short shrift, stating that these rights are trumped by the duty of the state to defend the realm and protect national security (*Harrow Community Support Limited v The Secretary of State for Defence*, 2012). This unusual example suggests that the home can be appropriated as a defensive outpost to bolster the resources of the police and the state, under conditions defined as 'exceptional' by the state itself.

Ironically, sometimes owners' efforts to protect their homes lead to conflict. The UK state agency Natural England designated a coastal area in Suffolk as a Site of Special Scientific Interest, where no interference with nature is allowed, although the cliffs are rapidly eroding and land is being lost to the sea. Peter Boggis and other homeowners whose property boundaries are now less than 100 metres from the sea built a kilometre-long sea defence. However, Natural England consider this to be unlawful activity at a Site of Special Scientific Interest and took them to court for non-compliance with planning law. The Court of Appeal decided against the homeowners, but said they were 'not unsympathetic to the plight of [Mr Boggis and his neighbours] who can see the cliff face remorselessly approaching the boundaries of their properties' (*Boggis, Easton Bavents v Natural England*, 2009: 41).

The game of outwitting UK planning authorities can sometimes take on more humorous aspects. A recent dispute concerned a large mock Tudor castle, complete with two round towers equipped with battlements and cannons. Robert Fidler, a Surrey farmer, built and concealed the entire edifice of Honeycrock Castle inside a haystack because he did not have planning permission. For four years he lived there with his family in the dark, attempting to establish that the building had stood for the required length of time without objection. However, the authority ordered the castle demolished once the haystack was taken down, and they succeeded in court, which put paid to Mr Fidler's ingenious arguments (*R (Fidler) v Secretary of State for Communities and Local Government and Reigate and Banstead BC* (2011)). To reinforce the point, the Town and Country Planning Act was amended in 2011 to give the courts greater powers in cases of 'deliberate concealment'. Perhaps Fidler can find consolation in the other castle which he owns, the seventeenth-century Fort Metal Cross, built by the British in Ghana to protect the local trade in ivory, gold and slaves (Hughes, 2008).

Confrontations between homeowners and planning officials can become bitter and personal, reflecting the strong emotions aroused by

4.2 Robert Fidler's Honeycrock Castle, UK

any threat to the home. In 1991, a shocking incident occurred in England, which fortunately has not been repeated since. Albert Dryden built a bungalow for his mother on land he owned but without planning permission. Following a lengthy dispute, the chief planning officer Harry Collinson arrived to serve Dryden with a court enforcement order requiring him to demolish the bungalow. As a mechanical digger waited to start the demolition work, Dryden opened fire with his gun. He killed Collinson, seriously injured two other men and was later jailed for life (BBC News, 2003).

In the USA, some confrontations between state officials and homeowners have turned into protracted states of siege, with defiant homeowners supported by members of patriot, militia and anti-tax movements attaining celebrity status. The 1991 stand-off at Ruby Ridge, Idaho, between Federal agents and Randy Weaver and his family and friends is a well-known example. Initially sparked by a charge of possessing an illegal sawn-off shotgun, the siege ended in three deaths. In 2007 the Browns of Plainfield, New Hampshire, attracted the same populist, libertarian support – including from Randy Weaver himself – when they were subpoenaed to attend court for income tax evasion. The Browns declared they would use deadly force to resist any attempt at arresting them for failure to appear in court. Their house was armed with weapons, ammunition, explosive devices and booby traps, and boasted a castellated turret providing panoramic views. All these measures were ultimately ineffectual against cunning and persuasion. In an echo of tactics that ended many a medieval siege the Browns were finally arrested by undercover officers they had unwittingly invited into the house, assuming them to be supporters (Great Dreams, 2007).

Tax officials have been less successful in getting owners at the world's most expensive residential block, One Hyde Park in London, to pay their council tax. The owners are proving very hard to trace, as the Land Registry ownership records include only details of offshore companies registered in the British Virgin Islands and other tax havens. A door-to-door search of the block is impossible because of the sophisticated security measures, including SAS-trained doormen (Boffey, 2011).

Gardens, trees and hedges

For those whose house is set back from the road, there is often an awkward space between the fully private house and the public space of the highway. By law, 'the occupier of any dwelling-house gives implied licence to any member of the public coming on his lawful business to come through the gate, up the steps, and knock on the door of his house' (*Robson and Another v Hallett* (1967: 412), although it was pointed out that occupants can always keep their front gates locked. The unfenced or unwalled gardens common in the less dense urban landscapes of the USA and Australia are privately owned; crossing the symbolic boundary between road and garden still amounts to trespass. The legal geographer Nicholas Blomley has explored the dual function of gardens as spaces both private and on view to the community and wider public (Blomley, 2005). When time and effort is expended on a beautiful garden, atavistic feelings of pride and ownership run deep; an irate Ohio homeowner shot dead a teenager who walked across his well-tended lawn (Associated Press, 2007) and, in Florida, another

4.3 One Hyde Park, London

death occurred in an argument over a dog allegedly excreting in a neighbour's yard (NBC Miami, 2015).

Hedges and trees, those apparently neutral and natural plants, play an interesting role in the sometimes violent ruptures associated with twenty-first-century home ownership. In a series of bizarre incidents, trees on public land have been attacked and killed by affluent home-owners in Australia and the USA, using poison, axes and chainsaws. In Sydney, where trees were blocking valuable harbour views owners felt they had a 'right' to them along with property ownership (Carson, 2011). In a similar case Madonna was ordered to trim her acacia bound-ary hedge to an acceptable height after her neighbour in the Hollywood

Hills took legal action and was counter-sued for trespass to Madonna's property (McMillan, 1990). Sometimes these disputes between neighbours have fatal consequences. Examples from the UK include a disagreement over a boundary hedge that led to the shooting of Llandis Burdon as he worked in his garden, by his neighbour of over twenty years (Paterson, 2000); and a long-running feud over a privet hedge in a quiet suburban cul-de-sac culminated in Robert Dickenson shooting his neighbour George Wilson, then hanging himself a few days later in his police cell (Britten, 2004).

Fast-growing Leylandii hedges that shoot up quickly to a great height have caused many disputes about overshadowing and loss of 'prospect', including one involving the film star Nicole Kidman who planted Leylandii around her 140-acre estate outside Sydney to shield her home from onlookers (Malkin, 2009). There is no legal 'right to light' or 'right to a view' that can be enforced; but local authorities may intervene when trees overshadow neighbouring properties. In Queensland, legislation to address 'nuisance trees' was considered, on the grounds that 'statewide consultation shows [these are] one of the major issues of contention between neighbours' (Bligh and Cameron, 2009). Provisions to control Leylandii and to mediate between adjoining property owners were inserted into the UK's Anti-Social Behaviour Act 2003, following a consultation paper that estimated 17,000 unresolved disputes (Department of the Environment, Transport and the Regions, 1999). Under this legislation a wealthy Scottish lawyer was ordered to reduce his Leylandii hedge by more than 10 metres following a long-running legal dispute with his neighbour (Spillett, 2015).

Neighbour problems

Fist fights and worse have been incited by another dubious 'right' associated with home ownership. Parking on the strip of road outside your suburban house is at best a matter of custom and practice, rather than one of property rights, but this makes disputes no less frequent or vehement. Affluence and social status do not provide immunity, as illustrated by wealthy New Hampshire neighbours Beverley Hollingsworth, a former president of the New Hampshire Senate, and millionaire lawyer Peter Hutchins. Their long-running parking dispute ended with allegations of assault, breach of privacy, mischief and stalking filed in court. The judge advised the parties to 'Reach deep within yourselves, grow as individuals, have some tolerance towards your neighbours, and show some respect' (Wang, 2005).

An increasingly common form of neighbour dispute centres on contested ownership or disputes over the exact location of the boundary between two properties, seemingly particularly serious when those properties are small. The strong emotions involved in ownership lead otherwise rational people to reject compromise and take matters to the civil courts, often incurring huge legal costs and resulting in permanent ill feelings between neighbours (Clark, 2005). One case involved twenty-two court hearings before one party was jailed for repeatedly defying an order to remove a fence unlawfully erected on neighbouring land. Considering legal fees, the net value of this narrow strip of land was £8 million an acre, the price usually paid for prime development sites in London (Clark, 2005).

The theme song for the incredibly popular TV soap *Neighbours* (composed by Tony Hatch and Jackie Trent, 1985) optimistically asserts that 'Everybody needs good neighbours / With a little understanding / You can find the perfect blend'; but understanding seems to be in short supply, and many homeowners are unwilling to mix with neighbours perceived as different. Paradoxically, in an increasingly individualistic society, neighbours matter more than ever because they may be counted among the risks against which homeowners have to guard themselves and their property. Lee Anne Fennell makes the point that neighbours affect the value of the owner-occupied home in this 'complex, inter-dependent world'; in consequence, homeowners often 'act both as castle-keepers bent on controlling their own space and as community crusaders bent on controlling everyone else's' (Fennell, 2009: 3). Nearby properties in poor decorative order and with unkempt gardens can wipe thousands off the sale price of a home. Rather than resolving problems amicably over the garden fence, these issues are increasingly referred to local authorities for adjudication.

Research into neighbour disputes and complaints indicates that the ideal 'good neighbour' is friendly and reliable, but keeps a proper distance, and above all, respects the property boundaries guarding the privacy and seclusion of their neighbours (Stokoe and Wallmark, 2003). At worst, neighbours can cause serious problems through thoughtless or even deliberate, maliciously disruptive conduct. Even then, the victim of this type of behaviour is unlikely to confront the nuisance neighbour directly, as there is no real social connection between them. This avoidance of conflict was described by Baumgartner (1988) as social control through moral minimalism; in such neighbourhoods third parties are needed to deal with disputes. For example, in Queensland, the state government's Dispute Resolution Centres dealt with over 500 cases of neighbour disputes in 2008–09 (Bligh and Cameron, 2009). A large UK study in the late 1990s examined problems that might end up as court cases and found that 15 per cent of all problems were related to housing ownership and occupation. This was the largest single category of problems, exceeding employment and debt, and surprisingly, 57 per cent of owner-occupiers reported suffering from problem neighbours, in comparison with only 25 per cent of tenants (Genn, 1999). This is one risk that apparently increases rather than is diminished by home ownership.

It is likely that the high rate of neighbour problems recorded by homeowners reflects frustration that property rights provide no solution to this issue. Legal action can be taken based on nuisance, which the law defines as any use of the neighbouring land that interferes with the homeowner's use and enjoyment of their own property. Legally, nuisance can take many forms, including dirt and smells in certain circumstances. The court weighs 'the right of the occupier to do what he likes with his own property and the right of the neighbour not to be interfered with' (*Sedleigh-Denfield v O'Callaghan*, 1940: 903). Lawsuits are rare due to cost, but the concept of nuisance resonates with most people. Some house-proud owners view bringing dirt into their homes as contamination and a violation of their most precious possession. In one extreme example, a homeowner in Texas asked two furniture deliverymen to remove their shoes before entering her pristine home. When they refused, explaining it was company policy to wear protective shoe coverings, she threatened to shoot them (United Press International, 2008).

Noise is the type of nuisance that elicits most homeowner complaints, invading from beyond property boundaries, upsetting the deeply held notions of privacy and control associated with home ownership. Sometimes disputes over noise can take a tragic turn; for example, a 2009 murder case in Melbourne, Australia, resulted from a neighbour's complaint about the 'disruptive racket' coming from a nearby house (Herald Sun, 2009). A search of any municipal website in Australia, the USA and the UK generally reveals guidance and advice for dealing with noisy neighbours (for a typical example, see Department of

Environment and Climate Change, NSW, 2008). UK official statistics demonstrate the scale of the problem of noise. In 2005, British councils recorded over 300,000 complaints about noisy neighbours, mainly concerning music, barking dogs, or young children, a fivefold increase in such complaints over twenty years (British Crime Survey, 2006/07). A majority of UK local authorities suggested that 'selfish attitudes' combined with 'a higher expectation of quiet' were the most common reasons for the rise in neighbour complaints, followed by 'incompatible lifestyles with neighbours' (Office for National Statistics, 2007: 152) and the rising use of gardens as outdoor rooms (Office for National Statistics, 2007). Against this background, a press report about a UK parish council chairman who shot dead his neighbour's dog to end its constant barking produced roughly equal expressions of horrified criticism from outraged animal lovers and public support from sympathetic homeowners suffering from similar noise intrusion (Rajan, 2008).

Celebrities are not immune from noise disputes, as can be seen from the long-standing feud between the actor Sean Connery and his New York neighbours over noisy renovation works, which led to court criticism of both parties for failure to reach a compromise (Hauser, 2007). In 2010, millionaire art collector Charles Saatchi and Nigella Lawson (his then wife, the celebrity chef and original 'domestic goddess') sold their home in London's exclusive Eaton Square to escape the noise of basement excavation and other extensive renovations carried out by the owners next door (McSmith, 2010). The journalist Ed Vulliamy (2013) laments the 'end of neighbourhood, in that sense of shared space and responsibilities to one another' caused by the gentrification of Notting Hill, London, when 'after the crisis for the rest of Britain in 2008, the bankers went berserk and basement bedlam began'. Wealth enables these very disruptive building works, in which super-affluent owners 'develop downwards' because in tight-packed cities, it is almost the only space remaining for ambitious new developments.

In an individualistic era, even innocent neighbourly acts such as calling round can be misinterpreted as a breach of privacy. Portable communication devices are used for much social planning 'on the hoof', but arrangements are usually made prior to arrival. New social rules of etiquette have reduced casual drop-ins by friends and acquaintances, rendering suspicious the unplanned-for knock at the door. 'Who can that be?', we ask when the doorbell rings unexpectedly, as though a lack of advance warning makes our visitor's intent more worrying. The change in attitude to tramps, hobos and travelling salespeople offers a telling illustration of how much more wary we have become over the past fifty years or so (for example, see Crompton, 1952). Rather than offering a cup of tea and some food, the more common reaction nowadays is irritation or fear. The residents of an affluent village described itinerant salespeople as 'saturating' their neighbourhood, hawking their wares from door to door, calling 'on spec, always wanting to do the driveway, or do your guttering'; this terminology speaks volumes about their suspicion and fear of 'the other' (Loader *et al.*, 2000: 72).

Apart from the annoyance they cause, there is a fear that such callers could be involved in a particularly unpleasant form of crime primarily targeted at vulnerable older people: 'distraction burglary', 'bogus calling' or 'burglary artifice' (Thornton *et al.*, 2003). These terms refer to the threat of home invasion by thieves at the door asking for work, pretending to be in urgent need of help or posing as officials such as police, council workers, or utility company employees. This crime tends to cause deep feelings of fear and trauma in victims who not only suffer loss and violation, but also blame themselves for allowing or inviting the criminal into their home, despite well-publicised security campaigns. The catchphrase used by the UK's *Operation Liberal,* the national intelligence unit for distraction burglary, is *'Not sure? Don't open the door!'*. Distraction burglary highlights how under certain circumstances the basic defences of the home can be circumvented by directly approaching the householder. The consequences of relaxing one's guard in this way underscore vulnerabilities on home ground.

The deep-seated fear of the 'cuckoo in the nest' that turns on the generous and unsuspecting homeowner has sometimes found expression in literature; Heathcliff in Emily Bronte's *Wuthering Heights* ultimately destroys the wealthy family that adopted him from the Liverpool slums. A more recent example is the self-invited guest in *Six Degrees of Separation* (play by John Guare, 1990; film directed by Fred Schepisi, 1993), fraudulently claiming to be a college friend of the homeowners' children who has just been mugged in Central Park. He skilfully manipulates them and breaches the social and physical edifice of their home. As with all successful fiction, such narratives touch a nerve and mirror (if exaggeratedly) real events. Media reports of real incidents are held up as warnings to us all: 'They groomed kind, decent old men, then bled them dry', was the headline for the story about two UK conmen disguised as builders in order to gain admittance, then befriend and extract money from lonely, elderly homeowners. One of their victims had his home repossessed for failure to repay a £100,000 loan incurred to pay for 'building work', forcing his 'move to a scruffy rented bedsit where he lives today'. Another victim was in the process of transferring ownership of his house to the same two conmen when they were arrested (Maitland, 2007).

Cyber risks to the home

At the same time as a generalised withdrawal from the wider neighbourhood into the home, the new information and communication technologies we enjoy there have made the home more vulnerable to a series of risks that pass beyond or between any physical defences. Electronic devices in the home bring with them the possibility of cyber intrusions directly into living rooms and bedrooms, rather than to the front door where the conventional intruder could be turned away. The alert householder must be on the lookout for the aptly named 'Trojan horse' and many other computer viruses designed to capture sensitive information and facilitate identity theft to access credit and illegally pay for goods and services. In theory, the home is where we can really 'be ourselves' and express our identities fully, but home computers brought with them the possibility of almost literally losing our identities as they leak beyond the household. It is widely known that use of the Internet, mobile phones and social networking sites carry their own risks, yet many people are content to place their images and life stories on social networking portals such as Facebook. We also generate counterpart cyber-selves from transactional data, credit cards, store loyalty cards and market research questionnaires. The risks of late modernity even extend to our sense of self, open to theft and increasingly vulnerable following the revelations of state-based sources of surveillance from Edward Snowden and others.

This fear is borne out: in the USA, an estimated 8.6 million households (7 per cent) suffered identity theft in 2010, up by 30 per cent from 2005, causing about $13.3 billion in direct financial losses (Langton, 2011). In most states in the USA, unlike the UK and Australia, households are under an obligation to report data breaches, so the data are more reliable. In 2010–11, the Australian Bureau of Statistics (2012) estimated personal fraud caused losses of $1.4 billion; in the UK, the total annual costs to individual computer users were estimated at £1.7bn for identity theft, £1.4bn for online scams and £30m for 'scareware' (Detica, 2011). The Crime Survey for England and Wales estimates that there were under 7 million criminal offences in the year ending June 2015; however this total does not include data on cyber crime. A pilot study undertaken in 2015 produced an estimate of 5.1 million incidents of online fraud, affecting 3.8 million adult victims in England and Wales in the previous twelve months (Office for National Statistics, 2015a). All three states run well-publicised initiatives against identity theft, spam and viruses, alongside a multi-million dollar private industry (1st Security, undated). These new corporate opportunities rely on the fact that householders cannot afford to stand still in the continuing, shifting battle against losses of data, identity and finances (Monahan, 2009).

While homeowners who are also parents have learnt not to relax their defensive vigilance even when their children are apparently safe at home, many parents misunderstand the nature of certain kinds of predation or may not be sufficiently aware of the risks to children using the Internet. Cyber-bullying is a very alarming type of victimisation in which the young person affected is targeted specifically at home, traditionally the main refuge from more conventional bullying tactics. Numerous studies suggest that less than one-third of parents actively monitor their children's use of the Internet (Strider *et al.*, 2012). Sexual predators use social media interfaces and chatrooms to solicit under-age sex, sometimes pretending to be children. In 2001 an Australian study found more than a quarter of adolescents surveyed believed they were recipients of sexual solicitation in Internet chat rooms (Stanley, 2001). In the USA, over 1.25 million reports were made to the CyberTipline in the years 1998–2012 relating to the possession, manufacture and distribution of child pornography as well as over 56,000 reports of online enticement of children for sexual acts during the same period (National Center for Missing and Abused Children, undated), while in the UK, an estimated 850,000 unwanted sexual approaches were made to children in 2006 alone (Fafinski, 2007). In some recent cases, predators used communication technologies to lure teenagers from their homes in the belief they were meeting someone their own age. This vulnerability has been exposed in the most extreme cases where teenagers have been raped and murdered by Internet predators in Australia (Breen, 2010) and in the UK (Carter, 2010). As early as 2000, internet-initiated rape comprised an estimated 7 per cent of all statutory rapes in the USA (Wolak *et al.*, 2008).

Another cause for anxiety among homeowning parents is the use of social networking by children to spread news of parties. In a few cases, so-called 'swarming' has occurred with invasions by online 'friends' leaving property owners picking over the destroyed shells of their homes. One British mother, whose daughter's party details were spread through messages on Facebook and via a Bluetooth alert, described the result as 'an absolute horror show', with the house overrun and the residents rescued by police (Pugh, 2008). Sixteen-year-old Australian Corey Delaney organised a house party in 2008 by advertising the venue on MySpace, which resulted in around 500 attendees and damage estimated at AU$20,000. This new type of risk to the home has been seized upon by the media to ratchet up the fears of homeowners, particularly following the stabbing of a teenager by gatecrashers at a house party in Sydney in 2011 (*Daily Telegraph*, Sydney, 2011). The press coverage in Australia highlights the transmission of homeowner anxiety about such 'flashmob' behaviour (Rheingold, 2002) through the media and by official agencies of social order. Standard police advice to homeowners is now that they should register parties in advance, put private security guards on the doors and prevent party invitations being issued via text message or social media.

Achieving privacy is made even more difficult these days as mobile phones and other everyday technological gadgets present a risk, particularly to celebrities. Pictures can be taken instantly and salacious gossip tweeted or texted around the world. Using the law to protect privacy has been shown to be counter-productive in what has become known as 'the Streisand effect'. This was named after Barbra Streisand who brought a lawsuit in 2003 to suppress publication of aerial photographs of her Malibu home, but by doing so drew public attention to the photograph, which was then downloaded almost half a million times. That privacy argument has been lost, and details of celebrity homes can now be easily accessed online. Almost inevitably, bringing the real and cyber worlds together has led to incidents such as the series of burglaries that took place in 2009, when jewellery, designer clothes and accessories worth more than $3 million were stolen from the Los Angeles homes of Lindsay Lohan, Paris Hilton and Orlando Bloom, among others. The celebrity victims owned so many possessions, they took time to notice that homes had been invaded and property stolen (O'Hagan, 2013). The perpetrators were a gang of five teenagers whose raids were planned by careful research in celebrity magazines and gossip websites, where they

gleaned details of appearance schedules, together with photographs and
Internet satellite maps of their victims' homes (Gardner, 2009). Dubbed
'The Bling Ring' by the *Los Angeles Times*, the gang also appeared on a
reality TV show. This bizarre example of art mirroring life mirroring
art has been exploited to the full, generating a book written by a *Vanity
Fair* journalist originally sent to report on the story, which in turn
formed the basis of a film directed by Sofia Coppola (Sales, 2013).

This risk also extends to less wealthy homes in the age of Google
Maps. The maps and street views now available allow criminals remote
'surveillance' of potential targets. A number of sources can be assembled
at leisure to determine hot targets, the best points of access and escape,
and likely rewards (O'Donnell, undated). The popular British newspaper
the *Daily Mail* described Google Street View as a 'burglars charter' when
it was first introduced (Derbyshire and Martin, 2008), and this was
borne out when a man accused of multiple burglaries in gated communities around Nevada told the US police that he and his accomplice
used Google Maps to identify and then target affluent enclaves (Hildebrand, 2010). Concerns about electronic surveillance and mapping have
given rise to extraordinary clashes between data providers and households. In Broughton, near Milton Keynes in the UK, a number of villagers gathered when they realised that Google's 'roving eye' car was
entering the area. The villagers reportedly formed a human chain to
turn away the car. In an ironic turn of events, news crews then raced
to the village to take pictures and broadcast images of the village to the
rest of the country (Barnett and Beaumont, 2010).

Conclusion

The human chain of villagers turning away the Google van must be
one of the more unusual examples of rare collective action by defensive
home owners. However, a communal electronic form of Neighbourhood Watch is available whereby homeowners install CCTV cameras
and monitor them together (Blake, 2011) and groups of activist homeowners sometimes band together in attempts to control further neighbourhood development to maintain their own property values. But
usually, as we have seen in this chapter, risks to the contemporary home
are perceived, experienced and guarded against at the individual level.
The ways the home may be disturbed or threatened are complex and
multiple, but are also subject to continuous evolution particularly as

information technologies advance. The home no longer represents an escape from surveillance. The association of the home with security, control, privacy and status, especially when owned rather than rented, has been partially compromised by the range of these diverse external risks. Of course, as we have seen, the reaction to these threats is an emphatically defensive posture, either through architecture, technology or the direct actions of owners. We have seen how fear and risks may be amplified by media coverage, and the next chapter further develops these themes.

5

Fear, crime and the home

The apathy of Sunday lay upon the streets. Houses were closed, with-drawn. 'They don't know,' he thought, 'those people inside, how one gesture of mine, now, at this minute, might alter their world. A knock on the door, and someone answers – a woman yawning, an old man in carpet slippers, a child sent by its parents in irritation; and according to what I will, what I decide, their whole future will be decided. Faces smashed in. Sudden murder. Theft. Fire.' It was as simple as that. (Du Maurier, 1959: 10)

The private home offers a fundamental vantage point; from its windows and screens we estimate a variety of risks and bear witness to a range of events that may trouble us or shape our domestic routines. One key example of such worry can be found in the ways in which a fear of crime, more specifically the possibility of burglary and invasion, generate defensive repertoires set in motion to protect the home and those inside it – locking windows and doors, checking outside and perhaps listening during wakeful moments in the night. These are neither illogical or exaggerated responses to potential risk – police agencies, among others, often advise that we should engage in these routines to stay safe and secure in our own homes. Yet despite this we may question the degree to which such worries are functional and whether they come to enforce a sense of lock-down or retreat into domestic space in the face of over-estimations of risk to ourselves and our households. In this chapter we consider these themes of fear and protection in detail.

   As Du Maurier's unsettling short story, quoted above, indicates it is often the possibility, however remote, of random or violent intrusion that lies at the heart of concern about the protection of the home.

Many people fear burglary and the possible terror of encountering an intruder in their home. We start here from these concerns before considering the wider politics and economics of responses to fear. In this context we argue that the home is a critical locus from which we need to understand the development of cultures in which risk has become both overstated and an organising feature of contemporary social life (Furedi, 2005). Ironically, and as the starting point for this book, we can observe how fear operates particularly for those who are most insulated from potential risks (affluent homeowners who are least at risk of burglary) or whose displays of prestige speak of such anxiety in the form of emphatic boundaries and gates that set them apart from everyday social contact. Our analysis here continues to develop some of the themes we have already explored – corporate incentives to unsettle and thus benefit from the sale of various security systems, governments looking to expand criminal justice mandates and political capital, to say nothing of the overwhelming prevalence of crime stories within media narratives.

For governments in particular the project to achieve extending forms of control and criminal justice functions is achieved through a disproportionate emphasis on crime (Melossi, 2008), rather than a concern with victims as such. It is crime that must be faced-down as a threat while generally paying less attention to the social origins and forces which generate these risks. Such arguments, also developed by Simon (2007) in the notion of 'governing through crime', offer useful frameworks through which we can consider the place of defensive homeowners. They are largely co-opted into the project of market-oriented governance which appears to guarantee personal gain while reducing its functional capacity to provide and support various systems of social and community security. This section of the population is in many ways compliant in a politics of work in which mortgages and other forms of credit must be serviced, they submit to crime and disorder agendas that extend their focus to risky others and national outsiders and, as we argued earlier, identify the home fundamentally as a tradeable asset that can be used to develop personal fortunes that enable reduced dependence on state and community supports. Seen in this way the home is, for many people, a methodology for achieving security and autonomy that is aligned with projects of statecraft and economic governance. It is the means, or the perceived means at least, by which the self and household hope to achieve a sense of security and independence. This

5.1   Steel gates and CCTV systems, London

position, between the state and household, is further 'braided', or inter-twined, with pro-market or neoliberal value systems.

We can elaborate these connections between governments, markets, homes and homeowners further by delineating this complex set of relationships as a kind of patchwork or archipelago (a tessellated forma-tion) of defended homes. These physical spaces are linked to prevailing ideological constructions of the home as defended market goods that facilitate an empowered and often aggressive form of domestic sover-eignty. This positionality has been privileged by successive governments, regardless of their political stripe, in which the autonomy, power and control of homeowners over domestic space is presumed, valued and courted.

Of course the impression of domestic sovereigns belies the often more illusory and ephemeral nature of such control. Simon (2007), for one, contends that one result of an emphasis on crime by government has been the production of what he calls crime-centred families. These domestic units operate as highly risk-aware household units, influenced by media representations of crime and the sense of the home as an investment that may be damaged or devalued by higher crime localities and other risks. Crime-centred families thus navigate a risky world via residential choices that are used as a form of risk management, or crime control. Here, seen through the lens of active private households, the sanctity of home life comes to feel increasingly neglected by traditional forms of state protection. Dangerous areas and risky people, as well as traditional concerns with the quality of services and other locational factors, form key elements of the management of domestic life and strategies for maintaining the integrity and security of the home more broadly, such as the installation of security systems. Developing these ideas, in this chapter we compile research data on crime, risk and fear and query the extent to which the domestic home has become a place of risk and violence. We also ask how these concerns relate to the changing uses, designs and strategies of the home more broadly and they tell us of a more emphatically aggressive stance in relation to such perceived risks.

Fear and the home

Burglary is in many ways a significant crime because the potential loss of possessions is only one strand in the wider story of its impact on those it affects. Burglary also generates a daily sense of risk and unsettling prospect, while its actual occurrence generates profound psychological impacts of fear, anger and the additional worry of the re-occurrence of an invasion of a private, secure and protecting domain (Mawby, 2013). The loss of possessions may generate an economic cost but, more pertinently, is the damaging of personal or familial identity (Chapman, 1999) that generates deep feelings of resentment and sadness. We have argued that social anxiety, inequality and profound economic changes work through the housing tenure relationships to produce a defensive and physically bolstered mode of domestic life. Here the metaphor of home as fortress can be used to invoke a mentality as well as more traditional physical elements of 'target hardening' and designs implemented by owners to other locales (Helsley and Strange, 1999). These processes are put in place in part because they have been shown to be effective (Mawby and Walklate, 1997) rather than simply being for show or ineffectual attempts at risk management. Certainly the widely observed decline in crime since the mid-1990s in Western countries can be linked in part to these practices. Yet, for many people, the navigation of contemporary life is no less fraught with anxiety and we should recognise the validity of these emotions which remain only loosely connected with statistics that suggest reductions in certain kinds of risk. As the editor of *Good Housekeeping* commented in 2007:

> Everybody has the right to feel safe in their own home and neighbour-hood. Maybe the Government are right and our chances of being the victim of crime are at a 25-year low, but this statistic is unlikely to ring true with the many people who have felt threatened on the street, forced to avoid certain areas, or frightened into keeping a weapon by their bed. There is clearly a rising culture of fear in our society and this needs to be addressed.

As realist criminology has continued to suggest, declining crime rates have not generated feelings of security within populations characterised by pockets of social distress, continuing risks of criminality (particularly for the poorest) and media systems focusing on extreme crimes which generate genuine anxieties (Hall and Winlow, 2013). In this context home ownership may offer a potentially effective method of achieving agency over particular kinds of risk to the home. For one thing, having the choice of homes on a market can be used to exercise choice over where to live, in what type of home and the lure of escaping to what are often perceived to be low-crime suburban areas (Fogelson, 2007), with other additional investments in home security also available as a route to greater security. Here the role of the state is understood by homeowners more as the guarantor of a favourable economic and policy context than as a sovereign acting to control crime directly. Here the state appears to have divested its roles and commitments around community safety and policing and instead focuses on more immediate mechanisms by which market privilege can be translated into private safety strategies for more privileged groups.

There is of course a long history to the politics and political economy of home ownership (see Chapter 2 this volume; Atkinson and Jacobs, 2016) but it seems increasingly clear that rising material inequality and social atomisation, generated by contemporary labour market conditions, has driven declining patterns of social association and mutuality (Winlow and Hall, 2013). In combination these processes have had the effect of installing private actors into key roles that help to fill the vacuum generated by the exit of the state yet who act in an unequal system in which not all have the resources to participate (Hope, 2000). The kind of jungle rules generated by this partial exit of the state from core security functions, emblematically referenced in private, rapid and armed response security systems, can be seen as an important factor that helps to explain the transition to fortress homes and neighbourhoods.

The kinds of fear we are discussing here can be placed into distinct streams of experience. Farrall *et al.* (2009) suggest two responses. The first relates to residents of high crime areas who have extensive direct and indirect experience of victimisation, for whom fear has tended to present itself as concrete episodes of worry. The second group are those living in more protected areas and whose experience of crime is less frequent, this group are less concerned about local incivilities or neighbourhood stability; 'fear' for this group appears more as a kind of 'diffuse anxiety'. Farrall concludes that fear of crime operates less as an irrational and misplaced impression of the scale of crime and more as a general barometer of social cohesion and moral consensus in society. Of course these latter contexts are themselves shaped by ideological and policy commitments, to austerity, markets and private institutions, which have led to modified responses by individuals and households.

Burglary generates anxieties and concerns that are particularly enduring, despite more than a decade of decreases in the prevalence of such crimes. A singular quality of burglary that sets it apart from other crimes is its capacity to make households feel unsafe and anxious 'all of the time' or 'some of the time' when compared with other common types of crime such as car theft, vandalism or assault (Ditton *et al.*, 1999). Thus the generalised anxiety that something 'could' happen, even in lower crime areas where risks are diminished, cannot be fully eradicated.

These reflections on the links between politics, inequality and the security of the self and home can of course be linked to the view held by some that fear of crime is a feature of societies where the general influence of normative consensus and agreements have fragmented

(Furedi, 2005), often in periods of rapid social change. Thus anxiety about local events and problems finds its wider expression in discussions about crime, and feelings of insecurity that raise suspicions of social others more generally. For Furedi, these perceptions may become intensified in national contexts where forms of social isolation and individualisation have become more embedded. To the extent that domestic fortresses appear as hermetically sealed units marked by social privatism and consumption practices, this thesis seems helpful in explaining the increasingly aggressive and defensive responses enacted by the affluent.

In becoming more like the proverbial castle of English law, the home presents us with an increasingly concrete manifestation of our fears, intertwined with ambitions for prestige and personal display. The kind of home produced by these conditions signals a paradoxical combination of refuge, control and status on the one hand, and an architecture of fear (Ellin, 1997) on the other. Following this line of thinking, Lucia Zedner (2003) has suggested that demands for security are essentially never-ending; there is a feedback effect between the security provisions we make, such as burglar alarms, toughened glass and so on, and the

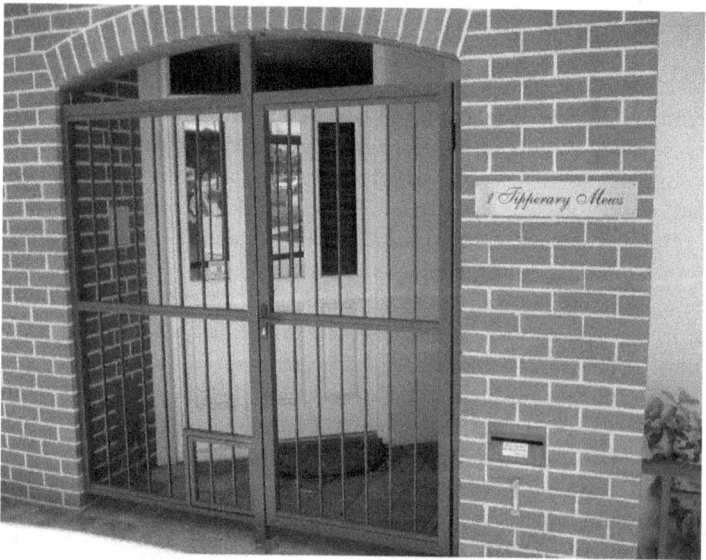

5.2 Locked grille over front door, Australia

way that these concrete measures remind us of our relative vulnerability. Repertoires of personal security in urban settings suggest increasingly cautious engagements with public spaces and areas seen as hazardous, with retreats back to fortress-like neighbourhoods or homes in suburban areas perceived to offer greater security or distance from the sources of risks (Atkinson, 2015). These conditions appear to generate a 'perfect storm' of social forces that shape emotional responses more attuned to worry about insecurity (Farrall *et al.*, 2009). In a context of ongoing economic crisis and reductions in social cohesion these social conditions appear to generate a worrisome backdrop for the private home as a key physical and psychical bulwark for anxious social subjects seeking to detach themselves from the social order.

Fear of crime, viewed from the domestic context, has been captured in a number of national survey instruments. In general we find that those living in deprived areas and rented housing experience the highest level of fear. These patterns are not particularly surprising, but the housing tenure of victims of burglary also differs markedly. Data from the Crime Survey for England and Wales of 2011 shows that while around one in fifty homeowners are burgled each year (1.7 per cent), for renters the figure is much higher – almost one in twenty for social renters (4.2 per cent) and 3.7 per cent for private renters. In this context, and we return to this point in the next chapter, the use of defensive measures like burglar alarms, stronger locks and double glazed windows are incentivised for homeowners, whereas tenants cannot install them in rented homes (Mawby, 2013). Research also shows that people in houses in wealthy areas feel safest, while young people, Black and Asian households feel most worried (Home Office, 2009a). Despite these socially selective impacts the number of people who feel that their own fear of crime has a moderate or high impact on their quality of life is more than a third (35 per cent). Fear of crime as measured by the Crime Survey for England and Wales of 2014 shows that almost two-thirds (61 per cent) believe that crime has risen across the country in the past few years (despite data showing that both recorded and self-reported measures of burglary and crime generally have declined) and almost a third (32 per cent) feel it had risen in their own locality. The tenure breakdown of fear of burglary specifically is interesting in revealing that around one in ten owners have a particular fear of burglary, one in six social renters (15 per cent) and one in ten (10 per cent) private renters. This suggests that the relationship between tenure and fear of crime, relative to the risks of burglary for each tenure, does not conveniently map onto these differences of position.

One of the most important indicators of prevailing levels of crime can be identified through those reporting feeling unsafe, even while in their own homes. In the UK, British Crime Survey data shows that over recent decades, such fear has declined from around 11 per cent of people in 1988 to 6.8 per cent in 2008. In Australia, around one in six (15 per cent) feel unsafe or very unsafe in their homes, though many more females are in this group (22 per cent female to 8 per cent male) (Australian Bureau of Statistics, 2012) and around a third of Australians feel that house break-ins are a problem in their neighbourhood (this rises to 40 per cent in Western Australia, Australian Bureau of Statistics, 2005). These figures suggest that there is something of a disconnect between declining levels of burglary risk while fear of intrusion and loss remain largely intact in many locations and for many groups, adding credence to the sense that the features of a culture of fear offer an enduring influence over social anxieties.

How effective are the defensive techniques employed in the homes we described in the previous chapter? Nearly two-thirds (62 per cent) of those households burgled in the UK *had* already installed additional security measures, though 97 per cent of those households not burgled had installed some security devices. Overall, the British Crime Survey showed that households with no home security measures were more than ten times as likely to have been victims of burglary than those with security measures like deadlocks on doors (25.0 per cent compared with 2.3 per cent). A quarter of burglary victims had a burglar alarm, 38 per cent had deadlocks installed, and over a third (36 per cent) had window locks. This suggests that technologies of this kind are essential, though by no means totally effective in reducing the risk of victimisation. Despite this it is still widely recognised that the use of basic measures including window locks and burglar alarms have been effective in reducing overall levels of burglary.

Burglary and invasion

William Blackstone wrote two hundred and fifty years ago that:

> nocturnal housebreaking [is] a very heinous offence: not only because of the abundant terror that it naturally carries with it, but also as it is a

forcible invasion and disturbance of that right of habitation … at the dead of night; when all the creation, except beasts of prey, are at rest; when sleep has disarmed the owner, and rendered his castle defenceless. (Blackstone, 1768: 223–228)

Though the language appears archaic we can still recognise and understand the strength of indignation combined with dread and anger at the invasion of the private home. Contemporary language used to describe the act of stealing objects from another's home varies slightly between countries. In Australia, the term that tends to be used is break-in; in the UK and USA, the term used is burglary, though the substantive meaning remains the same. When analyzing data on burglary it is important to distinguish between actual, successful thefts and attempts at breaking-in, and to demarcate between thefts from residential buildings and other, usually commercial or external, properties. Research on burglary (such as Mawby and Walklate, 1997) shows that perpetrators are highly attuned to the vulnerability of particular targets. Thus the defence of the home is dramatically linked to broader social inequalities that drive acquisitive crime, as interviews with burglars suggest (Wright and Decker, 1994). Certainly the risk of burglary is much more focused on those with few resources or incentives to defend their homes, as we show later in this chapter. The common pattern of predation on those with little by those with little has not, however, seemed to reduce anxieties about home invasion among higher income groups. The affluent remain motivated to abandon more open forms of neighbourhood for gated communities (Low, 2003). Their fortress homes function both as marks of distinction and as outward representations of hostility to the risks of burglary and social contact more generally.

Burglary is a significant crime in both material and emotional terms. In the USA, FBI data shows victims of burglary lost an estimated $4.6 billion in property in 2010 while estimates of the cost to the economy of burglary in the UK were estimated at around £4.1bn (Institute for Economics and Peace, 2013). Both this cost and material loss belie a much more important element of the occurrence of burglary: its profound and enduring emotional impact on victims, but also the fear of its occurrence in those who may not yet have been touched by the crime (Maguire 1980; Mawby and Walklate, 1997). Government surveys show that victims of burglary primarily experience a sense of anger, then shock, as well as more generalised worry about sleeping at night.

While the UK is often identified as a low crime society, data on burglary victimisation tells us that the UK experiences one of the highest levels of burglary victimisation of Western nations or of the 'advanced' economies, albeit one which has, as with others, declined markedly since the mid-1990s. The annual rate of burglary for the three countries that form our predominant focus can be given as follows: there were 230 burglaries per 10,000 people in the USA (previously the high was of 630 per 10,000 in 1994), 230 per 10,000 in the UK (in 2014) (Office for National Statistics, 2015b) and around 6.5 per 10,000 in Australia (Australian Bureau of Statistics, 2015). In terms of the basic volume of such crimes, there were 1.1m domestic burglaries in the USA (FBI data for 2015), 564,000 burglaries in the UK (Office for National Statistics, 2015b) and 196,000 break-ins for Australia (ABS, 2015). In the UK, police recorded data shows that burglary forms around a tenth of all recorded crime, with 2.4 per cent of people burglary victims in 2007–08 (this compares with 3.2 per cent for violent crime or 6.4 per cent for theft from vehicle).

National figures mask significant variation in the rates of burglary across states and their respective cities. For example, in the USA, New Mexico has the highest rate of burglary (87 per 10,000), and the FBI data shows that other southern and poorer states generally rank higher than the average. Notably, the New York metropolitan statistical area (which includes White Plains and Wayne counties) has one of the lowest rates at 27 per 10,000 (FBI, undated), the third lowest figure for the USA (other cities in the USA had quite divergent rates, such as Miami with 109; San Diego 56; Los Angeles 55),

In the UK, USA and Australia, the geography, tenure and type of house most at risk of burglary are similar. As well as homes in poorer areas (the 20 per cent most deprived areas in England had a rate of 368 burglaries per 10,000 households compared with 232 in 2013, Office for National Statistics 2015), for flats and rented accommodation risk is increased by living in a household with a single adult and children, with a young head of household, or if the occupants are of Asian origin. In the USA, the main groups identified as at risk of victimisation are central city residents, the young, persons with higher or lower income than average, nonwhites, and people regularly absent from home (British Crime Survey data 2007/8; Cohen and Cantor, 1981). In Australia, rented homes registered significantly higher break-in victimisation rates (4.7 per cent) than homes that were owned (2.9 per cent), which closely follows the British pattern (Australian Bureau of Statistics, 2015). This data portrays the pattern and prevalence of victimisation within and between national contexts as highly dependent on the social conditions of the time and the physical attributes of the home itself. In the USA, property crime occurs more often to those living in rented property. In the UK there were notable differences in the risk of burglary depending on where one lives in relation to overall levels of social deprivation. Despite these diverging risk patterns, shaped by geography, tenure and deprivation, public policy debates about the risks to the home continue to depict burglary as a significant risk, often without insight into the social and tenurial variabilities that drive differences in vulnerability to this form of crime. Thus, as Hope argues, the rich and poor have what he terms different risk positions (2001) in relation to this kind of crime that are embedded in the broader inequalities of capitalist economies.

National level data on burglary patterns masks wide variations in the distribution of victimisation between urban and rural areas, house types and social geographies. For example, data indicates that London had a burglary rate of 4.5 per cent (nearly one in twenty households are broken into each year), which was second out of 17 national capitals and second only to Istanbul at 4.6 per cent of households (International Crime and Victimisation Survey, dataset, 2005). Certainly, London leads the UK in terms of fear of crime, and yet assumptions about the incidence of such crimes are not borne out in reality – in particular, the burglary rate reported for New York was only 1.9 per cent, close to Sydney's rate of 2.2 per cent (van Dijk *et al.*, 2008), a point we return to later. Within the UK, London does not have the highest statistical risk of burglary at 130 per 10,000 households; instead, the highest was Nottingham at 180 per 10,000 (West Yorkshire and Manchester, both heavily urbanised and in general, socially deprived cities, also feature highly).

Historically, patterns of burglary rose in the post-war period, which is particularly evident in the national data for the USA and UK. Yet this also masks particular features and changes. For example, British rates of burglary are now roughly what they were in the early 1980s after reaching a peak in the mid-1990s and similar patterns can be detected in the long-running series data kept by the US Department of Justice. Work on the activities of burglars and the particular kinds of properties they target bears out some of the key theoretical treatments of increased crime in the post-war period, routine activity theory (Cohen and

Felson, 1979). This posited that much crime was predicated on the confluence of three critical factors: motivated offenders, suitable targets and absence of capable guardians.

Some analysts have argued that a number of factors explain the broader post-war pattern of property crime. For example, Hope (2001) suggests that the increasing pattern of women at work meant that homes were left 'unguarded' in ways that had previously been uncommon. Thus, a major tenet of routine activity theory, the absence of a capable guardian, became an increasingly common feature of the residential landscape. Hope also argued that rising affluence and the growth of valuable and potentially mobile consumer products (such as televisions that could easily and quickly be carried away) meant that more homes were worth more as targets. This point has changed quite dramatically in recent years with the reduction in the relative resale value of many of these products and their increased portability. Writing recently, James Treadwell has argued that many potential burglars have turned to other, more profitable avenues, notably online sales of illicit goods, as a result of these technological changes and the increased fortification of homes (Treadwell, 2011).

It is worth bearing in mind that despite real declines in burglary rates, contemporary rates of burglary in the West are high compared with the post-war period and have only declined from their peaks in the mid-1990s. Similarly, we need to be aware that for certain groups and locations, the risks of both victimisation and repeated forms of intrusion remain very important concerns and that these are often the consequence of lower household resources. Further, it is critical to recognise that the bulk of fortification practices, insurance options and defensive practices are deployed by those with most resources (Wright and Decker, 1994).

Data on British burglaries allows us to see the proportion of instances of contact with the burglars themselves – perhaps the greatest domestic terror. In just over half (53 per cent) the burglaries, the occupants were at home as it transpired (Home Office, 2013), though half of these householders (20 per cent) were unaware they were being burgled (8 per cent were at home and aware of the intrusion, but did not see the offender). In a quarter of all burglaries reported in this national survey, a quarter (25 per cent) of residents actually came into contact with or saw the intruder. Whether this figure is low or high is debatable. Within this group of victims, just over a third (38 per cent) experienced force or the use of violence (in half of such contacts, neither force nor violence was used). We can come to the broad conclusion that around 8 per cent of all UK burglary victims experience some degree of force or violence.

Repeat victimisation is a pivotal problem; in the UK, around 15 per cent of households are burgled more than once (Home Office, 2009a), often within a few weeks of the initial burglary because the perpetrator assumes that insurance claims will have been made and items of value replaced. This form of victimisation often reflects social geographies, applying particularly to low security areas. Repeat victimisation was recorded at a low of 13 per cent in 1981 and high of 20 per cent in 1999 (Home Office, 2009a). This problem has been used to improve policy interventions for addressing the profound vulnerabilities faced by groups in certain localities and income brackets much less able to defend their own homes. These issues force us to reconsider the important implications of Oscar Newman's work on defensible space, also influential in funding for target-hardening projects in the USA and UK. For example, in the UK, the Kirkholt project successfully reduced burglary to 25 per cent of its initial level by target hardening to prevent repeat instances (Pease, 1991). This was an area of public housing where burglary levels were *double* that for housing types at *high* risk nationally (homes were most vulnerable up to six weeks after first being burgled).

Fear and protection in gated communities

Where should we place the new emphasis on gated homes and communities within these discussions of domestic burglary and fear of intrusion and criminality? As discussed in Chapter 8, gating, of homes and neighbourhoods, has become a significant strategy in adding prestige to developments while offering the promise of a more or less crime-free neighbourhood. While fear of an aggressor tends to be directed at some distant other, someone that is not of the same community or locality, gating builds on this logic and places additional emphasis on the notion of a boundary between those inside the community (the good) and those outside (unknown/bad). However, such distinctions become increasingly difficult to sustain as gated communities grow in size and demographic diversity (Wilson-Doenges, 2000). Recent evidence shows that the social composition of such spaces is by no means restricted to the affluent (Plaut, 2011) – the increasing impression generated by recent US research is of an extending and fortified version of suburbia (Vesselinov and Le Goix, 2012). It now seems that the racial and tenurial diversity of these sites, to say nothing of their significant size in many cases, means that they appear to be evolving into something more akin to micro-societies or microcosms of much of the wider US urban fabric (Plaut, 2011). These shifts offer the possibility of anxiety being redirected and projected towards neighbours and community members, not least in relation toward the often bored youth within such spaces (Vesselinov *et al.*, 2007). The permeability of such spaces is also highlighted by the concerns of some residents towards their service staff and their potential connection to spaces seen as deprived and containing what are seen as lurking and potentially predatory criminal inhabitants (Maher, 2003). Not only are low-paid service workers the potential source of anxiety, those who guard and secure gated compounds have occasionally been the source of problems for residents (Atkinson and Smith, 2012) with at least one documented case of a guard killing the resident of a community in an unprovoked homicide.

To what extent can the risks of urban life be mitigated by living in a gated community? Research on this question has suggested that crime rates are no lower in gated to non-gated neighbourhoods when looked at in terms of similar socio-economic profiles (Wilson-Doenges, 2000). This study examined sense of community, perceived safety and crime rates in two high-income and two low-income areas in Newport Beach, California. In each income bracket both a gated and non-gated community were selected using census data and both of the low-income areas were public housing projects. Each pair of neighbourhoods were selected to have similar age, population density, size and housing profiles so that a range of hypotheses could be tested around perceived safety, community safety and actual crime rates. Crime data was collected for each community from the relevant police department including homicide, rape, burglary and car theft. The work showed there was no significant difference in perceived safety and actual crime rates between the high-income neighbourhoods (gated and non-gated). Between the low-income gated and non-gated communities there was also no difference in crime rates and no significant difference in sense of community and perceived safety.

Recent work on burglary in gated communities offers further evidence of a protective effect, albeit limited, from living in a gated

5.3 Entrance to gated community, Surrey

community (Addington and Rennison, 2015). The researchers considered two possible hypotheses. First, that gated communities might increase crime (by containing bored teenagers, or offering potentially higher rewards to the burglar). Second, that crime would be lower due to the presence of guardians and technologies that would protect residents from burglary. In their research they found that while around 1.3 per cent of households overall were burgled in the most recent year this was reduced to 1 per cent for the population of gated households. Addington and Rennison raise several questions about the effectiveness of gating due to the increasing diversity of populations inside gated communities while a further risk factor is that potential victims may be effectively contained or locked in with potential aggressors.

A misguided orientation or belief in finding total security appears to be amplified and misdirected by narratives around crime and harm within the media. Yet research to date indicates that residents of gated developments are not receiving substantial dividends, as we have seen, either in terms of perceptions (Low, 2003) or real rates of crime (Addington and Rennison, 2015). Property developers who locate the risk of violence in external, poorer and socially marginal communities offer problematic identifications of the roots of potential danger. In an analysis of all news reports over a ten year period Atkinson and Smith (2012) found more than fifty documented cases of homicides within US gated communities. It seems that three possible types of homicide in gated communities can be pinpointed – firstly intimate or domestic homicide which formed the bulk of cases (31 cases), community homicides in which the assailant was someone who lived in the same gated community (5 cases) and what can be termed 'breach' homicide in which the prototypical fear of an invasion of the home by someone from outside the walls or gates was responsible (21 cases), either by someone known to a resident or worker in the community (13 of the 21) or from entry by an unknown aggressor (8 of the 21 cases). It seems likely that increasing cases within such localities may end in tainting the premium derived from the apparent additional security of gated communities or feed the further fortification of homes within them to further escape the potential risks that may be found there. In any case, there remains the possibility that gating and other kinds of domestic and community design may facilitate or conceal forms of domestic and community violence. Certainly it appears that media narratives and developer pitches about the sanctity of high-income neighbourhood life close the social imagination to the idea that violence may indeed come from within the community or home itself.

The political economy of fear

Mass home ownership was supposed to herald the realisation of dreams of personal wealth, a haven for family life and a place of personal privacy and expression, yet 'fear is a larger part of our symbolic landscape at a time when the social terrain is comparatively routine, predictable and safe' (Altheide, 2002: 197). This conundrum has been addressed from a range of different viewpoints, with the broad conclusion that a culture or politics of fear has developed that has been conducive to expansionist visions for criminal justice and military systems (Melossi, 2008). Here these debates are linked specifically to the home, exploring why fear associated with threats to the home energises political and cultural debates so markedly. Turning first to such broader forces, the effects of neoliberal government and of a greater awareness of risk go some way to explaining the pervasive 'newly emphatic, overreaching concern with control and the urgency with which we segregate, fortify, and exclude' (Garland, 2001: 194).

Awareness of risk by no means ensures freedom from anxiety; for many, the release that might have been offered by a position of relative affluence, in terms of reductions in need and increased security, has in fact been met by a renewed anxiety, not least that privilege may be lost. As Garland suggests: 'For some, the crime problem has become a source of anxiety and frustration; an urgent daily reminder of the need to impose control, to take care, to secure oneself and one's family against the changes of the modern world' (Garland, 2001: 155). Certainly, governments have had to recognise that fear of crime is an issue of social concern that has to be taken as seriously as crime prevention and reduction. However, deeper treatments of these issues suggest that government and media systems are both implicated in generating fearful subjects whose concerns render them compliant citizens and political actors as potential saviours to these problems (Body-Gendrot, 2011).

The novelty of these mechanisms should not however be overstated. For many years it has been acknowledged that a failure to address fear of crime, particularly in relation to the home, has wider consequences. As Newman once suggested in his treatments of the relationship between housing design and crime: 'The home and its environs must be felt secure, or the very fabric of society comes under threat' (Newman, 1972: 51). A number of factors, perhaps most significantly the withdrawal of the state (also critically, in relation to policing), have generated a loss of confidence by citizens that the state will protect homes and property (Body-Gendrot, 2011). These concerns have been exacerbated by a gradual reduction in citizens' trust in the notion that forces of law and order might offer a less risky society. In place of that trust has grown an identification with the victims of crime, hence, the particular and popular support for the idea that homeowners should have a right to kill or incapacitate intruders (discussed in Chapter 7). Particular vitriol is reserved for enemies of the private home, both because of the obvious fear and anger generated by such invasions but also because of the wider sense that such risks are not faced down by public agencies (and despite popular support for low tax regimes that are implicated in generating such potential neglect by policing agencies).

In the competition to be tough on crime that emerged as part of the neoliberal agenda, misrepresentations in the media often go uncorrected if they suit political purposes. But is the media also responsible for heightening and distorting our fears and perceptions concerning the risks of being crime victims, as some have suggested (Fowler, 1991).

5.4 Target-hardened house, London

There are several strands to this complex question. For example, has the crime content of newspapers, TV programmes and other news outlets increased over recent decades? Are reports of particularly violent crimes now disproportionately covered in the media? Has the manner of crime reporting changed? What do major terrorist events do for the broader understanding of personal risk and fear more generally? In considering these questions we should note the difficulty of establishing a causal relationship between growing fear of crime and media consumption – in other words: 'do media crime stories cause fearfulness, or do more fearful people read or watch more?' (Reiner *et al.*, 2000). A UK survey in 2008 found that there was almost unanimous agreement among the

2,000 respondents that crime had increased over the previous two years. When asked to explain this opinion, 57 per cent said it was because of what they see on television and 48 per cent because of what they read in newspapers. Interestingly, there is also a 'trust gap' between the information and what the respondents believed, particularly where tabloid newspapers were concerned – 60 per cent of respondents had received information from that source, but only 20 per cent trusted its truthfulness (Duffy *et al.*, 2008: 5 and 42). The sense of a phantasmagoria of fleeting images of risk, worry and victimisation raise important questions about how to understand the nature of contemporary fear. In particular a kind of fear bind (the connection between fear of crime and media/political which may distort or exacerbate it) needs to be disentangled from a wider set of processes advancing commercial interests as security is pushed as the necessary or legitimate means by which such fear could be reduced. Social atomisation and individualism have become important social conditions that have fuelled these changing outcomes, leaving owners and renters more broadly adrift within a vacuum of responsibility for their relative safety. Rising social inequality and declining investment in the public realm do not seem likely to presage real reductions in social fear.

Conclusion

Following a path from the Cold War to the current war on terror, we can see a mutation in the kinds of insecurities outside the dual domestic context of home and nation-state. Into our homes are received the anxieties of a new age, relayed and amplified by constant news programming and political calls for action against criminals, outsiders and terrorists. War, gang violence, drug trade-related deaths, violent crime, community 'breakdown', degraded urban environments that promote fear and mistrust generate, in their mediated form on televisions and other monitors, a pervasive imagery that feeds a more general sense of unease. Visions of an external, dilapidated public realm, the space where civic and shared institutions operate and manage, are viewed largely from the home. It is in the home, above all other social spaces, that we witness terror, horror, cataclysm, disaster, decline, upheaval, change and crime. Decaying public housing or litter strewn streets are used on television and Internet news services as the visual signifiers of moral decline, personal danger and violent crime. This wider context is important in understanding the fears of those inside homes and how these fears translate into concrete actions of defence in a world where the assurances of the state, economy and society may feel eroded or ineffectual. More importantly these modes of defence and action operate within an unequal climate of resources and capacities that are focused on housing tenure. Yet it is not only local patterns of fear of disorder driving these conceptions; for writers like Young (2007), this process of 'othering' is also fuelled by macro-social and global changes implicit in capitalism itself. Thus patterns of destabilising and dramatic socio-economic change and pockets of profound, cosseted wealth render poverty and desperation as something spatially separate from and socially alien to the circuits and lifestyles of those secure in their own homes and jobs.

For those on higher incomes living in compounds and enclaves, a major result of anxieties about social difference and the risks presented by the poor has been a deep-seated wrath directed against potential threats to the sanctity of these spaces. An increasing physical retreat by an affluent and home-owning majority is part of a much deeper revolt articulated through the lobbying of political elites and which produces important effects on the management of public spaces and institutions outside the home (as detailed in Chapter 8). These efforts have a vengeful character, directed at the poor and marginal, are coordinated via a proxy war enacted by political actors – punitive welfare systems, the containment of poverty in public housing and the incarceration offered by the criminal justice system. The protected refuges sought by affluent owners thereby appear in ever-sharper relief against the poverty of other places and groups and as a kind of fortified archipelago. Within these conditions the domestic fortress arises as a physical, tenurial and social condition as well as a concrete space from which public faces can be more or less hidden within privileged domestic life and where the potential targets of criminal others can be protected.

6

Technologies of the defended home

If the worn floorboards and beat-up wicker furniture, the lattice and wisteria of the traditional porch have not been universally replaced by the lethal and graceful curlicues of razor ribbon, their place is being taken by the blinking red light of home alarm systems. (Busch, 1999: 113)

In this chapter, we argue that the recent increase in 'defensive technologies' has further turned homes into physical embodiments of negative emotions attuned specifically to home intrusion fears. In the next chapter, we explore homeowners' and the state's responses when defensive technologies fail to prevent intruders gaining access. The focus in this chapter is on architectural and other efforts to fortify the home, and how generalised anxieties translate into architectural motifs, aspects of design and technological features. The term 'technology' is used here to encompass the range of 'technical skills and achievements of a particular time in history, of a civilization or a group of people' (Brookes, 2004). It therefore refers both to the collective skills and achievements in the development of defensive techniques which are now pressed into the service of the individual homeowner, as well as to specific security measures aimed at preventing all kinds of home intrusion.

Many ordinary suburban neighbourhoods today, as much as in gated zones and affluent enclaves, display a remarkably exaggerated use of landscape and design to secure the home and control social access to it. In this chapter we explore the ebb and flow of fortification over time, situating different technologies in their historical contexts. As the great urbanist Spiro Kostof once observed, if we look back to the origins of urban development, we can trace the defensive qualities of many settlements, as well as their ceremonial and social aspects (Kostof, 1991;

Kostof, 1992). Domestic homes through history have displayed variations of architectural motifs connected with castellation and defence, but we suggest that the contemporary home under tessellated neoliberalism manifests particular forms of physical deterrence.

We know that burglary rates tend to be highest in Anglo-Saxon countries so it is not surprising to find higher investment there in home security devices. The widespread adoption of these devices is considered a major factor in the long-term decrease in domestic burglary rates (van Dijk *et al.*, 2008). Some of these measures are new products or scientific advances and others have long histories, so can be described as almost instinctive in their origins. They range from simple physical technologies such as deadlocks, window locks and security chains on doors, to more high-tech and expensive devices such as sensor or timer lights and burglar alarms. Interestingly, the first type of device is more effective in lowering the risk of burglary than the second type (van Dijk *et al.*, 2008). This chapter traces how even some of the more high-tech security solutions echo defensive characteristics of medieval castles.

Seeing history in the present

The modern home is the culmination of patterns of human settlement and construction over millennia, incorporating defensive elements recognisably derived from the very earliest dwellings. Possession of wealth remains important to ensure the hallmarks of home ownership: privacy, control, status. Celebrity responses to risks to the home have influenced the idealisation of ultra-secure home designs, and constant media exposure to the rich and famous – and their homes – affect popular aspirations about ideal architecture and features, which now include defensive technologies.

It is easy to assume today that the built environment is a given, almost natural aspect of our lives. However, we should remember that a crucial survival skill of our prehistoric ancestors was to find a shelter that provided both unimpeded views and a hiding place – the idea of standing one's ground to defend the individual home came later. The view ('prospect') afforded prior warning of an enemy's approach, allowing for flight if it was needed. The hiding place ('refuge') meant a secure retreat from danger. These two basic requirements for a place to build or reside are hardwired into the human brain (Stamps, 2005: 103). We seem to search instinctively for homes well placed to observe other humans or potentially threatening animals ('prospect') and which can provide a hiding place ('refuge') where others cannot see us (Appleton, 1996). Early defensive building techniques were likely to be collective (see for example Parker, 1976), epitomised in the enduring form of the walled city on a hilltop. Today, wherever cost and space are not an issue, deep preferences for homes with unimpeded views of the horizon are reflected in many housing developments. Popular rooftop penthouses and hillside homes come with high prices and social cachet. More everyday suburban communities are also planned to provide defensive sight lines. However, the aim of these newer developments is to eliminate unwanted or risky social contact for individual owners, rather than to facilitate effective collective defence as in previous eras.

The architecture of contemporary, ultra-secure homes tends to two extreme types: these might be termed 'spiky' and 'stealthy', which map onto notions of relatively aggressive or withdrawn designs and aesthetics. The different architectural approaches and styles are thus based respectively on fantasies of impenetrable castellation or the concealed or discreet presence of a refuge, providing retreat to private spaces inaccessible or less visible to others. Spiky architecture sends out a strong message: this building is supremely capable of defence, and an attack is not even worth trying – an architecture of intimidation exemplified in the increasingly visible 'forting-up' of homes and neighbourhoods (Dupuis and Thorns, 2008). The strategically defensive, alternative architecture of inconspicuousness, 'the stealth home' (Davis, 1992: 167) conveys that there is nothing worth pursuing behind a blank and unpretentious facade. In 2005 a residence actually called The Stealth House won the Royal Institute of British Architects' annual design prize, but perhaps the supreme example of stealth architecture is Dennis Hopper's Los Angeles abode, designed as an anonymous bunker with a corrugated-iron facade.

Both spiky and stealth architectural strategies are linked to status, privilege, wealth and tenure, in many cases sharing a sense of physical and social withdrawal, underlined by the ability to exclude unwanted visitors and other dangers. This insulation and sequestration is part of a process that pads already bunker-like spaces even further, with gates,

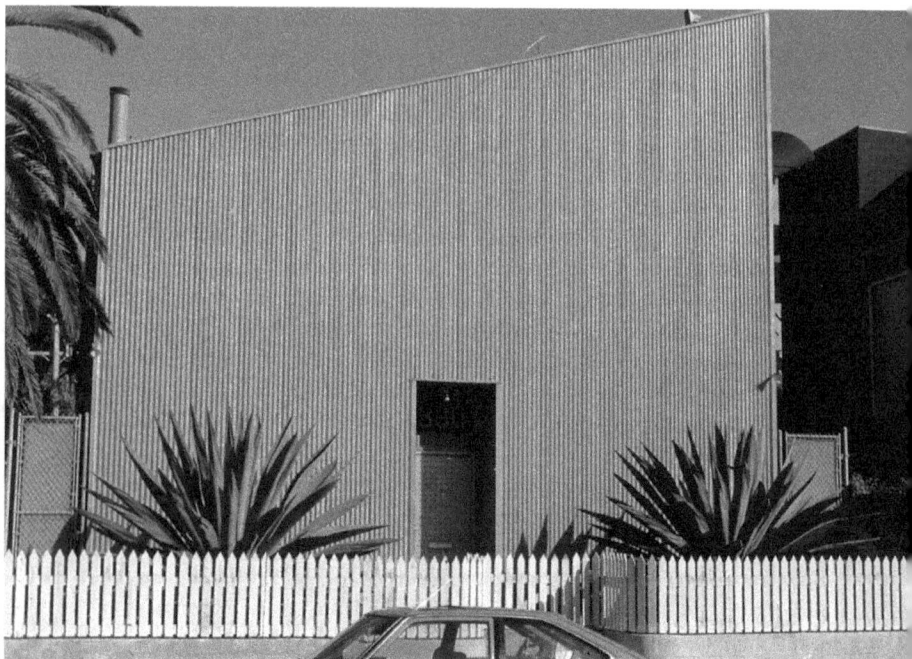

6.1 Bunker home, Los Angeles

guards and exclusive modes of transport, usually at the very top of the property market (Atkinson, 2015). The growth of the private security industry has been driven by what criminologists have identified as an enormous growth in private property (Shearing and Stenning, 1981; Jones and Newburn, 1999), alongside media coverage of the personal security systems of the wealthy, up to and including close personal security details and Hostile Environment Awareness Training for equipping the nanny to foil kidnap attempts (Rose, 2006). This social unease and the strategies to deal with it extend from the home into public space, often negotiated by cars, preferably with tinted windows to prevent the occupants from being 'on show'. Some go further than tinted windows; deluxe armour-plated cars are a status symbol fuelling the growth of this niche market and offering protection from bombs, gunfire and kidnapping (Economist, 2015).

The safest residence is perhaps one which doesn't seem to be there at all. This extreme version of stealth architecture is portrayed by a large and valuable house in Hampstead Heath, London, which conceals beneath the ground its extensive residential accommodation, triple volume living room, gym, home cinema and wine cellar. The agent selling it said, 'all the outside world sees is a subtle, yet beautifully engineered wooden fence' (Jamieson, 2015). This invisibility contrasts with the evidence apparent in most neighbourhoods in the UK, the USA and Australia, of an extensive array of mechanisms to manage the privacy and sanctity of domestic life: well-defined and seemingly impregnable boundaries, wood or metal outer doors, and burglar alarms. There exists a continuum between the technologies now normalised in suburbia and those of wealthier home owners, like the Corbi family, who use their own home in Los Angeles as a show house for prospective customers of their company, Strategically Armored and Fortified Environments (SAFE). In addition to more common defensive strategies, the SAFE house boasts biometric recognition software, earthquake-proof, steel-reinforced concrete caissons below ground, and a smoke system that can billow fog or a disabling and foul-smelling gas to disorient intruders; as Corbi himself says, 'If you saw this stuff in a movie you would think it is all made up' (Brennan, 2013).

Architecture as embodied anxiety

These protective technologies, from miniaturised cameras and closed circuit surveillance systems to panic rooms securely located and braced for lockdown in the event of home invasion, represent an embodiment of worry and fear, but also the logic widely relayed by security analysts that no level of security is too much. Such devices reveal widespread association of these newer, symbolic aspects of home with cultural values, especially the relation of gates with prestige, for example (Duncan and Duncan, 2004). In this environment, defending the home against risks from burglary to natural disasters such as fire is now the responsibility of every homeowner; so, too, is preparing suitable action plans for all occupants of the home if risk becomes reality (Hay, 2006).

The contemporary fortress mentality, as many observers point out, is by no means restricted to 'dangerous' districts, implicit in the idea of home as haven for the working classes over fifty years ago (Rainwater, 1966). Sophisticated surveillance techniques and security devices have

6.2 Watchtower and cameras in Detroit

become widespread and ever more prevalent in the most affluent districts. In terms of physical adaptations for protection and defence, home owners are correct to compare themselves favourably with tenants on the grounds that, as owners they have the incentive to fit such defences. Many new working-class homeowners in Bristol said they could now 'do more' to their homes (Gurney, 1999b: 1714). Mary Douglas (1991) argues that the idea of home begins with imposing order and control on space, while Porteous (1976: 383) observed that 'the average citizen appears to expend more effort personalizing and defending the home than any other level of fixed personal space'. It is not only effort that is expended; higher levels of home defence also cost money, and this generates inequalities in security and exposure that relate in general to income levels, wealth and tenure. These designs and physical measures form the bedrock of the tessellated neoliberal urban system – highlighting an interconnecting archipelago of defended residences that speak as much of prestige and market advantage as they do of a nurturing home environment.

Rykwert considered the growing extent to which homeowners are turning their homes into fortresses as a means of appearing to set themselves against their neighbours, but also transforming their homes into much less homely, perhaps uncanny sites, antagonistic to more traditional cultural interpretations of home. As discussed in Chapter 3, while homes protect and accommodate the bodies and minds of their residents, they can also be places of internal and external insecurities. We further suggest that the communicative power of architecture is not only effectively directed outwards to deter potential risks, but also has an effect on the fears of residents within the home. The drive to add more security and layers of defence can never be enough to ward off anxiety and insecurity all together. This undermines what may be the central promise of domestic life, that the home embodies 'the place of Peace; the shelter, not only from all injury, but from all terror, doubt, and division', as John Ruskin expressed it in an 1860 lecture. However, he continued, 'so far as the anxieties of outer life penetrate into it, and the inconsistently-minded, unknown, unloved, or hostile society of the outer world is allowed by either husband or wife to cross the threshold, *it ceases to be home*' (Ruskin, 2006: 116, emphasis added).

Not only is the home incapable of excluding all the fears and concerns of the outside world, every 'extra lock on the entry door ... makes the world look *more* treacherous and fearsome, and prompts still *more* defensive actions that will add still *more* vigour to the self-propagating capacity of fear' (Bauman 2006: 143, original emphasis). Fear breeds fear, so even if physical withdrawal can be achieved, empirical research suggests that anxieties remain significant even in 'secure' gated communities (Low, 2003). The impossibility of achieving peace of mind through defensive architecture is more bizarrely illustrated by the efforts of Sarah Winchester, wealthy heiress to her deceased husband's fortune, acquired through the patented rifle of the same name. Fearing retribution by the ghosts of those killed by the firearm, Winchester built a 160-room, seven-storey Victorian mansion in California. Yet even this structure was not enough to protect her; Winchester continued to make adaptations. The building work included creating labyrinthine hallways, incorporating false doors and building stairways that reached into ceilings to prevent the angry spirits from finding her. The adaptations and extensions continued until her death in 1922, apparently in the belief that the act of construction might appease the ghosts (Ignoffo, 2010).

More mundane fears cause 12 million Britons to lose sleep, concerned about home security; a quarter of those get out of bed at least once a week to double or even triple-check the door and window locks (Swinton Insurance, 2015). Home insurance is one of the non-negotiable demands made of homeowners in increasingly affluent western societies. Meeting these demands boosts the profits of security companies, whose products hold out the promise of a secure home and are required by insurance companies profiting from fears of home invasion and property loss.

Control, privacy and individualism

When asked to draw a house or a home, western children typically produce the image of a two-storey, detached building with a pitched roof, chimney and fenced garden. This is a version of the English cottage, the image of home taken to the American and Australian colonies. Over time, this nostalgic ideal developed into the aspiration to own a 'single-family house set on its own piece of land, isolated from its neighbour' (Newman, 1972: 3). Concern with privacy has become intricately connected with the control which only property ownership promises to deliver. Now the aspiration is for each household member to 'have a separate room, and even a separate telephone, television, and car, when economically possible. We seek more and more privacy, and feel more and more alienated and lonely as a result' (Slater, 1990: 12). This same privacy is widely recognised by economists as a crucial factor in boosting property prices, along with location, quality of the building itself, and sufficient surrounding space to ensure freedom from noise and other perceived irritations of contemporary life. Certainly, a vista and prospect adds value to the contemporary home. We might call owners of hilltop homes 'lords of all they survey', suggesting both an echo of the ancient need for prospect and the status it brings and also antipathy to social contact.

The shift from neighbours as potential allies in collective defence to sources of risk and annoyance to individual home owners is a relatively

6.3 The Winchester House, California

recent one. Although we are no longer living collectively in hilltop forts, it is worth remembering that even castles, apparently emblematic of the ultimate impregnable individual home, originally embodied hierarchical relationships that were reciprocal. As well as owing allegiance and protection to their feudal superior, in dangerous times the local population was entitled to take refuge in the lord's fortified residence. It is therefore not surprising that 'the distinction between a castle and a fortified city is not always clear' (Tracy, 2000: 6). Echoing this theme in the 1970s, relatively recently, Oscar Newman defined his concept of defensible space as 'a living residential environment which can be employed by inhabitants for the enhancement of their lives, while providing security for their families, neighbours, and friends' (Newman, 1972: 3). Newman viewed with concern the shift to individualism. Observing changes in the lifestyles of higher income groups, and trends to more private security, he commented: 'When people begin to protect themselves as individuals and not as a community, the battle against crime is effectively lost ... The move of middle- and upper-class populations into protective high-rises and other structures of isolation ... is just as clearly a retreat into indifference' (Newman, 1972: 3).

In the twenty-first century, the era of reliance on a community of neighbours appears to be well and truly over, as those able to afford them seek homes not contaminated by close proximity to others. This relates to much broader sociological observations that suggest we now view ourselves as highly atomised individuals who prefer not to get involved with problems of disorder outside the home in the face of state withdrawal from public services. Yet in a time when the home is seen as a source of wealth and an asset, the neighbourhood has regained its importance as a key factor in home value. This is why, for example, the British residential property website Zoopla allows prospective purchasers to research the neighbourhood profile down to the detail of the tenure breakdown, employment statistics, family types, residents' interests, and even what newspapers they read.

Alongside aspirations to emulate the ultra-secure homes of the rich and famous, there is also the need to 'keep up with the Joneses', our neighbours, in matters of defensive technology. If your house is the only one on a street without a visible burglar alarm or electronic gates, you may feel not only vulnerable to risk, but diminished in social status. An article on the annual International Builders' Show in 2004 reported that a new wave of hypervigilant homeowners saw how their peers were protecting their homes and were therefore buying into the new technologies to defend their own. New products were actively sought to meet the demand generated by the diffuse climate of fear, indicating heightened consumer anxieties (McKee, 2004).

Architecture of its time

The growing trend towards the fortification and enclosure of contemporary domestic life is also influenced by the fear and uncertainty experienced in other spheres of our lives, against which the home remains a kind of refuge. We can thus examine home architecture in its temporal context, noting how characteristics and emphases change according to whether the world or the more immediate environment is at peace or embroiled in warfare and crime (Gardiner, 1976). Here we also trace the ways defensive features symbolise status and prestige and their links to privacy and control, features which are central to current understandings of home ownership.

The importance of prospect and refuge for collective defence can be seen from pre-Roman European hill forts to the later walled city-states of Northern Italy. Similarly, in North America, vestiges of a number of pre-colonial examples of defensive settlement patterns remain today, from fortified enclosures under the control of powerful chieftains in the Mississippi region to more lightly built palisades in the north-east (Milner, 2000). As benign settlement by the Pilgrim Fathers turned to colonial occupation, forts were constructed to keep out the indigenous population and later still as symbols of the newly formed state's social power. These strongholds also featured mounds and stockades. Interestingly, early colonial settlers in North America described Iroquois longhouses as 'castles', although they were actually temporary bases for hunting and raiding (Rybczynski, 1986) rather than homes fortified to impose control over people and territory. This misapprehension illustrates the grip that European medieval forms continue to exert on the imagination, then and now.

Returning to our focus on individual rather than collective defensive architecture, we note that throughout history 'spiky' technologies of the home have been primarily associated with the rich and politically powerful. The ability to pay always confers access to the most effective forms of domestic security. The halls of important leaders, original forerunners of today's defended private homes, could be fortified and defended in times of danger, although most have left very little trace as they were constructed of wood. One exception is the *brochs* of north-western Scotland, small, high, stone round towers built between 700 BC and 100 AD. Still visible, *brochs* incorporate elements of both prospect and refuge, but there is insufficient archaeological evidence to determine the balance between defence and deterrent (more likely, as there is little evidence of attacks) or impressive family homes for tribal chiefs with high status (Armit, 2003). *Brochs* are thus an early model of the long-standing links between prestige and defence.

After 1066, there was sudden and frequent usage in Britain of the Norman French term *castel* (Liddiard, 2005). There were two types of castle: the royal, built to defend the king's authority and territory, and fortified private homes, built by Norman lords on land granted by the king as reward for services and loyalty. The feudal system was introduced to England at the same time, with important implications for the legal basis of landholding. The monarch had an interest in encouraging the fortification of private castles to deter potential rebellion, but there was a risk that such imposing and defensible buildings could also become bases for challenging the king. Therefore, a 'license to crenellate' (crenellations being battlements) was required, an early form of development control by the monarch and a check on potential challengers or insurgents. Yet crenellations quickly became an important indicator of status rather than a primary defensive measure (King, 2007; Coulson, 1994).

The Norman lords granted smaller estates to their own knightly tenants – who in turn built themselves smaller defensive homes. In this tiered set of relationships and castle-building aspirations, we see the forerunners of today's citizens who equip their homes with defensive features according to their budget, imitating the homes of wealthy celebrities. From the fourteenth century onwards, there was a gradual architectural shift from defence to domesticity, even in the homes of the powerful and wealthy. However, anachronistic defensive architecture was often still used to indicate status, such as Castle Drogo in Devon which was built in the early twentieth century and which has a huge working portcullis. Many stately homes in Europe held on to defensive aspects long after the possibility of direct attack warranted such designs and changes in military technology rendered them obsolete. For example, the dramatic garden fortifications found at eighteenth-century Castle Howard, a castle in name only, were modelled on defensive earthwork techniques more often used on the battlefield. The castle's architect Vanbrugh later designed Blenheim Palace, whose 'corner

6.4 Fifteenth-century Oxburgh Hall, part fortified castle, part domestic home

turrets hint at fortification and the military victories the palace com-
memorates, but they are decorative, not functional' (Cragoe, 2008: 15).
Such motifs and designs remain popular with those able to afford large
designer homes.

In eighteenth century England, Neoclassical architecture associated
with the Enlightenment and a relatively peaceful Europe had become
the height of taste. This was an era of harsh punishments for trespass
and property crime; many convicted criminals were placed out of sight
and mind through transportation, punished and co-opted to the colonial
project. With a more general reduction in violence, there was no need
for the external design of the Neoclassical home to make reference to
any defensive functions. The interiors, even those of relatively modestly
sized homes, featured rooms designed for gracious comfort. This style
was epitomised in the grand terraced town houses in Bath and in
various 'stately homes' set in large estates. However, the serene design
was protected by the basement area, 'seen as domestic moat, defended

with iron railings' (Vickery, 2008: 154). Capability Brown designed landscaped gardens for his wealthy clients' country estates, the 'must have' symbol of high social rank. Their boundaries developed from the ditches which had been used in English deer parks since Norman times, into the ha-ha. This sunken invisible inverted fence first popularised by Charles Bridgman was widely used to demarcate and protect the domesticity of the garden from a slightly less tame area where livestock might roam.

During the Neoclassical period homes became associated solely with family occupancy, as the impact of the industrial revolution gradually separated work from domestic life, both spatially and temporally. Gothic revival architecture, which became popular from the early nineteenth century, represented a significant change of direction. Now the external design of English houses across all classes looked increasingly to the defensive features of medieval castles for inspiration. Homes built in the Victorian period sprouted pointed arches and gables, crenellations, turrets, pinnacles, external stair turrets, tracery and leaded windows. An explanation for this change in architectural style may be found in the social context: this was an era of growing industrialisation and mass migration from the countryside by impoverished and landless rural labourers following the Enclosure Acts. Crime rates increased and familiar social structures appeared to break down. The idea of respectability acted as a bulwark against the horrors of social and sexual degeneration with the home becoming 'a place of constant struggle to maintain privacy, security and respectability in a dangerous world' (Hepworth, 1999: 19), and this struggle was reflected in the architecture of Gothic revival homes. Augustus Pugin, its chief exponent and designer of Victorian suburbia as well as the London Houses of Parliament, expressed nostalgia for the medieval period, which for him exemplified an idealised, socially ordered society, based on religious principles (Pugin, 1836).

An influential example of defence deployed in home design is clearly seen in the series of 'case study' houses built in Los Angeles during the 1940s and 1950s following a competition by *Arts and Architecture* magazine. In the first half of the twentieth century, the West experienced two devastating wold wars. The Stahl House, designed by architect Pierre Koenig, perhaps the highlight of this series, expresses not only the confidence and affluence of the period, but also its anxieties. It is an iconic example of 'stealth' architecture, presenting an almost blank, bunker-like facade that conceals a swimming pool and luxurious living

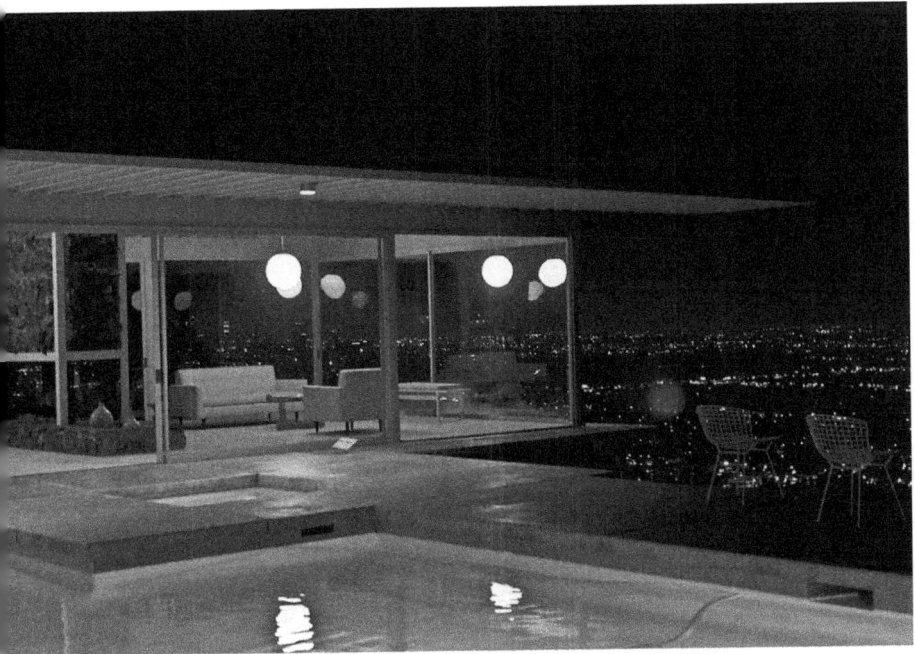

6.5   Case Study House no. 22, Stahl House

space. The protected and secure positioning of the Stahl House, isolated and high on a ridge, distils the principles of prospect and refuge as do many of the archetypal dream homes in the case study series. The vistas seen in the famous photographs of the homes were available only to the owner and invited guests. Consider also that Koenig had been trained during the recent war as a flash ranging observer, calculating the positions of enemy gunfire on the battlefield by triangulation. Case study house #22 and its architectural cousins may be seen as expressions of the soldier's ideal point of trigonometrical estimation; anticipating distant threats from a domestic interior, perfectly positioned above the risks of the city below as a wonderful exemplar of prospect–refuge theory in architectural execution.

   John Lautner, one of Koenig's contemporaries, also designed several homes similarly located among the Hollywood hills, which appeared as the lairs and 'cool' backdrops for films like *Diamonds are Forever* (the Elrod residence) and *Lethal Weapon* (the Garcia residence). Some of Lautner's homes were almost inaccessible to all but their owners – the residence he called the 'chemosphere', designed much like a concrete ball atop supporting struts on a steep hillside, could only be reached by a funicular railway. Ironically, architectural biographer Barbara-Ann Campbell-Lange (2005) noted how Lautner's devotees sometimes trespassed onto the grounds of the homes to see the ultra-modern designs, a harbinger of today's celebrity stalking and voyeurism centred on their homes.

Castles as metaphors, aspirations, dreams

Castles, which epitomise spiky architecture, retain an enduring popular affection; a conversion of the ruins of a twelfth-century fortress into a holiday home won first place in the 2013 Royal Institute of British Architects Stirling Prize (Waite, 2013). The defensive architectural features of castles are still instantly recognisable today. Often encircled by a water-filled moat, access to a castle was dependent on a lowered drawbridge. Forbidding curtain walls, broken only by arrow slits, were topped by crenellated battlements to provide shelter for defending archers. The portcullis, a large gate made of metal and wood, dropped down inside the fortified gatehouse to secure the castle against invasion. Towers and turrets '[thrust] skyward, draw attention to themselves, conveying an impression of strength power and wealth ... their height [making] them easily defensible' (Cragoe, 2008: 142). Carr Hall Castle, featuring battlements, turrets and arrow-slit windows and a ten-acre deer park, easily won viewer votes in the UK television programme *I Own Britain's Best Home*. The previous owner of this castle said he received 'lots of comments about the place, [but] the one I've heard most is "An Englishman's home is his castle"' (Carrhall Castle, undated). While this enduring metaphor conjures up the well-known image of a castle to explain the abstract idea of a home, its repeated use and acceptance over time structures our perceptions and is embedded in our commonsense view of the world (Lakoff and Johnson, 1980).

The castle metaphor is powerful precisely because it embodies connotations of defensive sovereignty and enclosed space; as 'a mode of thinking about home-ownership, it attaches great importance to the actual and assumed rights of people to defend their property, whether this be in relation to visual, spatial or aural breaches of a metaphorical moat'(Gurney, 1999a: 1713). The reference to home ownership, rather than renting, is deliberate; this tenure enables the occupants to adapt and control their home. Owners interviewed by researchers often search for ways to express their feelings about their home and keep falling back on the home-castle metaphor: 'it's just the best way to explain it really, it's just the way I'd sum it up. I know it's a cliché but it's true' (Gurney, 1999a: 1712). Despite its apparently narrow reference to Englishmen, the same castle metaphor is widely used in Australia and the USA. It gives its name, for example, to the Castle Doctrine in the USA, which is further examined in the next chapter, and to the Australian film by Eric Bana referred to in Chapter 4.

Homes of all shapes and sizes across the world may be described as 'castles', but most owners only metaphorically refer to the privacy, prestige, space, strong boundaries and security that characterise castles. Even so, imitations of and references to defensive medieval features are visible in many homes constructed far more recently. These may be both genuinely defensive and an accepted way of displaying wealth and prestige. This suggests an interesting thought experiment: *What kind of home would we live in if resources were unlimited?* Considered with care, such an exercise reveals deep preferences and desires. The connections between our personal and psychic development and aspirations for our home are extremely complex. Carl Jung applied his psychological theories of the process of individuation, the path by which we come to know ourselves more fully and thus relieve ourselves of troubling thoughts and habits of thinking, to an understanding of the meaning of home. In his memoirs (Jung, 1955; 1961), Jung relates how his own home was designed and constructed at Böllingen, Switzerland. Jung's sympathy with the vernacular styles of primitive African huts led to its circular design. The initial structure was extended four years later by building a private room where he could paint or meditate and the key to which he kept with him always. Later still, Jung desired an area of fenced-in land. The building was subsequently named 'The Tower' and bore a remarkable resemblance to a romantic medieval castle. One can read a further layer of meaning into this story of creation, belonging and exclusive possession, manifest in the built form of Jung's 'dream home'. The process was highly suggestive of the work of the subconscious, as he freely admitted. Jung concluded that the completed home provided him with what he felt to be 'a symbol of psychic wholeness' (Jung, 1961: 225).

External defence technologies

Early warning systems using people stationed at or beyond the property boundary can be traced back to the earliest times. Lookouts on the battlements of medieval walled cities and castles have contemporary equivalents in increasingly sophisticated electronic domestic surveillance systems, installed in a quarter of US homes today (Parks Associates, undated). Live images can now be streamed to the homeowner's smartphone, tablet or web browser, with footage stored in the cloud. Some systems incorporate motion-detecting wi-fi 'eyes' to enable night vision and even more impressively, hi-tech sensor systems can 'learn' the home's daily routine through monitoring activity and noise levels, alerting the owner if something unusual occurs. One surveillance system includes infrared cameras that can identify and locate a potential human intruder up to 15 kilometres away, even if that intruder is well-hidden or obscured by smoke (Brennan, 2013). However, tensions between neighbours can lead to long-running disputes over the use of CCTV cameras. Some visible defensive markers like castle sentries are deliberately designed to be seen from outside the boundary, to deter unwanted intruders. Amongst the simplest of visual deterrents are signs facing outwards from the property that warn of rapid, in some cases armed, response to any intrusion by private security companies – or warning of dangerous dogs roaming the property. The deterrent 'Beware of the dog' sign has a long history, as seen in the floor mosaic which warns 'Cave canem', found in the entrance hall to the second century BC Roman House of the Tragic Poet at Pompeii, Italy. In some cases, this theatrical manipulation of home defence is given a humorous twist, as with the sign from a large Australian house in Figure 6.6 below.

Dog warning signs are often used as a substitute for the actual ownership of animals, just as the dummy burglar alarm box is used to suggest the presence of protection where none exists. The long-standing problem of how to exercise control when the residents are absent has been at least partially solved by indoor timed light switches, giving potential burglars the impression of human presence. Burglars view outdoor motion detection lights, which alert unwanted passers-by of

6.6 'Mad dog', variant on warning sign

observation, as effective deterrents; just over half of all UK homes now have such lighting systems (Office for National Statistics, 2013b).

Visual forms of defence and deterrence have been historically complemented by simple but effective aural technologies. Gravel on the external approach to larger homes effectively enables owners or servants to monitor the sound of invading footsteps. Inside the seventeenth-century Nijo Palace in Japan are beautifully crafted 'nightingale floors' (*uguisubari*) in the corridors, which when trodden on make a sound like birdsong to betray the intruder to waiting guards. Real livestock also make effective warning systems. Geese are better at scenting humans than any other animal and cackle loudly at any approach. Similarly, in England and in India, peacocks were used as a decorative and upmarket alternative to geese; remote Australian homesteads used them to warn of intruders. In one of Sidney Nolan's series of paintings about the life of outlaw Ned Kelly, a policeman approaches a small house where Ned is hiding while a seemingly innocuous peacock stands outside; it 'was accustomed to making warning cries at the approach of any stranger' (Sayers, 1994: 12).

For millennia, people have kept a dog to guard their property, and dogs are still the most popular aural and physical deterrent today. There are over 80 million dogs in the USA (American Pet Products Association, 2014), 8.5 million dogs in the UK (Pet Food Manufacturer's Association, 2013) and an estimated 4.2 million dogs in Australia (RSPCA Australia, 2014). At the top end of the security market, specially trained dogs change hands for eye-watering amounts and are deployed as domestic guardians (Rose, 2006). Yet dogs may also be a source of domestic terror, with people attacked every year by dogs belonging to their families, to friends or to neighbours. Serious injury or even death may result, with children being particularly vulnerable and although the majority of injuries are not serious, victims can suffer emotional trauma. This is a high price to pay for home protection, alongside various drawbacks such as barking dogs and disturbed neighbours, which may also lead to further disputes. Dogs not properly trained and cared for may also present other problems to the proud homeowner with architectural and design changes potentially required, for example, by partitioning rooms or closing doorways to restrict dogs to yards or designated rooms (Ellin, 1997: 123).

Research suggests that most criminals avoid breaking into homes with either a human or animal presence, often ringing doorbells to check first (Mawby and Walklate, 1997). The growing feminisation of the workforce means there is often no traditional human guardian at home during the day, and in the absence of an animal to raise the warning, the burglar alarm is now the most used aural technology to protect the home from invasion. In the early 1990s, only around one in ten British homes had a burglar alarm according to the British Crime Survey in 1993; twenty years later, in 2012, the proportion had risen to one in three homes (Office for National Statistics, 2013b). In the USA, around 21 per cent of homes have electronic security systems (Rose, 2006). There are a wide number of variants, from high cost systems connected to private security companies that often send out silent alarms unbeknownst to intruders, to the more common types that trigger startling noises and lights, possibly also alerting the local police station. However, apart from the cost to public services, burglar alarms, like dogs, bring their own unintended problems. In 2002, US police responded to around 36 million alarm activations in 2000, at an estimated annual cost of $1.8 billion (Sampson, 2007). One British study discovered user error accounted for half of all alarms going off (Gill and

Hemming, 2003); bad weather and false detection can also trigger alarms. It is estimated that over 90 per cent of false alarms are caused by equipment failure or user error (Metropolitan Police, undated). Of course, the nuisance of continually ringing alarms leads to complaints by neighbours. A further problem is that researchers in Australia and the USA have shown that sophisticated wireless home security systems can be easily hacked, disabled or jammed by creating false alarms, even when password-protected, so homeowners may not be as well protected as they imagine (Security Sales & Integration, 2014).

The physical property boundary that demarcates public from private property is the first line of defence for the homeowner. Yet, as Christopher Falkenberg, former American Secret Service agent turned security specialist for high-net-worth homeowners, points out, 'The exterior has always been the holy grail because you could never really protect it without 24-hour guard service' (Brennan, 2013). These concerns are reflected in the residential choices of the very wealthy in cities like London; greater protection is identified in the city's suburbs, where walls and gates are more often deployed. Ironwork gates with artistic scrollwork used to indicate status; the next step was for a more defensive and closed design, perhaps topped with spikes; now the trend is increasingly to install solid ironwork gates or concrete barriers to provide an absolute deterrent. Close protection is also available at a price; the SAS-trained guards at the exclusive One Hyde Park development in London, for example. But however poor or affluent the owner, the home is primary territory and when threatened, it is likely to be defended with intensified territorial behaviour (Brower, 1980). Thus, perimeters are secured as much as possible and pushed outwards; front gardens are sacrificed nowadays so that cars can be locked safely inside the boundary fence with security details housed in separate dwellings within the perimeter, in the most extravagant examples. The increased use of entry-phones at the perimeters of increasingly secured individual homes represents a marked step-change in defensive technology, and yet another attempt to control home boundaries at the farthest point of entry.

Built into the fabric of the home, the door is far more vulnerable to an intruder than is the surrounding wall. Castle portcullises were designed to be impregnable when closed, as are their modern-day equivalents: kevlar-lined, bullet-resistant doors (Brennan, 2013). The oldest door lock discovered dates back around 4,000 years, from the Khorsabad palace ruins near Nineveh in Mesopotamia (Monk, 2009).

Locks have also been found in ancient Rome, Greece and Egypt and in the countries colonised by these empires. In Britain, the first commercially available domestic lock was patented by Jeremiah Chubb in 1818 in Portsmouth, winning a government challenge to invent a lock that could only be opened by its own key. Chubb's lever lock design was complemented by the pin tumbler lock created by Linus Yale in 1848, and household locks have changed very little since. Chubb and Yale remain household names, regularly tested by the skills of burglars and locksmiths. The contemporary climate of risk and fear has led to the addition of 'dead locks', whereby a bolt is turned to boost the integrity of a door already fitted with key-operated locks and thus slow intruders. Over eight out of ten UK homes now have double locks or deadlocks fitted on at least some of the outside doors, an increase of 13 per cent over the previous year (Office for National Statistics, 2013b). Yet the increased reliance on impenetrable locks and safes also increases the risk of more brutal attacks against key-carrying household members outside the home or by aggressive professional thieves who have pried system access codes from householders under duress. The house is, of course, most vulnerable to intruders when the front door is open. To combat this risk and the consequent anxiety it engenders, biometric technologies such as iris recognition or fingerprint scans for gaining quick and secure access to the home are becoming more prevalent. A former Israeli major-general in the Military Intelligence Directorate Ordinary now sells entry systems combining facial, voice and behaviour recognition technology, turning the home owner into an embodied 'key for your building in under two seconds' (Brennan, 2013).

The letterbox is also a particularly weak spot in the physical boundary of the home. Most British letterboxes used to be integral to the front door, but in recent years there has been a noticeable trend to reposition them at the front gate or in external boundary walls, copying the location of US and Australian mailboxes at the driveway end. This change signifies a growing unease about the letterbox as a chink in the armour of the home. These changes have been greeted with relief by the UK's Communication Workers' Union, for whom dog attacks have long been a serious worry. Comparison of the data on postal workers bitten by dogs is startling. The US Postal Service reports that in 2012, 5,879 workers were bitten (United States Postal Service, 2013), while in comparison, in the UK there were 23,000 reported dog attacks on

6.7 Australian Post Office warning sign

postmen and women over the five years up to 2013, with as many as 70 per cent of these attacks taking place on private property (BBC News, 2013).

The continued vulnerability of the home via letterboxes, even positioned away from the home, was brought to public attention by the anthrax sent through the US postal system in 2001. There was little possibility of detecting those responsible for delivering a chemical agent directly into homes. Nor could potential victims be protected, adding a sense of randomisation that amplified existing fears and exposed the weakness of traditionally 'defended' homes. The letterbox is also an unprotected site for anti-social conduct like inserting dog excrement or more serious arson attacks. Recent technological changes to mailboxes reflect these new fears. They include 'the Defender', a brick enclosure for mailboxes offered by the Mail Theft Solutions Company for $800 and Energy Technology Laboratories' cheaper 'Secure Mail Vault', with a wave-shaped mail slot to prevent anyone from reaching inside and a pin-code entry to the box for added security (McKee, 2004).

The external shell of the home also plays its part as a surveillance technology for the anxious homeowner. Fisheyes in doors allow for callers to be observed and filtered; windows can be fitted with one-way net curtains. Windows remain an obvious and vulnerable entry point into a home. In the UK the use of window locks has increased by 20 per cent to 88 per cent in 2012/13 (Office for National Statistics,

2013b), no doubt driven in part by insurance requirements. In contrast, bars and grilles over windows have decreased, probably because of fear of being trapped in a fire, from 7 per cent in 1994 to 3 per cent in 2007 (British Crime Survey, 2008). Modern technology available to affluent homeowners favours blast film to render windowpanes almost indestructible, backed up by unobtrusive detectors installed nearby to alert the owner in the unlikely event of a breakage.

Surveillance of 'the enemy within' the home

Suspicion of those personally invited into the home is increasing and extends even to long-term employees. Hollywood celebrities often attempt to guard their family privacy by requiring all household staff to sign non-disclosure legal agreements, also known as gag orders (Davidow, 2007). There is widespread use of domestic and often migrant labour in gated communities in the US, which has partially integrated poorer workers into affluent neighbourhoods at particular times of the day. These dependencies between rich and poor have also fuelled concerns about the potential for acquisitive crime opened up by employing poorer servants. In South Africa, the use of lockable refrigerators to prevent pilfering by domestic servants has been used for some years by distrustful employers. Surveillance may also be directed within at occupants of household spaces, with CCTV cameras turning the home into a micro-panopticon. Contemporary criminologists like Jock Young argue that these socio-technological shifts have created a palpable sense of mistrust; the home is one surveilled space nested within many broader scales:

> The cameras invade our corner shops, our shopping malls, the city centre, the residential estate, our factories and, finally, the home itself. The cameras move from surveying outside the home to inside the home so that the activities of babysitters, cleaners (and perhaps our partners!) can be surveyed and checked upon. (Young, 1999: 191)

The impact of these shifts in technology both matches and feeds broader concerns about the possibility of an 'enemy within' who cannot be trusted. It is telling that half of current or would-be users of home CCTV systems in the UK use them (or would do so) inside the home (*Which? Advice*, 2010). Home webcams streamed to the work desk can reassure absent parents that teenagers have returned safe from school.

More pertinently, they are used by a time-poor, cash-rich class fraction who contract-out their parenting – like surveillance for employees:

> These businesses [child protection] feast on an all-pervasive culture of fear, which create a mockery, alibi and distraction out of what they are really about – to remake the home as a citadel through the peddling of private protective technologies that reinforce it against various forms of intrusion. (Katz, 2001: 47)

Conclusion

Our homes have become the exoskeletons of the household, the hard external defences for the soft bodies within. Increasingly 'spiky' or 'stealth' home architecture reflects deep anxieties operating as systems of protection and social filtration. We have argued that these defensive technologies are contemporary manifestations of powerful underlying cognitive-social functions and histories, variably expressed in the building of homes according to prevailing social arrangements, the presence of particular threats and architectural fashions.

The forbidding quality of the built environment is also linked to housing tenure as physical modifications and investments are more likely to be undertaken by home owners and to a substantially greater degree by more affluent owners, the familiar pattern of tessellated neoliberalism. The desire to retreat into incubatory spaces where families and households seek to protect themselves also has the broader outcome of creating homes that are increasingly insulated from perceived and real risks. Yet we suggest that the dream of a completely cocooned home, a castellated fantasy, is not a dream of escape from danger, but its reverse: a gilded form of internment, accompanied by the background threat of crime and disorder and metaphysical insecurity. The recent increase in defensive technologies has turned homes into the architectural representation of our fears, from which we can never truly be free.

7

Withdraw, defend or destroy

We have previously suggested that the law is an effective defensive weapon accessible by affluent homeowners; here we look at the law that can potentially be used against those homeowners who inflict death or injury on home invaders. Although widely perceived as victims of crime, homeowners can themselves face prosecution and conviction – or be treated as 'have-a-go heroes' enforcing the law – depending on where they live. Governments set the standards of how much force, if any, it is acceptable to use against an intruder, and these legal rules currently diverge in Australia, the UK and the USA. The differences have been characterised as reflecting 'the comparative values that a particular society places on human life, and on property, privacy and dignity of the home' (Green, 1999: 40). In this chapter we examine these comparisons and the press and other campaigns lobbying for changes in the law to protect homeowners.

It is paradoxical that while governments have encouraged responsibilised homeowners to take defensive precautions against becoming victims of crime, individuals aggressively protecting private property are potentially usurping state powers to punish. Nearly one hundred years ago, Max Weber famously wrote that the state has a monopoly on the legitimate use of physical force and violence within its territory as well as the sole right to punish offenders (Gerth and Wright Mills, 1946: 77). For centuries, crimes against property carried the death sentence (Thompson, 1991), so householders using lethal force against intruders acted on behalf of the state and could arguably be exonerated. However, Getzler (2005) points out that the state monopoly on violence was always temporary and is now completely undermined by increased private security and the emphasis on individual responsibility. When faced with a criminal intruder, the homeowner cannot expect instant protection from the forces of law and order. Where is the line to be drawn between legitimate self-help and the responsibility of government to protect citizens and enforce law and order? States which in effect have delegated to homeowners the right to punish offenders, have thereby reinforced the tessellated formations of ranked homeowners in defended homes.

The varying legal positions in the USA, UK and Australia illuminate the shifting nature of the relationship between the state and individuals who demand the right to protect their homes with lethal force. In this chapter we also examine the influence of the media and survey popular cultural references that invite or compel us to respond aggressively to threats to the home. The law applies to all home occupiers, whether owners or renters, but property owners fit better the 'ideal' format of respectable, law-abiding and innocent victims. Owning your home and exercising territorial control over it has now become strongly associated with 'a concern for the maintenance of law and belief in the possibility of its enforcement' (Newman, 1972: 206), while tenants are more likely to be seen as members of a feared underclass. For example, there was no public outcry and the case was barely reported in the UK press, when two council tenants were found guilty of murder. They had caught a burglar red-handed in the tower block where they lived and had beaten him brutally before leaving him for dead (*Birmingham Post*, 2008).

The emotional significance of the home and deeply held ideas about domestic sovereignty have long given credence to vengeful calls for defending the home against those violating its sanctity. Four celebrated cases, all resulting in death by shooting and in murder charges which changed or challenged the law, provide the examples threading through this chapter. Two of these exemplar incidents took place at isolated farmhouses. In 1957, an Australian poultry farmer named Gordon McKay rigged up a system of alarms to warn of intruders, then killed a thief, shooting him in the back as he fled from his farm in Glenroy, Victoria. In 1999, under similar circumstances in the UK, a Norfolk farmer called Tony Martin shot at burglars as they ran away, killing one and seriously injuring the other. Two other significant cases in this chapter took place in gated communities; they were not about home invasion but about perceived threats to the security of an entire domestic complex. An Australian case from 1983 involved two residents of a courtyard development at Ascot Vale, Melbourne, Victoria, where Fadil Zecevic became infuriated by Harold Triebel's habit of leaving the security gates open. During one of their many arguments, Triebel stabbed Zecevic and threatened him; Zecevic went to fetch his own gun, and on his return shot and killed Triebel. In 2012, in the gated community of Retreat at Twin Lakes, Sanford, Florida, a neighbourhood watch volunteer named George Zimmerman followed the unarmed teenager Trayvon Martin because he thought him suspicious. An altercation ensued, during which Zimmerman suffered minor injuries and shot Martin dead.

Commentators on these cases and on many similar incidents almost inevitably make use of the 'home as castle' metaphor. Public opinion can swing behind homeowners who kill, treating them as folk heroes and as victims, rather than as criminals. Gun ownership, as in these four cases, often determines whether homeowners withdraw or confront those who threaten the security of home, and guns produce lethal outcomes in many such confrontations. We consider the combination of rates of gun ownership with different legal approaches to defensive home ownership, noting that most US states give homeowners the right *not* to be a victim, to fight back against home invasion with lethal force (Farmer, 2006).

Fear and loathing, fight or flight

Burglary is often reported by householders as an experience of pollution (Chapman, 1999: 141). It is a crime combining all three types of territorial infringement identified by environmental psychologists: invasion, violation and contamination (Altman, 1975). Owners who suffer burglaries often also feel a sense of shame at failing to defend homes and loved ones. This homeowner speaks for many, following a burglary at his house in a 'leafy, Georgian square in north London': 'I was in shock and dreaded opening the front door for months afterwards. I couldn't admit to this or the feelings of inadequacy, to my family, which I felt unable to protect' (Pollinger, 2005).

Despite the security measures discussed in Chapter 6, if the homeowner is faced with an invasion, the instinctive reaction is typically either 'fight', defending the home by directly confronting the invader, or 'flight', either inwards to a panic room or escape from the home.

So-called panic rooms are a variant on the timeworn strategy of retreat to an inner bunker, like medieval castle keeps 'defending the citadel with outward layers of security from a central core' (Woolsey, 2007), or the 'priest holes' of principal Catholic homes in sixteenth-century England whose entrance and location were disguised to conceal persecuted priests from officials seeking them out in the name of the king. Panic rooms also echo wartime bunkers such as the Anderson shelters built in 3.6 million UK gardens during the Second World War (James, 2003: 623).

The modern panic room is perhaps the ultimate protection for a household, and gained considerable publicity from the 2002 film *Panic Room* starring Jodie Foster. Ultimately, as her character in the film has to leave the safety of the room and confront her assailants, the message once again is that we can never be fully secure in our homes. In the years since the film was released, panic rooms have become more widely available, but top of the range custom-built safe havens can be extensive and elaborate. These are often unimaginably expensive, but promise to make the home a defence against all ills, including nuclear war. Water and power, plus entertainment and medical facilities are all supplied; one optimistic estimate is 'that families could survive in the best planned of these luxurious strongholds for up to three generations' (Brennan, 2013).

An alternative form of flight is escaping the home through a secret tunnel, as if fleeing a besieged castle. One CEO benefiting from private security expenditure is John Marshall of Commonwealth Studios, whose home is both gated and equipped with an electronic warning system. Despite these apparently impregnable boundaries, the Marshalls have been warned to resist the instinct to protect their home. They should leave their on-site security staff to deal with intruders, and withdraw to safety through a concealed escape route (Jones, 2009). These secret passageways are constructed by specialist builders, for example, the Creative Home Engineering Company, which creates about forty-five clandestine exits annually (Brennan, 2013). In this way, the very wealthy are protected from having to defend their homes at all, with temporary retreat seen as one of the most effective forms of defence.

The overwhelming emotion concerning housebreaking is anger, experienced by those with direct experience of this crime and even by others merely asked by researchers to think about it (Ditton *et al.*, 1999). Anger is much more common and more widespread than fear, but a high proportion of respondents reported both emotions. The Royal College of Psychiatrists point out that it is incorrect to assume 'that the two emotions of anger and fear are distinct. In medical reality they are not. Physiologically anger and fear are virtually identical' (Law Commission, 2004: 53). When real and immediate danger is experienced, 'a series of complex bodily changes alert the actor to the possibility of danger' (Ferraro, 1995: 95). At the moment of an actual confrontation between homeowner and burglar, cortisol (the 'stress hormone') floods the body and mutes the usual process of making judgements.

This is borne out in the first-hand accounts of those who fight rather than flee. A writer noted that the 'fury you feel when your private space is invaded and despoiled is extraordinary'; she found herself in hand-to-hand combat with the intruder who managed to invade her home 'despite thick security glass, window-locks, London bars and motion sensitive lights' (Craig, 2007). Similarly, an elderly home owner described his feelings when an intruder with an (imitation) gun appeared in his bedroom: 'When I saw him in my house I was damned annoyed and if you are so angry you don't have time to be scared. I would have been delighted to have done him substantial injury' (Carr-Brown et al., 2004). It is clearly difficult in the heat of the moment to distinguish between defending the home and the desire to punish intruders. There is a thin line between legitimate defence of the home and a visceral desire for revenge against an intruder, a tipping point when protection and deterrence becomes intent to do harm in the eyes of the law.

Homeowners as victims

In this neoliberal era when state resources are stretched thin, the home has become paradoxically both the site of ultimate control for its owner and a site of vulnerability. Here we look at how reporting of crime in the news media has combined with popular culture to shape our understanding of homeowners who kill in defence of the home. We tend to identify with them as victims, 'representative character[s] whose experience is assumed to be common and collective, rather than individual and atypical' (Garland, 2001: 144).

The perfect recipe for contemporary crime stories dictates that 'the victims are innocent likeable people; the perpetrator is an uncaring brute. Details of the crime, while shocking, are easy to relay' (Glassner, 1999: 24). This formula can be observed in use by criminal justice officials at press conferences. For example, the Detective Chief Inspector in charge of a 2004 murder investigation, when a home owner was killed by the intruder he surprised in the family kitchen in the middle of the night, said: 'Robert Symons was a loving and devoted husband and father. He was ambushed and wickedly murdered in his own home by a man whose only intention was to save his own skin' (Law, 2006). In the same year, a burglar disguised as a postman gained entry to the affluent Monckton family's home in Chelsea, London, then murdered Mr Monckton and attacked his wife, witnessed by their nine-year-old daughter. Prosecutor Richard Horwell told the court: 'Every house-holder's nightmare became a reality for the Monckton family' (Muir and Butt, 2005). This awful event can be related to our own everyday life experiences, and we identify with the victims (Altheide, 2002: 16). The more we see and hear about the same scenarios such as violent break-ins, the more familiar they seem and the more likely to happen to us.

Crime stories that capture the public imagination often also represent what many feel to indicate a significant form of social crisis (Glassner, 1999: 24). Politicians and officials in the criminal justice system in tandem with the media amplify moral panics of this kind. According to Macek (2006: xix), US news networks are 'fixated on underclass deviance and misbehaviour'. Barry Glassner (1999) suggests that news reporting makes it easier to focus anxieties on 'other' groups than on more deep-seated social issues and problems. Thus George Zimmerman suspected Trayvon Martin on the basis of his race and clothing. A news-paper report of the Symons murder referred to an unbridgeable social chasm: 'The victim and the man convicted yesterday of his murder fol-lowed paths that should never have crossed' (Law, 2006). Tony Martin was frequently presented as a respectable property owner, confronted by burglars with long criminal records who were also gypsies, an ethnic group within English society that has attracted fear and hatred from the settled population for centuries (Vanderbeck, 2003). Crime stories cir-culate in social life (Carrabine, 2008) and gain further significance when they provide moral outrage shared by respectable society. Another common feature of contemporary crime news reporting is 'a sense of randomness. This promotes incredible anxiety and fear' (Altheide, 2002: 136). Homeowners fear they will be unable to exercise the control that lies at the heart of home ownership. As if to emphasise this, media reports often include details of security measures at homes that have been invaded. The Moncktons' house was described as 'like a fortress – heavily and obviously protected by various security systems' (Muir and Butt, 2005). Yet even these defensive measures, well beyond the budget of most homeowners, were not enough to protect the wealthy victims.

The risks attached to threats to the home are reflected in and encouraged by the way these themes are presented in films, TV and other forms of popular culture. Many iconic films such as *Straw Dogs* and *Panic Room* focus on outsiders attacking the home. In *The Outlaw Josey Wales*, for example, revenge for home and loved ones is the driving force. The viewer becomes complicit in the hero's brutal actions, 'interpreted as utterly distinct from villainous violence, and characterized as "retribution", "punishment", "justice", "heroism", and so on' (Young, 2009: 8). The hero must take the law into his own hands because the state fails to respond adequately to violent crimes. This theme is also reflected in the development of cinema and TV crime dramas. In the 1980s and 1990s, 'the dominant images of American cities and urban space circulating through Hollywood film ... derived their shared fantasy about contemporary urban reality largely from the conservative interpretation of street crime, gangs and the "underclass" that became so prominent in news reporting and public discourse during this period' (Macek, 2006: 203).

We may be passive viewers of television and cinema, but we are active participants in electronic games. The retreat into the privacy of the home, and then within that into the privacy of an individual family member's room, has accompanied an increase to six hours or more on average spent each week in 2014 playing video games, in the UK and in the USA (The Statistics Portal, 2015; Aamoth, 2014). Some 42 per cent of Americans play video games regularly (Entertainment Software Association, 2015), so it becomes worth considering what kind of games are being played. The most popular have photo-real graphics and a first-person perspective, allowing players to control the action, often immersed in the game's violence as the central character (Adams and Rollings, 2006). For instance, in *Hitman: Blood Money* (a well-known game produced by Eido Interactive in 2006), the player takes the role of Agent 47. In the game scenario 'A New Life', Agent 47 must eliminate a gangster under FBI protection in a secure gated community on the west coast of America. The player/protagonist is licensed to cause mayhem, violence and death, reversing the usual association of gated communities with definitive shelter. The creators of this game exploit underlying fears about 'killers in our midst' and incorporate them into its play, exaggerating and emphasising the gated community and its confined surroundings.

These cultural developments may help explain the iconic appeal of exemplar cases that combine victimhood with violence and revenge in the emotional site of the home. Gordon McKay and Tony Martin, both living in isolated farmhouses, typify the vulnerable homeowner, self-reliant and facing a hostile world. Like many contemporary home-owners, both felt abandoned by the police. On several occasions, Martin's house and farm buildings were broken into and his property stolen. At McKay's farm, a thousand chickens were stolen over three years. No intruders were caught or punished. Similarly, George Zimmerman felt he had to take action himself to secure his gated community. He reported his suspicions to the police about Trayvon Martin, a black teenager wearing a hoodie. When he was told to wait for an officer to arrive, Zimmerman responded, 'Fucking punks ... they always get away' (Walker, 2013: 5), and took direct action himself, with fatal results.

Guns and other weapons

Weapons are usually involved when a homeowner, rather than becoming a passive victim, fights back against an intruder and causes death or serious injury. There is a sharp division over types of weapon between the USA on the one hand and the UK and Australia on the other, due to rates of gun ownership and regimes for licensing firearms. In the USA, there are approximately 300 million privately owned firearms; the number of firearms is reportedly increasing by over 10 million annually. The 100 million gun owners in the USA represent just under half of all US households (National Rifle Association – Institute for Legislative Action, 2014).

In Australia and the UK, where gun ownership is more tightly regulated, the rate of gun ownership is much lower. The firearms regulations in both the UK and Australia restrict who may own and use firearms, what types may be purchased and safe storage requirements. There are over 2.75 million registered firearms in Australia, owned by more than

730,000 individual licence holders or around one-tenth of households (Library of Congress, 2015). In England and Wales, police have issued over 650,000 licences, covering over half a million firearms and almost 1.5 million shotguns, generally considered to be less dangerous as a 'long arm' and therefore harder to conceal (HM Inspectorate of Constabulary, 2015). In both Australia and the UK, tragic events have provided a spur to initial regulation: the Hungerford and Dunblane massacres by gunmen in the UK in 1987 and 1996 respectively, and the Port Arthur massacre in Australia, 1996. Further regulations continue to be introduced. Chapman's (1998) analysis of the struggle for firearms regulation in Australia shows how public outrage and press campaigns dedicated to getting Australia 'off the American path' pushed government to embrace gun control, despite fierce resistance.

Proposals for gun control in the USA meet vociferous opposition, even though 'over the last three decades public mass shootings have claimed 547 lives and led to an additional 476 injured victims' (Congressional Research Service, 2013: 2). The American public attitude to gun control has in fact changed markedly over the last half century, although in the opposite direction to Australia. Polls conducted by Gallup indicate that, in 1959, 60 per cent of respondents favoured a ban on handguns, except for use by police and other officials, while in 2009, 71 per cent were opposed to such a ban (cited in Schelzig, 2009a: 39). It has been argued that gun sales in the USA have steadily increased since the mid-1980s in parallel with increasing references to 'fear' in the news media (Altheide, 2002). Between 2007 and 2008, there was a 9 per cent increase in gun purchases in the USA, 'about the time the housing bubble popped in parts of the nation', which caused widespread anxiety about increased property crime (Kunkle, 2008).

In the USA, guns are bought primarily for defending the self, family and home, whereas in Australia and the UK, the vast majority of licensed guns are used for rural activities like vermin control, hunting and clay pigeon shooting (van Dijk et al., 2008). Jennifer Carlson's (2015) study of US men suggests they carry guns in response to insecurities generated by socio-economic decline and anxiety about the inadequacy of state protections against crime. Many American men identify themselves as 'citizen-protectors' in order to assert their masculinity, assuming the role of home and family defender. In a society that made such early choices to enshrine militarism as a component of civic life, it is difficult to undermine or alter ingrained notions of self-protection. This worldview of inherent preparedness to use lethal force is exemplified in a book on developing a 'tactical mindset' by a former US policeman:

> When confronting an assailant, our thought should not be, 'Oh my god, is that awful man breaking into my house? Is that a real gun in his hand?' Instead it should be, 'I see him breaking into my house, he has a gun, and I'm ready for him. Boy, has he made a big mistake!' Attitude makes all the difference (Suarez, 1998: 6)

The National Rifle Association (NRA) plays on these themes to oppose any form of gun control and, as we will see, pressing for the right to use lethal force in home defence to be enshrined in legislation. The NRA claims over four million members and is widely reported to have a budget of over $300m. The Second Amendment to the US Constitution, 1791, is emblazoned across the NRA website: 'A well regulated militia being necessary to the security of a free State, the right of the people to keep and bear arms shall not be infringed'. The Supreme Court in the cases of *District of Columbia v. Heller*, 2008 and *McDonald v. Chicago*, 2010 has confirmed that the Second Amendment protects an individual's right to possess a firearm – these decisions were hailed by the NRA as marking a great moment in American history.

The connection between the availability of guns and rates of gun crime is not only 'one of the most contested issues in criminology' (van Kesteren, 2014: 53), but continuously at the forefront of public debate. Homicide rates are decreasing in Australia, the UK and in the USA. The latest figures show 4.5 murders per 100,000 people in the USA (FBI, 2013), with firearm violence accounting for about 70 per cent of all homicides from 1993 to 2011 (Planty and Truman, 2013). In Australia, the comparable homicide rate was 0.13 per 100,000, over twenty times lower than in the USA (Chapman and Alpers, 2013). The homicide rate is even lower in the UK, where there were 580 victims in 2012–13, of which only 5 per cent were killed by shooting (Office for National Statistics, 2015b). Most guns used in crime in the UK and in Australia are probably unlicensed. As the UK Parliament carefully explained:

> there is no direct correlation in recent UK history between levels of gun ownership and gun crime trends. However, it is fair to assume at least in part that this demonstrates the success of the licensing regime, in place since 1968, which enables the authorities to satisfy themselves

that those owning firearms are fit to do so (Home Affairs Committee, 2010: Para. 35)

Handguns remain the weapon of choice for criminals. In the USA, an estimated one-third of all firearms are legally owned handguns, a popular option for home and self-defence. However, it is at least debatable whether guns make homeowners feel safe. The decision to arm yourself to protect your family and your home can carry a terrible cost, as the risk of theft and accidents in the home is ever present. Wealthy and discerning gun owners can purchase secure gun cabinets featuring biometrically operated openings hidden behind paintings or disguised as old iceboxes (McKee, 2004), but too often, unsecured guns cause tragedies. In just one example a teenage girl from Dallas was accidentally shot by her brother in August 2010. The children's godfather was quoted saying that their father 'kept a gun in the house for protection, it's a rough and rugged neighbourhood'. This was a family home under siege: it was described as having 'black metal bars on the windows. The front stoop is completely enclosed in bars' (Trahan, 2010). Guns arouse strong emotions; in American culture, they are a means of protection, but also of random accidents and calculated acts of aggression.

The 'Castle Doctrine', 'Make My Day' laws, and 'Stand Your Ground' legislation in the USA

We have shown earlier how the home can be seen as an essential part of identity. It is therefore not easy to make or maintain the distinction between defending oneself and loved ones, and defending one's property from threat or attack. In the USA, this conflation between self and home is reflected in the law, particularly in legislation passed since the 1980s. The 'Castle Doctrine', referencing that famous phrase from *Semayne's* case, has always applied in the USA. It was eloquently summarised in this 1914 judgment, the source of the resonant phrase 'Stand Your Ground':

> It is not now and never has been the law that a man assailed in his own dwelling is bound to retreat. If assailed there, he may stand his ground and resist the attack. He is under no duty to take to the fields and the highways, a fugitive from his own home. (J. Cardozo in *People v Tomlins*, 1914)

In that judgment, the attack that can be resisted with fight rather than flight is an attack against the 'man assailed in his own dwelling', not an attack against his property. Fast forward to 1985, and Colorado introduced the first so-called 'Make My Day' legislation. This protects people from any legal consequences, criminal or civil, who use even lethal force against a home invader, regardless of whether they felt threatened (Wilbanks, 1990). The legislation was named after the 1983 film *Sudden Impact,* in which Clint Eastwood's character Dirty Harry says to the 'punk' he has arrested, 'Go ahead, make my day', daring him to provoke a shooting. The use of this well-known film catchphrase to refer to home defence legislation again illustrates the close relationship between popular culture and law. In 1990, it still seemed worthy of press comment when Francis Boutcher, a Colorado homeowner, was not charged with any criminal offence (Johnson, 1990). Although his own life was not being threatened, Boutcher shot teenage burglar Laureano Jacobo Grieigo Jr in the back of the head as he tried to escape through the front door. Boutcher benefited from the 'Make My Day' legislation.

Other states followed Colorado's lead, often prompted by public pressure. In Oklahoma, the legislation was rushed through only weeks after a 1987 incident in which a homeowner confronted two men and killed one who had broken into his garage during the night, using the gun kept beside his bed. The spread of Castle Doctrine laws across the USA is due largely to sustained pressure from the NRA. According to the NRA, at the time of writing twenty-five states, mostly in the south and west, have introduced 'Make My Day' legislation. Chief NRA lobbyist Chris W. Cox described their legislative campaign as 'a co-ordinated approach to respect that human, God-given right of self-defence by law-abiding Americans. We'll rest when all fifty states allow and respect the right of law-abiding people to defend themselves from criminal attack' (quoted in Schelzig, 2009b).

The NRA then pushed for extended 'Stand Your Ground' laws, first enacted in Florida in 2005 (Florida Statute § 776.013, 2005), which by 2014 had been adopted in thirty-three more states (American Bar Association, 2014). This legislation exonerates the use of lethal force when you believe you are facing a threat to your physical safety, whether inside your home, your car or in a public place, regardless of any alternative such as safe retreat or using lesser force. Although George Zimmerman opted to plead not guilty to the murder of Trayvon Martin on the basis of self-defence, his trial took place in the charged atmosphere around this legislation. He was acquitted of all criminal charges, leading

7.1 Castle Law Home Security Yard Sign. Tell the public you are informed and prepared!

to some public protests, outrage expressed by civil rights leaders and intervention by President Obama (Walker, 2013: 5–6).

Intruder death and serious injury inflicted by homeowners now seem commonplace in the USA and mainly go unreported in the press. They are classified in law as 'justifiable homicides', so numbers are not recorded (National Research Council, 2004: Chapter 5). However, media reports show how far the 'Make My Day' provisions have been stretched. In Florida, Gregory Stewart was awakened early one morning in 2009 by an unarmed, drunk young man knocking at his front door. When the man, Billy Kuch, refused to leave, Stewart shot him in the chest, but no charge was brought against him (Rooth Law Group, undated). In another example from 2014, Houston firefighter Sam Keen was shot dead by his neighbour who thought he was trying to get into her house as he returned home in the early hours after a night out (DeJohn, 2014).

The weight of public opinion in the USA is behind homeowners using maximum force against intruders, despite concerns expressed by criminal justice system professionals. The US National District Attorneys Association claims prosecutors no longer have discretion to consider whether the force used was reasonable or whether the use of deadly force was justified (Jansen and Nugent-Borakove, 2007). In states with 'Make My Day' legislation, there has been no deterrent effect on crimes such as burglary, robbery and aggravated assault, but an 8 per cent increase in homicides (Cheng and Hoekstra, 2013). The American Bar Association's Task Force examined all the available empirical evidence on 'Stand Your Ground' laws. It found the law is not being applied consistently, even within the same state, and the likelihood of racial disparity in determining justification of lethal force is significantly higher in states which have passed the legislation. In these states a white person shooting a black victim is 350 per cent more likely to be found justified than if that same person had killed a white victim (American Bar Association, 2014: 20).

Despite these concerns, defensive home ownership in the USA has been bolstered by the constitutional right to own guns and by legislation sanctioning their use against intruders, so that lethal force can be used even where the threat is negligible. The three catchphrases used for the current US legal position, the 'Castle Doctrine', 'Make My Day' and 'Stand Your Ground', offer a heightened historical and cultural legitimacy to homeowners who act as judge, jury and executioner.

Common law, common problems?

Unlike their counterparts in the USA, Australian and English homeowners have no constitutional right to bear arms. Firearm regulations only permit those with legitimate reasons to own guns and store them in their home, including many farmers like Gordon McKay and Tony Martin. In both countries, the courts and legislatures struggle to clarify and stabilise the law applicable to defensive home ownership. Media and public opinion concerning threats to the home and the right to defend it are showcased in landmark court decisions and changing legislation.

England and Australia share a starting point in the common law, which has no special rules for the defence of property. However, homeowners who wound or kill an intruder in their own legitimate self-defence are not committing a crime, provided they do not use an unreasonable degree of force. The courts accept that a person being attacked cannot 'weigh to a nicety the exact measure of his necessary defensive action' in the heat of the moment (*Palmer v R*, 1971). Certainly, at the moment of confrontation with an intruder, a homeowner is hardly likely to be worrying about his or her legal position. But if an intruder dies or is wounded, the Australian or English homeowner may be arrested and face lengthy police questioning, followed by anxious delays until the decision is made to prosecute or not, and then perhaps a stressful trial before a jury decides whether the action was excusable as self-defence. It seems then that though the law supports those challenging intruders in cases of self-defence it lacks some clarity and predictability, as shown in our exemplar cases of Zimmerman, Zecevic, Martin and McKay. This suggests that social conversations around the lack of rights of householders may continue where this ambiguity remains, despite the law appearing to broadly support the use of force when it is needed.

Gordon McKay was convicted of manslaughter rather than murder, and the Australian appeal court reduced his sentence from three years to eighteen months (*R v McKay*, 1957). He was freed immediately by the Governor following 'an outcry in the press based, it is true, on ignorance and sentimentality' (Morris, 1960–62: 50). The decision that McKay was not a murderer, despite using excessive force to protect his property, changed the common law of Australia. However, thirty years later, the High Court considered the case of Fadil Zecevic, who killed his neighbour in their gated community, and the court reinstated the original common law position: the degree of force used in self-defence (or in defence of property) must be reasonable in the circumstances (*Zecevic v Director of Public Prosecutions*, 1987). Zecevic's name is associated with this legal principle still cited today, but there was no media outcry about his case; he did not conform to the model of the homeowner as sympathetic victim.

In contrast, when Tony Martin was convicted in 2000 of murder and received the UK mandatory sentence of life imprisonment, the media fanned the flames of public outrage (see Atkinson and Blandy, 2007). US observers were nonplussed; in their country, Martin's actions would hardly have seemed noteworthy, let alone criminal. The argument that Martin acted in self-defence and in genuine fear for his safety was rejected by the court. There was evidence that Martin had publicly advocated shooting criminals. He was lying in wait for the burglars he shot with an unlicensed gun, his Rottweiler dogs were roaming loose around the farm and his home, the memorably named Bleak House, had been deliberately booby-trapped. In 2001, new psychiatric evidence was submitted on his behalf that allowed the Court of Appeal to substitute a conviction for manslaughter (*Martin v R*, 2001). Martin was released after four years in prison; in 2003 he returned home to police protection and a hero's welcome.

The role of the media and public campaigners for new legislation that the courts would be obliged to follow, rather than following the common law rules, have had an effect in both the UK and Australia. However, the media and popular opinion is not always in favour of allowing greater leeway for homeowners to defend their property with lethal force. Australia's Model Criminal Code (Parliament of Australia, 2009) exonerates anyone acting in self-defence or to protect property, responding reasonably to circumstances as they perceive them. However, those acting only to protect property (rather than defending themselves) will not be exonerated if they *intended* to kill or to cause serious injury. This exception seems to acknowledge the danger of heightened emotions evoked by threats to the home while preserving the balance between state and homeowner. Yet Australian states and territories, keen to appease the defensive homeowner lobby, have not necessarily followed the Model Criminal Code (for an overview, see Tasmania Law Reform Institute, 2015). For example, the Queensland Occupants (Home Invasion) Protection Act 2002 is modelled on US-style protection for homeowners. In an official bulletin introducing similar legislation, thirty news reports were included about incidents where homeowners had killed or injured intruders (Sampford, 1997). The Queensland legislation was clearly a response to public and media debates about the respective positions of homeowner and home invader.

In 1998, the New South Wales Parliament also declared its policy 'that its citizens have a right to enjoy absolute safety from attack within dwelling-houses from intruders' (Home Invasion (Occupants Protection) Act 1998). That legislation made no distinction between self-defence and the defence of property. However, unlike the populist US pro-gun lobby, here the press was concerned that the new law would encourage people to keep loaded guns by their beds, commenting that the legal 'requirement for the safe storage of guns must still apply and should be enforced' (Sydney Morning Herald, 1998). That law has now been replaced by legislation less favourable to defensive home ownership (the NSW Crimes Amendment (Self-Defence) Act 2001).

The effect of legislation which focuses on the state of mind of the homeowner at the moment they face an intruder, is that each case must be considered on its merits taking into account the individual circumstances. This leads to delays and uncertainty, well illustrated by the case of Donald Brooke who in September 2011 was confronted by burglar Azzam Naboulsi in the lounge of his home at Yagoona, New South Wales. Brooke stabbed Naboulsi, who was armed with a stun gun. When Naboulsi later died there was 'a groundswell of public support' for Brooke as the victim homeowner potentially facing a manslaughter charge (Cuneo, 2012). It was not until four months later that the police notified Brooke that they would recommend to the coroner that no charges be laid because he had acted in self-defence; and not until December 2013 that the NSW Director for Public Prosecutions made the final decision that no proceedings would be brought – arguably a very long time to wait. The convoluted legal language of the official press statement explained that 'the available evidence is not capable of excluding beyond reasonable doubt the possibility that Mr Brookes (sic) acted in self-defence' (Office of the Director for Public Prosecutions, 2013). The law is clearly difficult to apply.

England has also seen several recent reviews of this area of law, with a trajectory towards ever greater leniency for homeowners. Tony Martin's conviction in 2000 provided the catalyst for a campaign for US-style legislation, which was lent further force by the brutal murder of homeowner John Monckton in 2004. In 2005 the Government decided not to introduce new legislation. The Home Secretary explained this by saying: 'I believe in that old adage "an Englishman's home is his castle" … the current law provides that … but needs to be better explained to all concerned' (BBC, 2005). This familiar rhetoric was part of government activities designed to reassure homeowners that they were entitled to self-defence. The Director of Public Prosecutions briefed the press that an 'informal trawl' through prosecution records had found only eleven prosecutions for attacking intruders in the past fifteen years, of which only five had resulted in convictions (Crown Prosecution Service, 2005). A public leaflet advised that 'the more extreme the circumstances and the fear felt, the more force you can lawfully use in self-defence', while warning that actions motivated by 'malice and revenge with the intent of inflicting punishment through injury or death' could never be considered reasonable self-defence (Crown Prosecution Service and the Association of Chief Police Officers, 2005).

The Law Commission of England and Wales was also asked to review defences to murder, to calm the furore surrounding the Martin case. It published two reports (Law Commission, 2004; 2006); the later report was illustrated by a cartoon of a pyjama-clad householder wielding a baseball bat against a masked burglar armed with a knife (Figure 7.2). The UK government continued to hesitate over a major change in the law. In 2009 it introduced a provision to reduce murder to manslaughter where someone loses self-control as a result of fearing serious violence or from a justifiable sense of being seriously wronged; it would not apply to anyone motivated by a 'considered desire for revenge' (Coroners and Justice Act, 2009). The provision about self-control has not yet been tested in court, but when giving judgment in a case where a burglar had killed the homeowner, the Lord Chief Justice stated that: 'If either of these men was justified in losing his self control, it was the deceased [the homeowner]' (*R. v Dawes*, 2013: 66). It therefore seems

7.2 Householder confronts night-time intruder, as illustrated in *Murder, Manslaughter and Infanticide* (Law Commission, 2006)

likely that a homeowner who killed a burglar would face the lesser charge of manslaughter.

The media has subsequently forced the UK government into repeated efforts to reconcile vengeful and vocal homeowner interests with the need to discourage violent self-help or revenge. In 2013, the government explained that it was anxious to counter 'public perception that the law is balanced in favour of the intruder ... [and is] committed to ensure that people have the protection that they need when they defend themselves against intruders' (Ministry of Justice, 2013). Attempting to appease a vociferous press and section of the public, the Crime and Courts Act 2013 exonerates householders who use a 'disproportionate' (although not 'grossly disproportionate' level of force) when defending themselves against intruders in their homes. Although the new provision does not, as in the USA, apply if the householder acts only in defence of property, criminal justice system professionals opposed this measure when it was first introduced. This was characterised as 'state-sponsored revenge' by Tony Martin's defence barrister, and the Criminal Bar Association's chair called it 'sanctioned extrajudicial execution' (Gibb, 2010). The law will remain difficult to apply in practice, even though the new Act has further tilted the balance towards the individual homeowner over the punishment of intruders.

Conclusions

The prevalent discourse of fear and crime that adheres to the home, which is fanned by media and government and reflected in popular culture has distorted risk assessment and increased homeowners' sense of victimisation. This is particularly acute when individual sense of identity is conflated with the home. This chapter has traced the rise of a victim culture for homeowners which allows pent-up aggression against threatening and despised 'others' to be legitimately discharged in defence of the home. We have argued that this underlies the violent or lethal response of some homeowners to intrusion, and the popular support for these actions.

The proper role of the state in dealing with crime is now seriously in question, as courts and legislatures across the USA, Australia and the UK wrestle with the issue of relinquishing the power of punishment to individual homeowners. Campaigners for law reform in Australia and the UK demand legal protection for those who violently defend themselves against burglars, pointing to the clarity of the law in the USA and much lower burglary rates there. For some US commentators, the comparative defencelessness of English and Australian homeowners stems from unreasonable restrictions on the ownership of firearms and the law's failure to protect the rights of those who defend their homes. The idea of householders as domestic sovereigns now appears to have real purchase in the US states whose laws permit lethal force to be used against intruders, yet fear of crime remains for many homeowners.

8

The fortress archipelago

We have made a series of observations about the ways the home has become an increasingly defended site. Though we should recognise the variability of 'forting-up' at the level of the individual home in this chapter we offer what we see as an intuitive and evidence-based analysis that extends our suggestion that a range of economic, social, political and technological forces are re-shaping the experience of individualism and home ownership today. We can advance further the argument we have developed by drawing out these trends and patterns in urban and domestic life. It is now notable, for example, that we can identify homes which have several layers of security within and around them – armed people, in defended homes, living in gated communities within segregated and heavily policed cities. These layers and structures of home defence on the ground of many cities and urban spaces form the basis of our explorations in this chapter, as we seek to understand more about the social, political and spatial position of the home within arrangements of defence and outward rejection, developed in order to protect and secure householders.

Patterns of social control and surveillance have both widened and deepened considerably since writers like Cohen (1979) first considered the ways that policing by the state operated within and around cities and the state at that time. Recent work on the changing nature of public space (Minton, 2012), the privatisation of many city spaces (Blomley, 2010) and urban crime and security systems (Coaffee and Wood, 2006) offer nuanced pictures of the interplay between scales and arrangements that have been put in place to ensure more fully secured and locked-down spaces. In these contexts, we have also witnessed new and more aggressive forms of social control intended to socially cleanse and pacify neighbourhoods and streets and prevent signs of social disorder emerging (Beckett and Herbert, 2009). We argue here that the deeper result of these changes has been to create new forms of policing and state/ private surveillance systems which are connected to an archipelago of districts and homes containing the politically vocal and materially affluent. In short, an essential driver for demanding safe, predictable and orderly environments has been generated by the way that such groups have made strong and effective demands for personal autonomy, reductions in disorder, private or enhanced policing aligned with government priorities.

Such governing through crime, as Simon (2007) terms it, has generated local legal ordinances (within cities and gated communities) to reduce potential threats to their position. Yet, as we have argued throughout, these tessellated spaces of ownership and material means are also shaped and produced by modes of government which promote market solutions and mechanisms in all spaces of social life. Thus we can identify the melding together of political ideology and social values with physical homes and security systems as a cluster of relationships. We cannot make sense of defensive home ownership if we strip away the wider forces and systems of which it is ultimately a part.

In this chapter, we connect the apparently benign politics of home and safety with the kinds of aggressive stances and actions taken by policing and other agents of social control located at some remove from the home, at essential borders and points in these wider systems. Many of the forms of social control permeating the scales and layers around the private home, and the ways that more aggressive forms of pacification and control emerge in spaces around it, are indicators of the nature of the contemporary home and its important place within political decisions about allocations of resource by the state. This 'domopolitics' (Walters, 2004) (literally, politics of the home) also operates at numerous scales and is threaded through a number of important social and political institutions. As we argue later in this chapter, home has become an important building block of much larger tessellated mosaics that engage concerns with economic boosterism (the growth and desirability of ownership as a signal of success and personal security), social control (the pacification of public spaces as though they were extensions of the living room and other key domestic spaces) and in-group identity (the play of migration politics and the concerted

8.1 Bunker module, Australia

policing of borders and boundaries at the edge and within the nation state).

   We can identify numerous defensive layers (panic rooms, gated neigh-bourhoods, bordered homelands) akin to Russian dolls that are used to help protect the home and wider socio-political constructions of home and national territory. Such layers of defence have been created in order to defend the constituent parts of the body politic, itself primarily identified as respectable homeowner/voters. So the role of this chapter is to further outline the relationship between the territorial core of the home (Porteous, 1976) and a wider set of arrangements that are nested within each other like a series of semi-porous membranes (Bottomley and Moore, 2007) that produce an almost foam-like space (Klauser, 2010) with connected yet discrete units of secure homes and neighbourhoods that combine to form a much larger system designed to insulate the affluent from risk. These conjoined spaces are fundamentally aligned with the dominant values of unfettered autonomy, calm and predictability. These can be identified most strongly in productive, owning and self-determining agents; their apotheosis is the homeowner. In short, the domestic fortress is a model of residence, but also an index or sign of the wider extent of prevailing market orientations, inequality and neoliberal political manoeuvres more broadly. This era is characterised by a range of privatising and socially controlling apparatuses aligned with desires and plans for ownership that cross the majority of the population and which thus enjoy significant legitimacy within popular social discourse despite inequalities which prevent the realisation of these ambitions. The fortress home is thus not simply a type of home but also a model of control that connects both to and from political, policing and managerial discourses operating at a wider series of scales. While the private home is formed by these forces its constitution as a physical product or space in a grounded setting is the manifestation of ideological commitments to secure affluence. This chapter begins with an analysis of the connections between the home and the neighbourhood, before examining the wider relationship between the home and urban spaces. Finally, we examine the nature of a contemporary domo-politics and the growing archipelago of secured domestic spaces in terms of a contemporary political economy of the home.

Layers of defence

One of the main features of contemporary residential landscapes is the emergence of increasingly securitised layers of defence around the home in addition to the kind of target-hardening measures undertaken in relation to the home itself. The proliferation of gated residential

8.2 Gated residential units, London

developments is a strong visible example of the tendency to create protective and secure spaces that shield the private home from intrusion, as well as producing higher value landscapes by developers and prestige-seeking owners (Low, 2003). This securitised residential landscape has become normalised in many regions globally, where it is now the most prevalent type of new-build construction in many cities and areas. Even in countries like the UK where traditional streetscapes have historically emphasised open spaces, social encounters and porous neighbourhood designs (Schoon, 2001), we find more gated compounds and ever-larger gated communities that cocoon and insulate the homes within them.

Deep-rooted desires for security and privacy have increasingly been realised through the expanding fortunes of the affluent and the parallel growth of gated developments. These changes further amplify the ways in which previously public spaces have been enclosed, pacified and attached to private residential environments (Minton, 2012). The new-found popularity of gated communities in the UK and other countries suggests such rationales and market logics have proliferated; secured micro-enclaves are constructed to add value to 'dangerous' locations by appearing to protect against property and car crime in central locations, while adding further value to property in more suburban locales. The result of these new trends in home design and neighbourhood planning has been to create a new yet relatively discrete landscape which, in countries like the UK, is more or less alien to the traditional forms of streetscape and urban life.

Gated communities are certainly not a new phenomenon, and there are parallels with the private streets and squares of eighteenth-century London and the city states of sixteenth-century northern Italy. Yet walls and gates within cities are a new and distinct feature of developments which are increasingly extensive. The effect of such changes has been to assist in a marked process of privatising public streets and exacerbating forms of segregation in which the affluent are more or less physically and socially closed-off from other social and identity groups in the city. Gated communities thus highlight the ways in which the private home and notions of ordinary domesticity can become powerful and subordinating ideals of community governance – that which lies outside is deemed deviant from or dangerous to those spaces which have been successfully pacified in this way. Meanwhile many new neighbourhoods are made to conform to notions of predictability and control and cater for an increasing range of social functions as their scale and commercial spaces increase. For example, in one Australian study (Dowling *et al.*, 2010), 22 per cent of residents in a gated community in the centre of Sydney said that all of their social activities could be satisfied within the estate.

Why have these changes taken place? Aside from the obvious observation that gating and fortification responds to a desire for social prestige, protection from harm and developer profitability, the move to gated communities also demonstrates a much deeper form of social escape and attempt at what recent urban studies have described as a partial exit (Andreotti *et al.*, 2015) from shared spaces and municipal goals. Again, this suggests that physical space and its structure is important in thinking through connections to a broader social politics which is increasingly antagonistic to shared forms of provision and insurance and more predisposed to private solutions and services. The logic of neoliberalism is thus further accepted and internalised because of the way that urban space and homes are created and maintained as private spaces, with systems of security and maintenance largely unrelated to those provided by a withering state that was previously the guarantor of personal and community safety.

Rising inequality and personal wealth have helped to fuel the purchase of increasing levels of total privacy and bespoke security services

8.3 Steel shuttered house, Detroit

(Atkinson, 2015). These services have helped to produce a more prickly outward appearance to many neighbourhoods that appears intentionally intimidating to those with ill-intent, perhaps, but also generating a wider unease in those encountering the kind of security landscape permeating many locales. The highly securitised landscapes of what in other respects are quite ordinary spaces in many towns and cities can be seen as a kind of solidification or visual manifestation of fear among the affluent, whose reference points are anxieties about violent crime and invasion, but also a general move away from social contact more broadly that permeates the biographies of the affluent and disconnected (Elliott and Lemert, 2006). Private services and policing supplant and provide further impetus to escape traditional modes of local government provision and accountability.

Daily patterns of movement from and to gated communities can be understood as a time–space trajectory of segregation, in which maximal separation from different and potentially intrusive or dangerous groups is maintained even beyond the boundaries of these secure developments (Atkinson and Flint, 2004). Forms of mobility are engaged which allow shielding from risks or social contact, such as the example of the powerful car with tinted rear windows, chauffeur-driven cars or taxis which allow shuttling between aerial nests in urban systems increasingly designed to allow the wealthy to circulate in unhindered and discrete ways – private highways, underground parking systems, premium cabin and transportation services. As Flusty (2001) identified, this is a kind of 'interdictory city', produced by high-income group anger and acted upon by politicians, police forces and related institutions concerned with the management of disorder, difference and the sources of potential harm to property and persons that results in designs and management systems that seek to displace the poor and the dangerous.

Many gated neighbourhoods are now constructed along defensive lines, and this has arguably produced a more unsettled urban culture, indicative of a predisposition to face down possible risks and close off more casual or random social contact. More deeply, such arrangements also suggest the emergence of an embattled and fearful mindset among the wealthy (Atkinson, 2015). Writers like Low (2003) and Maher (2003) indicate that far from unworried freedom, life in gated communities includes the psychic costs of exaggerated concerns with security routines, anxieties about invasion and the identification and exclusion of non-residents. When outside such protected bubbles, the sense of vulnerability also appears marked, especially for young people. The more time spent in the home, the more the environment is synonymous with control and predictability and the less residents appear to be at ease when traversing spaces outside the home, as Setha Low observes: 'Residents' fear, worry, anxiety, and paranoia are constructed out of a discourse of fear of crime and others that resonates at many scales including the local, regional, and national' (2008: 252).

Domesticating public space

While new themes of a hostile and surveillant quality to city life have been identified by many commentators, these changes have also re-emphasised the meaning of home as a space of emancipation from such forms of risk and control. Nevertheless, home remains a refuge that requires labour and maintenance to ensure it remains safe, and as writers like Low (2003) argue, to leave a protected home in a gated neighbourhood is to sally forth into a less predictable world beyond the gates. The implication of creating neighbourhoods and homes that feel like secured districts in a sea of less stable social encounters is significant – what happens to notions of home, civility and the social itself under conditions where urban space is segregated, controlled and splintered into these domains, managed or owned by diverse private individuals and institutions (Graham and Marvin, 2001)?

What some see as the apparent social disorder lying outside protected residential zones, itself produced by forms of social disinvestment and welfare retrenchment, have helped to legitimise the ways the affluent have divided themselves from more deprived groups through gating, guarding and 'forting-up', and the rise of aggressive responses to poverty by states and citizens. Gating begets gating, so the fortress home percolates through the urban fabric and generates hostility between class positions. People with problems are seen as social actors making flawed choices, rather than resulting of inequality and systemic forces. This all too convenient form of social politics and scapegoating nevertheless produces narratives of good and bad places, areas to be avoided and spaces that offer refuge from an envying class of yobs, skivers and the criminal. If anything, these anxieties are further enhanced by the kinds of racist and religiously inflected discussions of social and national change that have emerged particularly in recent years as migration and terrorism have been discussed more frequently and indeed more often connected as problems that should be addressed. Yet, just as these social influences make a retreat indoors more desirable, we can also see how the rules and scripts of private, domestic life have been relayed outwards to spare our public selves the risks of exposure. These messages are articulated by both homeowners and wider publics, demanding that politicians, law enforcement agencies and new private institutions now managing public spaces exclude particular risks and risky groupings.

These patterns of control can clearly be identified in measures to combat anti-social behaviour in the UK, the ordinances preventing begging in many US cities, and in the zero-tolerance policing responses to disorder in many countries and cities globally. In this context, the home is a critical nexus, a point where social and political flows converge between the values internalised and attached to the home and those values overlaid onto urban politics, managerialism and policing. What is particularly marked is how these values (control, freedom from

8.4 Forting-up, London

interference and privacy) are bolstered by those of the market, making control and autonomy over space the critical foundation of a market-legal conception of the home and increasingly of the rules of conduct and encounter acceptable in public space (Blomley, 2010).

Despite our reading of what might be thought of as purely a retreat into the defended home it is also important to see how this withdrawal has strengthened expectations about how public encounters and problems should be addressed, both by private individuals and collective institutions in spaces outside the home. The feeling that we have located some form of liberation in our homes has generated amplified attempts at annexing and pacifying public spaces and making them similarly safe and predictable. As Sennett (1974) argued, social actors often anticipate potential threats by fomenting demands for safety and comfort in spaces external to the private home. Thus we find how broader ideas and norms, of social and political individualism, have been important in generating stronger demands for a public sphere that offers unfettered and risk-free spaces for private social actors. Vocal calls for collective action around sanctions against those deemed to be at the root of public risks have been generated by a growing sense of broadened personalised responsibility, and the feeling that collective or state-based responses are not available or effective, particularly as this relates to personal safety. As David Sibley has suggested:

> In effect, rules that might be applied in the well-ordered private space of the home are extended to public space, so that all space becomes *heimlich* [homeland or home] for the powerful. The idea of public space as a space of difference, of encounters with strangers as well as with familiars, is erased. (Sibley, 2005: 158)

The patterns and general values of domestic social life, or what goes on behind closed doors, have become directed outwards and are now articulated through the goals of political life. The fundamental principles of domesticity have become scripts for running and organising public space as well as the expectations of (higher income) users of these spaces. Apparently, civilising scripts undergirding our expectations of the private home emerge outwards as rules and norms for action and expectations in shared spaces. The effect of this is to append public space to the regimes of behaviour and taste of the home and the emanating social values of this institution, particularly as this relates to higher income groups. In short, the control of public space is generated and demarcated by higher income groups to whom policing agencies and political actors are fiscally and electorally beholden. The result is that public spaces, commonly streets, city squares and iconic spaces, are managed by emphasising new rules of conduct, becoming more like extensions of the public 'front' room of the home by the enforcement of 'civility', designing-out difference and poverty, ordinances against profanity, drunkenness and so on.

Writers such as Blomley (2010) show these regimes at work in new Canadian city ordinances; new rights against impeding pedestrians were enacted so that being approached in a public space is equated with a kind of personal interference and infringement. Similarly the work of Mitchell (2003; 2005) finds such processes in the USA effectively raised the bar of legal precedent so that in some jurisdictions the person on the street is now accorded the same rights of 'quiet enjoyment' as domestic residents in their homes. In such circumstances, bodies located

8.5 Fortress suburbia, Vancouver

in public spaces become identified as those not at home or out of place, rather than being constructed as essentially equal and public citizens. Such legislation shifts the terms of citizenship and the right to the city while deepening the sense that the domestic home has become the lynchpin of political debates about the constitution of sociality, discourses around public interaction and acceptable conduct. While the home is a founding element of these new debates and rules, we also need to expose the implicit understandings of private property and inherent inequality upon which such notions are founded. Access to 'public' space has thereby been increasingly defined in relation to a common understanding of what the private home means and thus, what public space should mean – a space in which private individuals meet on terms consonant with their market power and standing rather than as equal citizens.

John Hannigan (1998) has argued that the kind of cities and public spaces we now inhabit are places of fantasy and escape more than ever before. Many cities currently have central entertainment districts, places of spectacle, public art to inspire the walker-by, to say nothing of the widespread development of night-time economies. Yet Hannigan's central argument is that these spectacles and sources of excitement are ultimately insipid simulations of a more authentic form of urban life and about which we feel much greater anxiety. The response to our desires for excitement has therefore been channelled into creating spaces with a sense of exhilaration, without allowing risks to intrude on these experiences. Hence, we see what Goldberger (1996) called the rise of urbanoid spaces that appear to be like real urban space, but which are ultimately imitations of real examples and which emphasise forms of consumption over social encounter. Driving these shifts is the sense that the sterility of daily life generated by pronounced social affluence again raises demands that spaces outside the home are safer so that moments of potential exposure, such as getting out of cars, crossing streets, accessing shopping areas, are made more fully secure.

The changes we have described here have generated socially sanitised forms of urban life that imply that regimes of public expectation and taste generate what Jonathan Simon describes as 'hypercontrolled' spaces, where outward waves of enclosure and safety are sought and the production of:

> a standard of security and comfort that virtually no external environment can sustain, unless that external environment itself becomes a larger internal space. As the family is placed in ever more nested security, the goal is redundancy. Locked inside SUVs, parked in a secured garage, locked inside a 'gated' and privately policed subdivision, the contemporary suburban family is arriving at an 'equilibrium' as circumscribed as the much-feared career criminal, locked inside a high-technology armoured cell within a super-max prison. (Simon, 2007: 203)

The increasingly insulated form of private and public life formed under these emerging conditions inaugurates what Mike Davis (1992) terms a process of 'padding the bunker'. These processes of risk management in the built environment privilege the security of places and homes for the affluent and their consumption habits while marginalising politically and socially unacceptable groups. Cities are thereby partitioned in ways that apparently lift up or abstract richer groups from the fabric of the city, further ghettoising and containing the poor. Underneath the kind of lives and circuits experienced by the wealthy and social elites, the middle classes have been increasingly exposed to violence and the visibility of disorder since the 1970s. These shifting patterns help to explain what Garland (2001) terms the rise of a 'culture of control', where crime is the primary lens for viewing social life, producing increasingly aggressive and illiberal responses to questions of transgression and incarceration. These feelings of ambient uncertainty in so many lives raise the value of those social anchors and physical shells to which we tether ourselves or climb into for comfort and security.

A key political driver for many of these changes can be identified in the feelings and fears of high-income groups in many western societies as they have become suffused with the kinds of anger and resentment previously thought to be reserved for the poor and working class. As Young (2007) describes it, a coruscating fury in this class is generated by relatively new insecurities in work, the prospect of a fall from status and longer-established fears of crime. This emotional condition has bolstered vengeful drives to secure modes of punishment and sanctions directed at proxies for the real sources of these fears – the poor, working-class, minorities, foreigners of one kind of another and identifications of criminality which are overlaid onto all of these identities. The resulting programmes devised by various tiers of government have taken the form of extensive social surveillance, the retrenchment of welfare programmes and the social cleansing of spaces outside the home in the cause of protecting respectable society and boosting prosperity.

This context of tessellated neoliberalism has generated the provision of nests to which fear-fuelled retreats can be made, as well as demands to make spaces outside the home safer and less prone to random or troublesome encounters. The intervening spaces of the city are subjected to aggressive policing methods, largely directed towards an intolerance of social difference and even the lowest forms of disorder (such as behaviours like non-consumption or congregation) and the celebration of spaces offering the possibility for unfettered consumption activities. In many western cities, spaces that were municipal and shared public spaces have been reworked to adopt regular and corporate forms of policing and the shutting down of functions and pursuits that were freely available (such as public benches, parks and fountains and even some streets). In response to this, the current manner of managing many city shopping centres or malls suggests the adoption of domestication strategies to tame the perceived riskiness of these places (Flint, 2006). The turn toward competition for footloose capital at the level of cities and regions has also underpinned the resulting social scarification of public space, pursued in order to promote safer spaces that appeal to corporate executives and creative workers.

The legal basis of private home ownership and its influence now extends through cities, their public spaces and neighbourhoods (such as so-called 'common interest' and gated residential developments) and the leasing of what was once public space by civic authorities to private developers (now seen in cities like Melbourne, Sydney, Los Angeles, New York, Birmingham and Sheffield among many others) to produce new forms of 'privately owned public space'. Such shifts signal broader changes in the way we conceive the place of the self in relation to domestic and public space, as well as how we deal with otherness in spaces outside the home. Instead of socially diverse, exciting and authentic street spaces, we have created 'non-places', substituting our associations of danger with anodyne, riskless and bland spaces of consumption activity, but through which the private living room has become a template for the design and control of public spaces. Perhaps Richard Sennett (1974) is right to suggest we are happy to tolerate the bland qualities of our public spaces in return for the reward of our autonomy within the home itself. We move ever more emphatically to reside and preside over domestic spaces, while using the scripts and discourses of these familiar home territories as the underpinnings of public expectations and management techniques that offer what might be identified by some as more civilised spaces in which to live, shop, work and play.

A wider politics of domesticity

References to 'home' add force to a range of metaphors about place and the claim of social groups to it – identifying who we are, who belongs, who should be included, and by extension, those who should remain beyond the pale (the external fence of the Anglo-Saxon home). These metaphors are commonly found in the relatively recent language of national homeland security in the USA and that of borders in the UK. The idea of a domopolitics (Walters, 2004), a politics of the home, homeland and their ascribed values, has become widespread in public

8.6 Fortress home inside gated community, Istanbul

language and discussions. In such discourse, the everyday play of national and wider regional identities are inflected with ethnic–national group-ings and designations of otherness and exclusion, notably within debates about migrant workers and immigration provoked by new levels of international population instability. While the impression we have sug-gested here is of people hunkering down inside homes padded and modified to offer greater security, these sites are also located within wider arrangements, scales and socio-political narratives that speak of homes and home-like spaces which require protection – using the metaphor of home as a means of recruiting support and action, usually in order to strengthen security in various ways.

Many commentators thus argue that at each of these corresponding scales, national and international security systems focus on questions of national–ethnic identity, disruptive flows of people (Aas, 2011) and concerns about terror and insurgent local urban populations that lead to more entrenched identities and defensive routines to protect home-land spaces. The net result of these changes is that in the name of offering calmer and more pacified core territories, the spaces around the home have become more socially inhospitable, particularly for the socially vulnerable. Perhaps the most obvious of such changes is the use of European borders to control the flow of migrants deemed to be intrinsically criminal by virtue of entering the home-like space of the region. At a local level, the implementation of city curfews and private policing regimes (Minton, 2012) against young people and more aggressive policing routines in general provide notable examples in many cities (Beckett and Herbert, 2009). Across these scales, the idea of governing can be linked to the management of a home: 'Homeland Security is not only a matter of articulating the domestic sphere to a national and global crisis/threat but of developing and acting upon a set of technical strategies from the domestic sphere as a response to this broader crisis as a threat to a Homeland.' (Hay, 2006: 352)

The end result of these narratives is to increasingly mobilise social thinking around the idea that social welfare is a private or personal responsibility. These themes take us full circle and back to ideas of ontological security, household well-being and the insurance of the household against future threats. It is a short step from these deepening and extending beliefs to metaphors of households tightening belts and household management, frequently deployed as the conceit through which market-oriented governments embark on cuts to public services as they maintain privileges for owners and the more affluent. The message remains clear: there is a nexus of interests between political aspirations to govern, the courting of aspirant populations and neoliberal principles of market exchange and privatism pursued throughout social domains and institutions and which returns us to gated communities and the clusters of gated mansions and homes that, in combination, generate long defensive facades.

Domesticity, the domain of the household accorded territorial rights of expulsion of non-members, forms a powerful script or organising social narrative. There is a consonance between neoliberalism and the rights and values of homeowners that can be traced to the desire for unfettered social and economic exchange, the inalienability of these rights, and the celebration of affluence and the home as a commodity, which 'has overrun' exceeds its status as a place of residence and personal development. Access to these 'bubbles of security' and consumption practices has been largely determined by relative affluence. Yet with precarious living no longer restricted to the low paid (Standing,

2011), insecurity of being, anxiety and the search for metaphysical assurances or distractions have created further social atomisation. This is often expressed through a desire for an authenticity of the self, sometimes manifested through consumption. The anxiety at the core of these ways of social life further feeds the growth imperatives and logic of neoliberalism: work hard, buy your own home, and seek whatever assurances you can, with little regard for others because ultimately we are on our own.

A significant result of the shift into market societies siince the 1980s (Currie, 1997) has been the alignment of owner with state interests and an overlay of defensive arrangements in which the state acts to privilege and second-guess the needs of a home-owning constituency, shielding it from fears of social otherness and external threats. These values find physical expression in fortified homes, calls for unfettered private lives, the withering of social institutions and supports, the rise of gated communities and calls for the privatisation of policing and controls over public spaces. All of these sites and practices offer economic gains to those capable of seizing the remaining commons, while espousing the need for vigilance and fear over the development of more pro-social routines and investments. As Winlow and Hall (2013) forcefully argue, the social domain has been partially evacuated, leaving the idea of the social as a hollow metaphor and the realisation that despite imperatives to combat social exclusion the affluent wish to move out of relationships into spaces of private seclusion. This logic is even more pernicious than it appears at first blush. Since growing inequality has appeared at a time of increasing wealth and government supports for the affluent, the decline in the public realm has become more palpable. These shifts feed a fortress mentality propagated by anxious and angry citizens imagining the prospect of urban insurgency and riots, degraded public spaces and chasm-like inequalities. Under these conditions, property has become a sign of security and an envied position, thus feeding a logic of protection. Read in this way, fortification, gating, border controls, and migration policies become defensive, exoskeletal scales built around an archipelago of affluent owners in homes and castellated neighbourhoods.

The move into secure and private spaces and affiliations toward private responses has been given a contemporary twist by Lieven De Cauter (2004), who refers to these shifts as a process of 'capsularization'. This term expresses how the home and other aspects of our urban

systems fit together in the context of urban and social anxiety that sur-
rounds us. In our daily lives, we inhabit the capsules of cars, urban
enclaves, cocoon-like homes and gated communities in order to feel a
sense of shelter and to enable our movement through complex transportation and information technology systems. The impression De
Cauter conjures is of the seamless integration and overlay of these protected modes of social action that ultimately give rise to 'an architecture
that functions like a space capsule, that creates an artificial *ambiente*,
minimizes communication with the outside and forms an isolated environment of its own' (2004: 150).

The ascent of a more emphatically interior domestic life suggests
that 'real' urban places have been partly exited in the search for
enclosed spaces, pods and capsules in an attempt to maintain personal
security. Our lives inside are thus maintained in spaces that provide
the appearance of social life, but are ultimately illusory since our ambition is to suspend and limit the intrusion of the real and more unruly
world outside. There is a deep social misanthropy implied in this
process of capsularisation, wherein the home can become its own kind
of resort or 'all-in' destination, constructed to satisfy demands for protection. High definition television, digital audio, surround sound, and
the photo-real graphics of contemporary videogames increase the
home's capacity to offer virtual compensations for the messier reality
outdoors.

From the 1960s onwards, sociologists like Richard Sennett have
argued that there is a marked tendency by the affluent to move away
from unruly urban space in search of predictability and order. The
concept of order appears as a potentially powerful means of explaining
a range of interrelated social transformations. The increasingly emphatic
rejection of the public sphere begins perhaps in Sennett's (1974) description of the *émigration intérieure* by the French aristocracy as they shunned
public political life, instead returning to the comforts and privacy of
their estates. Similarly, Lasch's (1995) work on what he termed the revolt
of the elites interpreted these issues in a more explicit spatial frame. He
observed that there was a growing trend in American cities for corporate and political elites to move out of the public realm and its associated
institutions. In both examples and especially in relation to gated residential development, the actions of elites suggest that their vision of
domesticity requires a precise combination of control and comfort,

attributes they no longer associate with collective forms of consumption and experience outside the home.

The growth of home ownership has been complementary to the growing market orientations and political projects mounted by both right and centrist political parties globally over the past few neoliberal decades. It was particularly during this time that forms of personal prosperity and control came to be seen as antagonistic to collective provision, and more generally, the public realm itself. In this context, the prototypical affluent western home with its new and multiple satisfactions manifests as a central site for endless consumption. In talking of such values, we can refer to an ideology of home ownership (Saunders, 1990) that stressed personal liberties, maximum autonomy from intrusions in the home and which saw the private home largely as a tradeable asset. These values drive a narrative or understanding of home as a particularly private, inviolable space, within which its residents appear as consumer sovereigns.

The broader point we can make here is that the social values and politics of the home are grounded in the spaces and localised practices of the home itself and the new kinds of territory that have been spawned around it. Here we return again to the idea of these grounded and concrete formations of the defended home and neighbourhoods as a tessellated neoliberalism in which the values of the market are expressed through the interlocking spaces of these domestic fortresses and fortress neighbourhoods. In these spaces, we find private individuals, rather than citizens, who embrace or are subconsciously the receptacles of ideals of private rights, defensive enjoyment, personal investment, profit-making and an understanding of the role of government as a system dedicated to the celebration and expansion of the privileges.

The idea of nesting suggests the building of a nurturing space, yet it can also refer to residence of an object or person within a broader scale or container. Both uses of the word can be deployed in relation to the model of contemporary home ownership we elaborate here – a model in which the home acts as social insurance and a form of defence/containment within larger spatial scales that also works to exclude and control anxiety-inducing populations and risks. We are now able to visualise a society around us comprising nested scales of defensiveness. Writing at the turn of the twenty-first century, J. G. Ballard in his book *Cocaine Nights* had already elaborated a vision of what the residential life of such a society might look like in his description of a gated residential compound on the French Riviera as offering 'the logic of Goldfinger's lair raised to a planetary intensity'. As Setha Low has argued:

> Most people want to feel loved, safe, and secure at home. But the strategies being used to accomplish this security – building higher walls and adding trained guards and security patrols to gated communities, improving home surveillance technology, adding both a private and public police presence on city streets and in neighborhood complexes, creating safe rooms, stockpiling supplies for a terrorist attack – produce a new level of reactivity. (Low and Smith, 2006: 252)

These new spaces of governance and privacy have generated anxieties about new forms of social exclusion and the lack of accountability of new security apparatuses operating within them. The film *La Zona* highlights these localised uses of force and defence in the absence of effective state structures. The film shows the residential life of a gated community, positioned like a wealthy citadel over a city filled with abject poverty, an image of an archipelago of affluent bunker neighbourhoods in a sea of urban poverty and exclusion. A bungled burglary leaves a resident and two of the intruders dead, with the other intruder, a boy, seeking refuge in the basement of one of the houses. The film addresses crucial themes in contemporary urban life: neoliberalism's legacy of profound inequality and the enmity between those in and outside its reward system. Director Rodrigo Pla has stated that the film is about the painful social trajectories traversed by those symbolically left outside the new affluent and fortified zones created by economic growth alongside persistent social inequality.

Not only do the kinds of spaces presented in *La Zona* represent the physical manifestation of wealth in the built environment, they also offer concrete distinctions between the class positions and resentment of those excluded outside and those holed-up within. As Pla argues, the very obvious social split between rich and poor symbolised by gates, guards and walls, drives the impression that the poverty outside can be explained through flawed individual choices and personal deficiencies rather than the unfair workings of the social and economic system. The effect is the production of a middle class that is both fearful and aggressive, signed up to projects for controlling the spaces and people outside their front doors.

Conclusion

A number of broad trends have generated novel spatial orderings of public and private life in which the home is a key component, space that allows us to think more broadly about many of the changes occurring within cities and within national political frameworks. These changes have led to a kind of nesting of nesting – a search for 'cosy' and safe homes away from social risks that lie at the centre of numerous outer defensive scales and new institutional arrangements, in which armed owners live in toughened homes with panic rooms, inside walled developments, in cities with aggressive policing regimes and pervasive surveillance systems. The background to these forms of social and spatial division are forms of social inequality – of wealth, opportunity and human security – all of which have intensified under market-oriented modes of governance. At the heart of this complex ideological, physical and social amalgam rest multitudinous ego-centres, the defended homes of the affluent that form the bedrock of these methods of exclusion and containment, which we have termed here tessellated neoliberalism. This is surely De Cauter's capsular civilisation writ large.

We have observed not only how homes have become increasingly defended, but also how neighbourhoods, cities and nations are also organised as home-like spaces, constructed in ways designed to repel those deemed not to belong. Home lies at the heart of a broader spatial order across which methods of control, the filtering of bodies and insulating social and political practices operate, around and beyond the home itself. Yet despite ideological fervour for the idea of the home as an insurance against future insecurities, the global events of 2008 highlighted the role of housing in a new form of crisis and led to the loss of many millions of homes globally. Perversely, the resulting social outfall has been a milieu in which owning a home appears ever more appealing as a retreat from the uncertainties of public life and in which the state has only more emphatically sought to protect the interests of those who own their own property.

Although this might seem a story of loss and appropriation, much of any nostalgia for a more collective way of life has been submerged in the headlong pursuit of private affluence. These new conditions have brought widespread boosts to the living conditions for many and we should note the difficulty of challenging such powerful ideologies; resistance has been marginalised and neutered by social atomisation resulting from assaults on ideas of society and the meaning of citizen-ship. Seen in this light, the fantasy of escape to the fully protected home offers the promise of safety, but also a space of possible incarceration. In seeking to get away, we end up run-to-ground, fixed in place behind gates, walls, locks, buttressed doorways and windows. So the flight into the expansive interior universes of many new homes also presents us with a vision of such spaces as sites of cyclical detention – where para-doxically we move from being holed-up at home to being at relative liberty in more or less public spaces.

9

Complexes of the domestic fortress

The core of our argument has been that across architectural, technological, social, political and legal domains we can observe how it is that many private homes have become a kind of domestic fortress, designed in more or less overt ways to avoid social contact and to repel real or imagined potential intruders. While the fears upon which these changes have been built are not illusory, they have helped fashion mentalities and dominating built environments that speak of widespread attempts at escaping social contact and risk. We have also made the perhaps slightly more subtle observation that continuities and new features also exist in this social and physical landscape, which must be part of our understanding how domestic and urban life now operates in more socially withdrawn, market-oriented and private-leaning societies.

Despite the history of castles, private squares and urban policing, there is something identifiably new at work in the landscape of gated communities, CCTV and doorway cameras, elaborate home security systems, guards and gardeners, powerful cars and remote control gates. As a social and technological system, this landscape combines to facilitate a mode of living we hold to be qualitatively different from earlier modes of urban and domestic life. These observations, as we have seen, connect with a range of criminological, legal, sociological and geographical analyses of key changes that now facilitate a more defended mode of home ownership. Fuel to these changes is the increasing circulation of myths and realities of a wide range of risks, many of them now more invasive due to the penetration of information technologies into the home, among a panoply of other political and economic factors generating more fearful social actors.

9.1 Safe house, Poland

In many ways, the private home today has been enrolled in political projects that are antithetical to forms of social cohesion and municipal objective. The home has become alive with defensive apparatuses aiming to prevent wider social contact, for fear that this might expose us to risk. While we should still acknowledge that the home and in particular those homes that are owned or being bought by their inhabitants are places of nurture and self-realisation, they are also places from which deepening social mistrust and an embodied, concrete form of anti-sociality is being formed. These themes are not new, as Disraeli argued long ago: 'In the present state of civilization and with the scientific means of happiness at our command, the notion of home should be obsolete. Home is a barbarous idea; the method of a rude age; home is isolation; therefore anti-social. What we want is Community.' (Disraeli, 1845)

In identifying and naming the domestic fortress we are perhaps helping to identify a distinctive model for living seen in the fortified private homes and gated residential developments which now dominate many cities and districts globally. These signal widespread inequalities, subjugating, materialistic and market-oriented political systems and the promotion of fear by media systems. It is clear that a significant constellation of forces and actions are both focused on and increasingly vigorous in relation to the defence of the homes we inhabit.

Home ownership, affluence and the logic of property exchange and wealth have remade our sense of home into a construct laden with dreams of autonomy, privacy and release from anxiety. Yet inside the daily life of so many domestic lives, the reality is much less clear. The rise of the domestic fortress implies a hardened and secured exterior; it evokes the use of socio-legal instruments and policing systems to shore-up these defences. It is also attached to a wide-ranging routinisation of behaviours directed at the security of the household itself, disproportionately targeted at potential threats as well as conflating security with social standing.

Gated development appears attractive since it superficially offers a break against the ambient anxiety pervading contemporary life. But against the complexity and reach of these forces, gates and walls ultimately offer little respite. Analysts like Lipovetsky (2005) suggest that the rise of a kind of social cult focused on the self is increasingly lived through the emancipatory offerings of the physical home – we seek freedom in solitude and less the company of others. This thesis of growing privatism, the celebration of the non-municipal, and its links to the project of personal desire and ambition is by now well-worn, yet this ideology is also embedded socially and in the physical walls of the homes we have described in this book.

The fragmentation of both public political systems under rising individualism has positioned the domestic realm as a place of retreat. In this context, the concept of a fortress-complex takes on two related meanings. First, we register the physical complex of the home as it is increasingly nested within abutting homes and neighbourhoods protected by gates and walls. Second, as a psychosocial dynamic within which the fearful become more firmly attached to the private home (by legal means of ownership, and by its policing and its physically protective qualities). These forms of containment and protection generate fixations on the bordered home and the impression of a rising feral quality to life outside. The resulting feeling of a buffer zone is further emphasised by the class basis of tenurial connections to property and control over entry to the home.

As we have elaborated at some length, the range of perceived intrusions into domestic life are multiple, complex and non-trivial – from the possibility of burglary, cold-callers by phone or at the door, even unwanted neighbours or political canvassers. Beyond these more prosaic intrusions lie many others, including Internet viruses, the threat of repossession, retirement and dwindling pensions, germs or contagion, natural disaster and so on. Such fears are not new. For example, we know that the Victorian gentry were significantly preoccupied by the threat of mobs, violent criminals, gangs and disorderly behavior resulting from the availability of cheap alcohol (Gurr *et al.*, 1976). Set against these threats are diverse forms of defence, by no means all physical but perhaps most often found in the presence of gates, alarms, locks and walls, but also legal frameworks prohibiting certain forms of behaviour, by zoning ordinances, pricing or designing out risky groups, by private security and public police forces, Internet virus guards, locks, keys, panic rooms, dogs, alarm systems and through the design of buildings that promote external surveillance. What we term the domestic fortress refers only in part to the physical attributes of homes (few truly live in anything directly resembling castles or fortresses) and extends to a range of social practices, legal frameworks, external forms of protection (such as the walls and gates of gated communities) and ultimately to the role of corporations and local and central states acting to protect the homes of their consumer-citizens.

Staying in, protecting the home base, has become part of an elaborate shift of social centrality. Fear of crime, home consumption of alcohol, televisions and home cinemas keep us more house-bound and entertained than previous generations. The emphatic focus of our lives towards this interior space reflects one of the crucial binds of contemporary social existence: an apparent release from traditional forms of community, obligation and identity has been partially supplanted by more atomised modes of living. We are more free to do what we want, insofar as our homes become the embodied expression of social identities, and more disinterested in contact with others or collective forms of provision.

The retreat into the safety of the home and related forms of social privatism is further extended by the retreat to sites behind gates and

9.2 Low-cost gated homes everywhere, UK

walls. So extensive are such changes in many national and urban contexts that it is possible to conceive of numerous archipelagos of enclaves
that generate new levels of social inaccessibility and desires for yet more
gating, policing and control in order to eliminate any further sources
of danger or risk. It remains a paradox of life in the affluent West that
venturing outside the home or neighbourhood gates may seem like
launching ourselves berserker-like into a zone of unpredictable social
encounters and a degraded public realm that either alarms or depresses
us. As J. K. Galbraith (1958) noted, our private wealth tends to come at
the cost of a public squalor that must be traversed as we move around
outside the home.

The distinction between safe and dangerous zones has been accen-
tuated by the development of tens of thousands of gated communities
globally, alley gates and innumerable other protective adaptations in
the UK alone. We find ourselves moving between micro-bordered
worlds from one safe zone to another – what de Cauter (2004) terms
a 'capsular civilization'. In the USA, armed householders live in
fortified homes, inside gated communities within cities aggressively

9.3 Secure apartments and parking, Australia

patrolled by militarised police forces. Nests of domesticity are themselves nested in an escalating series of scaled defensive arrangements,
up to and including the boundary policing by the nation-state itself.
A fear of personal harm and the pursuit of status have combined to
yield a built environment speaking to us of a more generalised state of
alarm, feeding the very rationale responsible for engineering such
citadel spaces.

In seeking to identify these relationships and features of contemporary home life, we are not suggesting that basic defensive routines are
somehow unnecessary, but rather that they are successively overstated
and set against a public realm that if dangerous, is made more precarious
because social investments have been reduced over time. Similarly, this

is not an argument against forms of familial or household privacy; many would acknowledge that respect for individual rights and freedoms is central to the development of autonomous and emancipated individuals. Yet these freedoms may be made stronger in societies where inequalities and social problems are countered more effectively (Wilkinson and Pickett, 2009). As the UN Universal Declaration of Human Rights – Article 12 states, 'No one shall be subjected to arbitrary interference with his privacy, family, home or correspondence, nor to attacks upon his honour and reputation. Everyone has the right to the protection of the law against such interference or attacks.' In large part, to be 'at home' means being in a space of personal autonomy, thereby shielding us from dangers over which official agencies have less control.

Henri Lefebvre (1991) once argued that the idea of a truly private life was anathema to the social core of our existence. He posited that a generalised search for privacy had become a major source of alienation in modern, everyday life because such aspirations essentially deny the social basis of our identity. Throughout this book, we have seen not only the strength of the drive for privatism and the defence of the home, but also how illusory and temporary the satisfactions derived from this flight into the interior may be. The kinds of trends we have identified here point to an escalating form of social neurosis, with more aggressive responses and defended homes, entwined with demands for greater security and the control of potential risks in large part propagated by our social and economic systems (Zedner, 2003). Our cumulative awareness of unsettling events on the global scale further presses down on the sense of our self and its vulnerabilities (Bauman, 2006). What many commentators view as a fully fledged culture focused on risk and fear is not simply something that is 'out there'; it is part of the daily routine of our lives, domestic or otherwise. This fear is embodied in how we scrutinise others in public spaces, take refuge in the predictability and certainty of our homes, and in the way we compulsively lock doors and windows – we have ingested and take for granted the need to do these things to make us safe, yet the end result is the enmeshing of our beliefs about danger and anxiety with a social climate that feeds these worries.

The dream home as prison

The idea of the dream home is attached to our subconscious desires for nurture, for the release of our desires and for freedom from fear. Yet our dreams of freedom, insofar as these are focused on our homes, imbue the home with qualities of constraint and relative incarceration. A central barometer for these aspirations is visible in the uppermost end of the property market, where money can be used to buy into the gilded jails of gated communities, walled mansions and even islands. Often, prestige and the need to 'escape' find their ultimate embodiment in castellated grand designs, like those of the Barclay Twins' island castle, Nicholas Van Hoogstraten's gargantuan, unfinished, stately home and mausoleum, Madonna's country mansion, J. K. Rowling's Edinburgh manse, Enya's castle in Ireland or Mark Zuckerberg's several mansions in Palo Alto, California, purchased in order that he not be overlooked by any neighbours. These physical expressions of affluence and enclosure are attached to deeper fears of penetration by envious peers or acquisitive criminals to be kept at bay by new castle gates.

What kind of ideal home is implied by these defensive arrangements? Surely there is a curious irony in the way that Jung's own dream home, in Bollingen, Switzerland, was constructed in the manner of a small and towered fortress. In his memoirs, he relates that his was a home that welled up from within his subconscious desires for a home that allowed him to realise the greatest sense of personal realisation and actualisation (Jung, 1961). In today's social climate, are we faced not only with the pressures of social fear, aspirations for symbols of status expressed in physical domestic design, but also deeper instinctual desires for

9.4 Jung's castellated 'dream' home, Switzerland

residential shells that might offer a similar kind of psychic armour? Even without a deep fear of crime many homes might still be shields to conceal private affluence and a distaste for social contact.

The search for safety appears more urgent today and demonstrates increasingly clearly how anxiety may result in the exit from and ceding of control over wider public spaces. The emerging sense is of a deeply complicated series of layers and flows – of privilege, of access and defence, and the rising militancy of the affluent as they face down the classes and groups perceived as threatening a particular way of life. In this sense, the domestic fortress is not simply a discrete space or mentality; it is a multi-layered, multi-site and multi-agency formation of technologies, ideals and actors, that combines to repel those who do not belong. What we have called the domestic fortress refers in this sense to the result of a wide range of historical, social, legal and political forces that combined in late capitalism to generate a form of home ownership containing a central paradox. This paradox lies in the way that the home offers financial health, a place of sanctuary and social reproduction, but is also the site of a proliferating range of fears centred on different forms of physical and networked invasion as well as deeper anxieties about our very being and continuity. This paradox is heightened by the state's tendency to rely on market solutions and the diminution of social capital and community supports that alleviated earlier fears. As Bauman's (2006) analysis suggests, we are caught in a trap of fear: if we do not fear the threats to the home, we become complacent but then worry about the consequences of not being fearful.

The internment of privilege we have described here has become a method by which fears of otherness and the unpredictability of the outside environment may be allayed (Low, 2003), but is also likely to have consequences for the further separation of social groups over time. As Low asks, how will those who are socialised in gated compounds distinguish between a safe and predictable sanctum and an unpredictable exterior where otherness outside the gates appears to present risks because of its unknown nature? This kind of residential seclusion is reinforced by the opening up of new possibilities for travel and trajectories shielded from interference by other social groups (Graham and Marvin, 2001), and eloquently described by J. G. Ballard:

> Secure behind their high walls and surveillance cameras, these estates in effect constitute a chain of close communities whose lifelines run directly along the M4 to the offices and consulting rooms, restaurants and private

clinics of central London. They remain completely apart from their local communities, except for a small and carefully selected under-class of chauffeurs, housekeepers and gardeners ... Their children only mix with each other at exclusive fee-paying schools or in the lavishly equipped sports clubs sited on the estates. (1988:12)

We cannot make this point without considering the prevailing levels of crime within particular frontier capitalist and formerly statist societies – gated communities generally started in more violent countries, many Latin American states, the USA and South Africa. In South Africa, where some of the most extreme examples of social violence occur, the process of fortification has been taken almost to its logical conclusion:

> They raise their low, picturesque garden walls by two, three or sometimes even four metres, and top them with spikes or glass chips; they unfurl razor wire ... along their perimeters; they add electric fencing, designed to shock when touched; they install automated driveway gates and inter-com systems ... to pass from sleeping to living to kitchen areas may involve unlocking three security gates ... If one house on a street installs an electric fence, the others feel pressurized to follow suit, afraid of becoming the most vulnerable property on the block. (Bremner, 1998: 8)

However, this embattled mentality has proved contagious on a wider scale, emulated by developers and owners in low crime rate welfare-capitalist societies: Australia, UK, and parts of Western Europe. Gated communities have been popularised around fears of crime, dreams of status and shifts in the real base of affluence that marked recent decades of economic growth and socio-economic polarisation – in effect, building walls around the economic positions emerging in these regions.

As Rainwater (1966) observed, the idea of the house as a haven from harm plays a heightened role for deprived households threatened by local disorder. Nevertheless, as resources and incomes rise, the ability to exercise such withdrawal and defence has accrued to those with the resources and legal rights to do so, often by banding together into club geographies that enable resources like security to be accessed in new forms of micro-statehood. These spaces support a wider social and spatial template of interaction, so the poor increasingly mix with the poor and the rich even more so, with the rich (Massey and Denton, 1993). Graham and Marvin argue that as fortified residential and work spaces are connected by private roads, private shopping streets and malls, CCTV and transportation. New secessionary spaces have been created allowing the affluent unfettered movement in which a 'set of processes are under way within which infrastructure networks are being "unbundled" in ways that help sustain the fragmentation of the social and material fabric of cities' (Graham and Marvin, 2001: 33). Put more bluntly, these shifts are deep, semi-permanent features of new social and physical arrangements in urban life today.

Daily patterns of movement from and to gated communities can be understood as mobile forms of segregation in which maximal separation from different and potentially intrusive or dangerous groups is maintained even beyond the boundaries of these developments (Atkinson and Flint, 2004). Travel in encapsulated modes of transportation and the relative security and social homogeneity of destinations creates both a sense of placelessness and perceived safety. As Sennett (1974) argues, this quality appears to be linked to a desire by citizens to avoid risks and 'exposure' in public space. Shielding technologies, like sports utility vehicles and gated neighbourhoods, have extended these barriers and help confer temporary feelings of safety. If anything, the increased insulation of these spaces heightens demands for predictability and safety when moving beyond front doors and gates in which similar levels of control, household autonomy and self-actualisation are desired.

Home economics and homo economicus

The home is a device for accumulation as well as protection. Although compromised by the economic crisis of recent years, unless the very fundaments of the American and European economies collapse, we will rush headlong into future waves of accumulation, crises and crunches. Our privately realised freedoms belie the deep inflection of our sense of self by the logic of markets and trade as home ownership has opened up the connection between home as a marker of identity and housing as a pyramid scheme of value creation. We have referred to these combinations of the spaces of the home, contemporary market-oriented politics as tessellated neoliberalism in which the home is a connecting node for ideological projects that see their realisation in the concrete manifestation of defended homes and the defensive orientations of social actors within these new fabrics. The private home contains powerful constituencies of owners who favour political projects conferring their relative security as owners, even as the security of social systems around them is made more fragile by these shifts.

Given the financialisation of housing assets and the unique character of capitalism since the 1970s (Harvey, 2005) so often described as neo-liberalism, we can see that a significant aspect of this political-economic superstructure is the building block of the tradeable asset of the home. This evokes the impression of tessellated building blocks that go to make up the wider economic system we inhabit. This was evidenced decidedly when the latest crisis of capitalism was provoked by the reduction in value of housing assets, rather than the locus of former crises in equities or oil. Homes owned by their residents form the building blocks of a broader political economy that privileges ownership and market exchange is celebrated as the foundation of freedom, democracy and economic growth.

Market principles undergird the financialisation of housing as a tradeable asset. This complex saga spawned new insecurities in tandem with overreach of the credit system. A chicken vs. egg element exists in this scenario, as home ownership has been deeply implicated in the construction of late capitalism's financial architecture, while the tenets of capitalism as freedom have also been aligned with support for the autonomy and importance of home ownership. As politicians and bankers collude to conflate political freedom with home ownership, the subsequent promotion of this tenure suggests that a property-owning democracy is an intrinsic good even where it symbolises rising social divisions and forms of human insecurity resulting from the gross promotion of market projects and orientations. The 'we' implied in these notions of a free national economy and community still tends to apply foremost to those who have, or desire to buy, their own homes.

According to Nicholas Blomley (1998), property relations – owning, buying, selling and trading – have become ontologically embedded within social relations. That is, we take these aspects of law and exchange to be so fundamental to our understanding of how society operates that they become almost invisible to us. These observations cut to the heart of debates about the role of 'the home' and of home ownership in advanced capitalist societies; ownership has been embedded into the broader play of the economy, but also within our social and political lives. These relationships are mediated by states, private corporations and finance houses. As the wealth attached to ownership has given rising numbers of households a stake in the tenure's protection and growth, so the micro-worlds of individual households have become more firmly aligned with political projects of the centre-left and right where they have both tended to recognise and feed desires for order, control and private wealth. This is not simply about a neoliberal makeover of the state into a purer market orientation or buttress, but rather that the home, in relation to its social and economic functions, is peculiarly enmeshed in a larger amalgam of forces that feeds regimes of accumulation and control.

If we view the state as a geodesic dome founded on neoliberal principles, then inside its frames we can observe the unit of the home within broader aggregations that form the political territories of the local and nation state. Notions of domestic sovereignty conjoin the ideologies of privatism and neoliberalism, thus sponsoring a wider political project supporting the needs and preferences of this vocal constituency over and above those it regards as potential intruders.

Ways out of the complex

Perhaps the central message of this book is a fairly depressing one. For many analysts, cities today are places of limited sociability as rising fear, consumerism and corporate imprints on city centre areas manufacture a sense of bland spaces fit only for consumption practices. Within these urban and suburban landscapes, a strangely aggressive ideology of home ownership and home-being, policing and local state-corporate control has materialised. In fact, western growth economies are predicated on these landscapes of consumers and owners and by a social logic that compels us to accept the spaces and the values on which they are built. In this landscape it may be challenging to locate those agencies, institutions and political actors who might advance positions of trust and ways of engaging with the sources of social fear, rather than seeking programmes that perversely feed the social conditions that may see crime rising, further punitive responses and privatised methods of incarceration. If we feel like prisoners in our own home, this is due in part to the kinds of emotions fomented by aggressive wars on welfare, crime and drugs which identify dangerous others and outsiders whom we should fear and who might represent a threat to our way of life. To take one example – how might concerted action to address inequalities and poverty tackle inter-generational, violent and related forms of crime that originate in exclusion from economic participation?

To make these connections is to go against the grain of the kinds of welfare, policing and justice policies relentlessly pursued by those

9.5 Braced door on apartment, Hong Kong

voted into power, often almost regardless of political stripe. The emergent actions delivered on our behalf criminalise, destroy, incarcerate and repeat dangerous patterns of behaviour that come back to haunt the constituencies made afraid by these groups. This bizarrely self-destructive pattern of social and political action has its logical impetus in the way we interpret social problems primarily as matters of choice, rather than of structural influence and constraint. So long as we pursue forms of prohibition, zero-tolerance action against the marginal and vulnerable while doing little to address inequality, these will be unending wars with only periodic and pyrrhic victories to mark out a perverse view of progress (drug busts, arrests, increasing incarceration of the dangerous).

Can we envisage a less defended form of urbanism and neighbourhood life than the one currently generated by the tendency towards fortification? The prospect of a way out of these situations brings us to a wide range of progressive interventions and the remaking of civil society that steers us away from the dominance of market ideologies across the social sphere. We live in a world where a culture of fear often trumps the possibility of some kind of architecture of happiness (de Botton, 2006). The home appears to offer financial return, sanctuary and the reward of domestic autonomy. However, the home is now also the locus of a proliferating range of fears focused on physical invasion, unwanted visitors, phone calls and even chat room interactions that threaten our children, all illustrating a progressive anti-social retreat into the private domestic realm.

These shifts privilege and secure the place of affluence and consumption while marginalising politically and socially unacceptable groups. The city has been partitioned and overlaid in ways that protect affluence (Rodgers, 2004), while further containing what is seen as the insoluble problem of urban poverty. These changes in the physical and social fabric of cities suggest that higher income groups are no longer as averse to the potential amenity of urban life; yet the risks associated with these locations must be managed to enable selective participation in the public realm. The growth of gated communities indicates this kind of management via an advancing crystallisation of the disconnection between affluence and the wider social geography of the city, based on a fear of crime as well as a desire for security, investment and privacy. Walls and gates within cities now support a more solid form of segregation physically and socially expressed in the dispersion and collection of different income and identity groups in the city. Gated enclaves highlight this position *in extremis*; the neighbourhood becomes a strategy for social insulation and social reproduction. Enclave and gated neighbourhoods 'follow' their residents around the city via patterns of avoidance behaviour and shielded modes of conveyance (Atkinson, 2008). This context creates a kind of 'solipsism of riches' (Young, 2007: 99), in which the wealthy have become increasingly ignorant of the social distress and danger outside these zones, even as middle and lower income groups are subjected to increased insecurity.

A crucial consequence of domestic fortification is what we term an ideology of defensive home ownership. We have emphasised the importance of the home's economic value and the way it leads to social repertoires aligning ownership with the maintenance and defence of those assets. Fear in the urban context has largely been theorised at the scale of the wider city, its publics, cultures and central spaces. We might argue that this focus largely ignores the building block of the home, often the focus of fear and the projection of social anxieties played out through political programmes. These programmes apparently seek to displace or destroy social groups defined as 'other'. This kind of defensive home ownership has developed in a period of affluence and anxiety, produced by a myriad of sources and that affects various areas of social life, including attitudes to neighbour relations and child-rearing, the creation of physical barriers in the home and at neighbourhood scales, and the use of territorial markers and socio-political action directed at excluding, zoning-out and otherwise avoiding difference and danger.

Conclusion

Sarah Winchester, heiress of the repeating rifle company, famously built a house over many decades with false stairways and corridors to thwart the spirits of those that might haunt her, killed by the weapons her husband had manufactured. Like Winchester's, many social fears among the affluent emerge in relation to those excluded or damaged by our social system, seeking the potential protections offered by the home. Perhaps the most important message of her laborious attempts at achieving psychic ease is that despite these efforts, this could never be achieved without some attempt at resolving the source of these fears.

A history of the defence of the modern home shows a trajectory from protecting feudal lords to gated estates and individual homes, to the embrace of personal responsibility for the defence of private homes. We can also appreciate that despite this changing the nature of many homes, many others do not fortify and exclude. Nevertheless, our project has been to observe trends, tendencies and extreme forms of social conduct that appear to signal deeper tendencies and problems. The resulting new built environment is symbolically important – it reveals these fears and the desperate desires of many to project status and their indifference to those around them.

In this book, we have argued that these interconnected and complex changes lie within the collecting pool of neoliberalism located at the scale of the home, which has cascaded down from the nation-state, to the city and then to domestic contexts. In an environment of support for unfettered markets and personal freedoms, this includes the perceived right to defend the home and to bolster its investment value. These defended homes function as the tessellated building blocks of neoliberalism – this process is mutually reinforcing and binding as values and rhetoric feed the project of ownership and as the affluent buy in to these political projects and values. The complex of the domestic fortress can thus be envisioned as the conflation of a series of social forces coalescing around home ownership, the economy, property sales and personal wealth. The defence of this territory offers a way of comprehending the kind of social and physical changes we see in the built environment of today's cities, as well as their means of management.

Our homes and where we live in them say much about who we are and the lives we lead. The lifestyle and real estate industries are now matched by sectors that specialise in selling protection from real and imagined harm. Unlike other forms of security, such as the political focus on national borders, domestic security brings us closer to our personal fears. In our homes, we not only feel aware of the security this shell offers us, we are often keenly aware of the vulnerabilities of our shell-dwellings and the fears we project onto the home. With rising wealth also comes expanding inequality, and this particular feature of societies like those in the USA, the UK and Australia has induced a more pronounced anxiety among the middle classes and social elites. The creation of a society that excludes entire groups from opportunity brings with it the threat of unrest, envy and anger directed at affluence and its symbolic domestic locations.

We can use the term domestic fortress to denote home set at the spearhead of a rather concealed 'front' from which homeowners enact strategies to maintain the safety of their occupants. But this term also embraces a deeper aspect of the social worry plaguing contemporary social life. In this light, the home is not only a place of aspirant privatism, but also a place of serious fear and anxiety of being, where an unsettling and uneasy tension manifests between the fruits of affluence (bigger homes, greater luxury) and concomitant personal responsibilities focused on childcare and policing. In an era of confusion, fluidity and social unpredictability, the home is valued for its role as a brake on change and uncertainty, going beyond prior notions of ontological insecurity (Giddens, 1991; Sánchez-Pardo, 2003). In the current context, destruction of various kinds – environmental, state projects, ways of life – has been raised to a planetary level, and the significance and integrity of the self has perhaps been cast in doubt. These anxieties now intersect with and reinforce local and personal worries as well as the apparent coherence and security in the face of these challenges.

We appear captivated by alluring dreams of safety while these desires have led us into the hollowness of defended shells. Instead of inhabiting machines of vivacity and self-realisation, we are under house arrest, imprisoned by fears in large part driven by the economic systems and inequalities around us. The bordering of private life today responds to a common conception of the self – instead of politics operating as the means by which common progress might be achieved, we accept a hierarchy of needs that stresses primal security and sustenance in which the role of state and community is diminished. Freedoms and limitations, core elements previously offered by a guarantor state, are now the work of the individual and small collectivities of householders. Naturally, we shun the jungle rules and disorderly nightmare of precarious life outside our front doors and find comfort in a world mediated and softened by distractions inside. Those outside provide evidence of either deficiency or their own choice not to join this vision; they are the ones to avoid, the ones who might try to get in. But we have forgotten that many of the greatest risks still come from inside.

The 2009 murder of Guerline Dieu and her five children by her husband in a gated community in Florida exposed an oft-overlooked weakness in the embrace of new securitised residential landscapes – gates and walls cannot save us from the commonest forms of violence and abuse. Not long before Dieu's murder, paramedics failed to save the life of a man suffering a heart attack in another gated community. A standard rescue was complicated by an unmanned gate with a pin code entry; the ambulance driver tried for three minutes to get through. County administrator Gary Kubic later observed that a total of thirty-two unmanned gates exist in Beaufort County, South Carolina, alone. What would otherwise have passed as an ordinary death provoked debate about the need for emergency override systems installed at barriers largely intended to keep trouble, rather than assistance, out.

A BBC documentary in 2006, *United Gates of America*, offered a rather disturbing portrait of life in a Californian gated community. It showed a homeowner committee that played down local references to murder and rape within the large development in order to maintain the value of homes. What remains startling about this case is that it reveals a broad logic that ranks human safety second to promoting an ideal image of security in the pursuit of property values, even by those residing within them. As developments become ever larger, they are imbued with social variety and lose their distinction from society at large and so, in subtle ways, the residential security landscape has become less distinct and separate from the risks it sought to wall out. Yet the point here is that even in homes bought with the ambition of total safety, threats either remain or are denied and thus produce increasingly neurotic responses to our contemporary social condition. In seeking to escape from other people and places we associate with danger and risk, we end up run-to-ground, behind gates, walls, locks and buttressed doorways, and none the happier for these choices.

References

1st Security (undated) *Distraction Methods of Burglars.* [Online] Accessed 23 August 2015. Available at: www.1stsecurityusa.com/distraction-methods-of -burglars/.

Aamoth, D. (2014) 'Here's How Much Time People Spend Playing Video Games', *Time*, 27 May 2014. [Online] Accessed 18 January 2016. Available at: http://time.com/120476/nielsen-video-games.

Aas, K. F. (2011) '"Crimmigrant" Bodies and Bona Fide Travelers: Surveillance, Citizenship and Global Governance', *Theoretical Criminology*, 15:3, 331–346.

ACPO (UK Association of Chief Police Officers) (2004) *Secured by Design* (London: ACPO Crime Prevention Initiative).

Adams, E. and A. Rollings (2006) *Fundamentals of Game Design.* Accessed 18 January 2016. Available at: http://wps.prenhall.com/bp_gamedev_1/54/ 14053/3597646.cw/index.html.

Adams, G. (2009) 'Jobless Father Kills Children', *Independent*. [Online] 29 January 2011. Accessed 20 August 2015. Available at: www.independent. co.uk/news/world/americas/jobless-father-kills-children-1519092.html.

Addington, L. A. and C. M. Rennison (2015) 'Keeping the Barbarians Outside the Gate? Comparing Burglary Victimization in Gated and Non-Gated Communities', *Justice Quarterly*, 32:1, 168–192.

Allon, F. (2008) *Renovation Nation: Our Obsession with Home* (Sydney: University of New South Wales Press).

Altheide, D. L. (2002) *Creating Fear: News and the Construction of Crisis* (New York: Aldine Transaction).

Altman, I. (1975) *The Environment and Social Behaviour: Privacy, Personal Space, Territory, Crowding* (Monterey, CA: Brooks/Cde).

American Bar Association (2014) *A Review of the Preliminary Report and Recommendations of the National Task Force on Stand Your Ground Laws* (Boston, MA:

American Bar Association). Accessed 18 January 2016. Available at: www. americanbar.org/content/dam/aba/administrative/racial_ethnic_justice/ aba_natl_task_force_on_syg_laws_preliminary_report_program_book. authcheckdam.pdf.

American Pet Products Association (2014) *2013–2014 National Pet Owners Survey*. [Online] Accessed 24 August 2015. Available at: www. americanpetproducts.org/pubs_survey.asp

Anderson, J. L. (2009) 'Countryside Access and Environmental Protection: An American View of Britain's Right to Roam', *Environmental Law Review*, 9:4, 241–259.

Andreotti, A., P. LeGales and F. J. Moreno-Fuentes (2015) *Globalised Minds, Roots in the City: Urban Upper-Middle Classes in Europe* (London: Wiley-Blackwell).

Appleton, J. (1996) *The Experience of Landscape* (London: Wiley).

Armit, I. (2003) *Towers in the North: The Brochs of Scotland* (Stroud: Tempus).

Associated Press (2007) 'Life Term for Killing Teen who Walked on Lawn: Ohio man said boy knew how he cared for his grass and provoked him', *NBC News*. [Online] 25 May 2007. Accessed 22 August 2015. Available at: www. msnbc.msn.com/id/18849855/.

Atkinson, R. (2008) 'The Flowing Enclave and the Misanthropy of Networked Affluence', in M. Savage and T. Blokland (eds), *Networked Urbanism: Critical Perspectives on Social Capital in the City* (Aldershot: Ashgate), pp. 42–58.

Atkinson, R. (2015) 'Limited Exposure: Social Concealment, Mobility and Engagement with Public Space by the Super-Rich in London', *Environment and Planning: A*, 1–16.

Atkinson, R. and S. Blandy (2007) 'Panic Rooms: The Rise of Defensive Home Ownership', *Housing Studies*, 22:4, 443–458.

Atkinson, R., S. Blandy, J. Flint and D. Lister (2002) *Gated Communities in England*. (London: Office of the Deputy Prime Minister).

Atkinson, R. and J. Flint (2004) 'Fortress UK? Gated Communities, the Spatial Revolt of the Elites and Time-Space Trajectories of Segregation', *Housing Studies*, 19:6, 875–892.

Atkinson, R. and K. Jacobs (2016) *House, Home and Society* (London: Palgrave).

Atkinson, R. and O. Smith (2012) 'An Economy of False Securities? An Analysis of Murders Inside Gated Residential Developments in the United States', *Crime, Media, Culture*, 8: 2, 161–172.

Atkinson, R. and B. Tranter (2011) *Outside Society? The Social Implications of Gated and Secured Neighbourhoods in Australia* (University of York/University of Tasmania: Working paper).

Australian Bureau of Statistics (2005) *Crime and Safety Australia, Apr 2005*. [Online] Accessed 22 August 2015. Available at: www.abs.gov.au/ausstats/ abs@.nsf/mf/4509.0

Australian Bureau of Statistics (2007) *Australian Social Trends 2007: Larger Dwellings, Smaller Households*. [Online] Accessed 23 August 2015. Available at: www. ausstats.abs.gov.au/ausstats/subscriber.nsf/0/423C5DCC0DC2E85ECA257 32F001CA355/$File/41020_Larger per cent20dwellings, per cent20smaller per cent20households_2007.pdf.

Australian Bureau of Statistics (2012) *Personal Fraud, 2010–2011, Report 4528.0*. [Online] Accessed 23 August 2015. Available at: www.abs.gov.au/ausstats/ abs@.nsf/Latestproducts/4528.0.

Australian Bureau of Statistics (2015) *Recorded Crime, Victims, Australia, 2014* (Canberra: Australian Bureau of Statistics).

Bachelard, G. (1958) *The Poetics of Space*. (First published in French as *La poétique de l'espace*.)

Bahrani (2015) *99 Homes* [Film].

Bailey, B. (2013) 'Mark Zuckerberg Buys Four Houses Near His Palo-Alto Home', *Mercury News* [Online] Accessed 14 December 2015. Available at: www.mercurynews.com/business/ci_24285169/mark-zuckerberg-buys -four-houses-near-his-palo-alto-home.

Ballard, J. G. (1988) *Running Wild* (London: Hutchinson).

Barnett, E. and C. Beaumont (2010) 'Buckinghamshire Village in Street View Fight against Google', *Daily Telegraph* [Online] 12 March 2010. Accessed 24 August 2015. Available at: www.telegraph.co.uk/technology/google/ 7422494/Buckinghamshire-village-in-Street-View-fight-against-Google. html.

Barranger, D. (2008) 'Laid to Rest Together, the Father and the Family he Killed', *Independent* [Online] 20 December 2008. Accessed 20 August 2015. Available at: www.independent.co.uk/news/uk/crime/laid-to-rest-together -the-father-and-the-family-he-killed-1204989.html

Basolo, V. (2007) 'Explaining the Support for Home Ownership Policy in US Cities: A Political Economy Perspective', *Housing Studies*, 22:1, 99–119.

Bauman, Z. (2005) *Liquid Life* (Cambridge: Polity).

Bauman, Z. (2006) *Liquid Fear* (Cambridge: Polity).

Baumgartner, M. P. (1988) *The Moral Order of a Suburb* (Oxford: Oxford University Press).

BBC News (2003) 'Further Parole Delay for Gun Killer' [Online] 12 December 2003. Accessed 21 August 2015. Available at: news.bbc.co.uk/1/hi/england/ wear/3313001.stm.

BBC News (2005) 'Tougher Intruder Laws Ruled Out', 12 January 2005. Accessed 18 January 2016. Available at: http://news.bbc.co.uk/1/hi/uk _politics/4167865.stm.

BBC News (2013) 'Killer Dogs' Owners in England and Wales Could Face Life in Prison' [Online] 6 August 2013. Accessed 24 August 2015. Available at: www.bbc.co.uk/news/uk-23578561.

Beaglehole, E. (1931) *Property: A Study in Social Psychology* (London: Allen & Unwin).

Beck, U. (1992) *Risk Society: Towards a New Modernity* (London: SAGE).

Beckett, K. and S. Herbert (2009) *Banished: The New Social Control in Urban America* (Oxford: Oxford University Press).

Bell, P. A., T. Green, J. Fisher and A. Baum (1996) *Environmental Psychology* (Fort Worth, TX: Harcourt Brace).

Bernasco, W. (2014) 'Residential Burglary', in G. Bruinsma and D. Weisburd (eds), *Encyclopedia of Criminology and Criminal Justice* (New York: Springer), pp. 4381–4391.

Bettelheim, B. (1976) *The Uses of Enchantment* (New York: Alfred A. Knopf Inc.).

Bettelheim, B. (1983) *Freud and Man's Soul* (New York: Alfred A. Knopf Inc.).

Birmingham Post (2008) 'Two Guilty Over Death of Burglar' [Online] 25 March 2008. Accessed 5 May 2016. Available at: www.birminghampost.co.uk/news/local-news/two-guilty-over-death-burglar-3963005.

Blackstone, W. (1768) *Commentaries on the Laws of England, vol. II* (London: Clarendon Press).

Blake, M. (2011) 'A New Social Network: Communities Use CCTV to Crack Crime Rise in Number of Communal Cameras That Allow Neighbours to Look Out For Each Other', *Independent*, 22 October 2011 [Online] Accessed 3 December 2015. Available at: www.independent.co.uk/news/uk/crime/a-new-social-network-ndash-communities-use-cctv-to-crack-crime-2328655.html.

Bligh, A. and D. Cameron (2009) 'New Laws to Help Quell Neighbourhood Disputes'. [Media Statement]. Accessed 22 August 2015. Available at: www.cabinet.qld.gov.au/MMS/StatementDisplaySingle.aspx?id=65238.

Blomley, N. (1998) 'Landscapes of Property', *Law and Society Review*, 32:3, 567–612.

Blomley, N. (2005) 'Flowers in the Bathtub: Boundary Crossings at the Public–Private Divide', *Geoforum*, 36:3, 281–296.

Blomley, N. (2010) *Rights of Passage: Sidewalks and the Regulation of Public Flow* (London: Routledge).

Body-Gendrot, S. (2011) *The Social Control of Cities: A Comparative Perspective* (London: John Wiley & Sons).

Boffey, D. (2011) 'Only Nine Pay Council Tax in Enclave for Super-Rich', *Guardian*, 26 November 2011 [Online] Accessed 26 November 2011. Available at: www.theguardian.com/uk/2011/nov/26/one-hyde-park-council-tax.

Boggis, Easton Bavents v Natural England [2009] EWCA Civ 1061.

Bottomley, A. and N. Moore (2007) 'From Walls to Membranes: Fortress Polis and the Governance of Urban Public Space in 21st Century Britain', *Law Critique*, 18:2, 171–206.

Bowlby, R. (1995) 'Domestication', in D. Elam and R. Wiegman (eds), *Feminism Beside Itself* (London: Routledge), pp. 77–85.

Breen, G. (2010) 'Teen's Murder Sparks Facebook Privacy Plea', *ABC News* [Online] 17 May 2010. Accessed 23 August 2015. Available at: www.abc.net. au/news/2010-05-17/teens-murder-sparks-facebook-privacy-plea/829850.

Bremner, L. (1998) 'Crime and the Emerging Landscape of Post-Apartheid Johannesburg', in H. Judin and I. Vladislavić (eds), *Blank–: Architecture, Apartheid and After* (Amsterdam: Nai).

Brennan, M. (2013) 'Billionaire Bunkers: Beyond the Panic Room, Home Security Goes Sci-Fi', *Forbes* [Online] 27 November 2013. Accessed 24 August 2015. Available at: www.forbes.com/sites/morganbrennan/ 2013/11/27/billionaire-bunkers-beyond-the-panic-room-home-security -goes-sci-fi/.

Brenner, N. and N. Theodore (eds) (2002) *Spaces of Neoliberalism: Urban Restructuring in North America and Western Europe* (Oxford: Blackwell).

Brett, J. (2003) *Australian Liberals and the Moral Middle Class: From Alfred Deakin to John Howard* (Cambridge: Cambridge University Press).

Britten, N. (2004) 'Man Shot Neighbour Dead in Privet Feud', *Telegraph* [Online] 13 January 2004. Accessed 22 August 2015. Available at: www. telegraph.co.uk/news/uknews/1451524/Man-shot-neighbour-dead-in -privet-feud.html.

Brookes, I. (2004) *Chambers Concise Dictionary* (Edinburgh: Chambers).

Brower, S. N. (1980) 'Territory in Urban Settings', in I. Altman, A. Rapoport and J. F. Wohlwill (eds), *Environment and Culture* (New York: Plenum Press), pp. 179–207.

Buchanan, C. and M. George (2011) 'Multi-millionaires Win Fight to Keep Gated Community', *Kingston Guardian*, 12 April 2011.

Busch, A. (1999) *Geography of Home: Writings on Where We Live* (Princeton, NJ: Princeton Architectural Press).

Cable, S. (2012) 'The Battle of Kate's Gates: Honeymooning Actress Told She Can't Have 6ft Barrier at 15th Century Home', *MailOnline* [Online] 31 December 2012. Accessed 21 August 2015. Available at: www.dailymail. co.uk/tvshowbiz/article-2255504/Kate-Winslet-The-battle-Kates-gates -Honeymooning-actress-told-6ft-barrier-15th-century-home.html.

Campbell-Lange, B. (2005) *Lautner* (Berlin: Taschen).

Carlson, J. (2015) *Citizen-Protectors: The Everyday Politics of Guns in an Age of Decline* (New York: Oxford University Press).

Carr-Brown, J., S. Lambart and R. Woods (2004) 'Burglary: Just How Scared Should We Be?', *The Sunday Times* [Online] 12 December 2004. Accessed 5 May 2016. Available at: www.thesundaytimes.co.uk/sto/news/uk_news/ article95581.ece.

Carrabine, E. (2008) *Crime, Culture and the Media* (Cambridge: Polity).

Carrhall Castle (undated) [Online] Accessed 22 August 2015. Available at: http://booking.carrhallcastle.co.England/history/.

Carson, V. (2011) 'Poisoners Run Wild – Tree Killers Stalk Suburban Giants in Quest for Views', *Daily Telegraph* [Online] 7 June 2011. Accessed 5 May 2016. Available at: www.dailytelegraph.com.au/news/nsw/poisoners-run-wild -tree-killers-stalk-suburban-giants-in-quest-for-views/story-e6freuzi -1226070541134.

Carter, H. (2010) 'Facebook Murderer who Posed as Teenager to Lure Victim Jailed for Life', *Guardian* [Online] 8 March 2010. Accessed 23 August 2015. Available at: www.theguardian.com/uk/2010/mar/08/peter-chapman -facebook-ashleigh-hall.

Chapman, S. (1998) *Over Our Dead Bodies: Port Arthur and Australia's Fight for Gun Control* (Annandale, VA: Pluto Press).

Chapman, S. and P. Alpers (2013) 'Gun-Related Deaths: How Australia Stepped Off "The American Path"', *Annals of Internal Medicine*, 158:10, 770–771.

Chapman, T. (1999) 'Spoiled Home Identities: The Experience of Burglary', in T. Chapman and J. Hockey (eds), *Ideal Homes?: Social Change and the Experience of the Home* (Abingdon: Routledge), pp. 133–146.

Chapman, T. and J. Hockey (eds) (1999) *Ideal Homes?: Social Change and the Experience of the Home* (Abingdon: Routledge).

Cheng, C. and M. Hoekstra (2013) 'Does Strengthening Self-Defense Law Deter Crime or Escalate Violence? Evidence from Expansions to Castle Doctrine', *Journal of Human Resources* 48:3, 821–854.

Clark, R. (2005) 'Get Off My Land (All 5ft of it)', *Telegraph*. [Online] 13 July 2005. Accessed 22 August 2015. Available at: www.telegraph.co.uk/finance/ property/3343181/Get-off-my-land-all-5ft-of-it.html.

Coaffee, J. and D. M. Wood (2006) 'Security is Coming Home: Rethinking Scale and Constructing Resilience in the Global Urban Response to Terrorist Risk', *International Relations*, 20:4, 503–517.

Cohen, S. (1979) 'The Punitive City: Notes on the Dispersal of Social Control', *Crime, Law and Social Change*, 3:4, 339–363.

Cohen, L. and D. Cantor (1981) 'Residential Burglary in the United States: Life-Style and Demographic Factors Associated with the Probability of Victimization', *Journal of Research in Crime and Delinquency*, 18, 113–127.

Cohen, L. and M. Felson (1979) 'Modernization of Risk, Social Change and Crime Rate Trends: A Routine Activity Approach', *American Sociological Review*, 44:4, 588–608.

Coke, E. (1604) *Semayne's Case* 77 Eng. Rep. 194; 5 Co. Rep. 91.

Coke, E. (1644) *Third Part of the Institutes of the Laws of England* (London: M. Flesger for W. Lee and D. Pakeman).

Congressional Research Service (2013) *Public Mass Shootings in the United States: Selected Implications for Federal Public Health and Safety Policy* [Online] Accessed

22 August 2015. Available at: http://journalistsresource.org/wp-content/uploads/2013/03/MassShootings_CongResServ.pdf.

Cooper, M. C. (1995) *House as Mirror of Self: Exploring the Deeper Meaning of Home* (Berkeley, CA: Conari Press).

Coulson, C. (1994) 'Freedom to Crenellate by Licence: An Historiographical Revision', *Nottingham Medieval Studies*, 38, 86–137.

Cragoe, C. D. (2008) *How to Read Buildings* (Lewes: Herbert Press).

Craig, A. (2007) 'The Thief Who Stole Our Peace', *Independent* [Online] 18 September 2007. Accessed 5 May 2016. Available at: www.independent.co.uk/property/house-and-home/amanda-craig-the-thief-who-stole-our-peace-5335146.html.

Craig, G., A. Gaus, M. Wilkinson, K. Skrivankova and A. McQuade (2007) *Modern Slavery in the United Kingdom* (York: Joseph Rowntree Foundation).

Crompton, R. (1952) *William and the Tramp* (London: George Newnes Ltd).

Crown Prosecution Service and the Association of Chief Police Officers (2005) *Householders and the Use of Force Against Intruders* [Online] Accessed 24 August 2015. Available at: www.cps.gov.uk/publications/prosecution/householders.html.

Cuneo, C. (2012) 'No Charges For Donald Brooke Who Fatally Stabbed Home Invader Azzam Naboulsi' [Online] Accessed 3 December 2015. Available at: www.news.com.au/national/no-charges-for-donald-brooke-who-fatally-stabbed-home-invader-azzam-naboulsi/story-e6frfkvr-1226242200976.

Currie, E. (1997) 'Market, Crime and Community Toward a Mid-Range Theory of Post-Industrial Violence', *Theoretical Criminology*, 1:2, 147–172.

Daily Telegraph (2011) 'Parents Urged to Deter Gatecrashers as Teen Stabbed at Party in NSW. Sydney, AU.' [Online] 18 September 2011. Accessed 23 August 2015. Available at: www.dailytelegraph.com.au/news/sydney-nsw/parents-urged-to-deter-gatecrashers-as-teen-stabbed-at-party-in-nsw/story-e6freuzi-1226140228497.

Davidow, A. (2007) 'L.A.'s Secret Service; Confidentiality Agreements Have Become Like Prenups Between Hollywood Elite and Household Help', *Los Angeles Times* [Online] 26 July 2007. Accessed 24 August 2015. Available at: articles.latimes.com/2007/jul/26/home/hm-confidential26.

Davies, M. (2007) *Property: Meanings, Histories, Theories* (Abingdon: Routledge-Cavendish).

Davis, M. (1992) *City of Quartz: Excavating the Future in Los Angeles* (New York: Vintage Books).

de Botton, A. (2006) *The Architecture of Happiness* (London: Hamish Hamilton).

de Bruxelles, S. and V. Elliott (2004) 'Madonna Wins Right to Keep Riff-Raff Out', *The Times* [Online] 19 June 2004. Accessed 21 August 2015. Available at: www.thetimes.co.uk/tto/news/uk/article1925097.ece.

De Cauter, L. (2004) *The Capsular Civilization: On the City in an Age of Fear* (Rotterdam: Netherlands Architecture Institute).

DeJohn, I. (2014) 'Houston Firefighter Shot Dead by Woman Who Thought He Was an Intruder', *New York Daily News*, 18 March 2014 [Online] Accessed 20 August 2015. Available at: www.nydailynews.com/news/national/houston-firefighter-shot-dead-woman-thought-intruder-article-1.1725621.

Department for Communities and Local Government (2009) *Preventing Repossessions: Fact Sheet*. [Online] Accessed 20 August 2015. Available at: www.communities.gov.uk/documents/housing/pdf/1380862.pdf.

Department for Communities and Local Government (2015) *Statutory Homelessness, Live Table 774*. [Online]. Available at: www.gov.uk/government/statistical-data-sets/live-tables-on-homelessness.

Department of Environment and Climate Change (2008) *Dealing With Neighbourhood Noise* (Sydney: Department of Environment and Climate Change).

Department of the Environment (1971) *Fair Deal for Housing White Paper* (London: Department of the Environment).

Department of the Environment, Transport and the Regions (1999) *Consultation Paper. High Hedges: Possible Solutions* (London: Department of the Environment, Transport and the Regions).

Derbyshire, D. and A. Martin (2008) 'Google "Burglar's Charter" Street Cameras Given the All Clear by Privacy Watchdog', *Daily Mail* [Online] 31 July 2008. Accessed 24 August 2015. Available at: www.dailymail.co.uk/sciencetech/article-1031861/Google-burglars-charter-street-cameras-given-clear-privacy-watchdog.html.

Detica (2011) *Cost of Cyber Crime*. [Online] Accessed 23 August 2015. Available at: www.baesystemsdetica.com/uploads/resources/THE_COST_OF_CYBER_CRIME_SUMMARY_FINAL_14_February_2011.pdf.

Disraeli, B. (1845) *Sybil or The Two Nations* (Oxford: Oxford University Press).

District of Columbia v. Heller (2008) 554 U.S. 570.

Ditton, J., J. Bannister, E. Gilchrist and S. Farrall (1999) 'Afraid or Angry? Recalibrating the "fear" of crime', *International Review of Victimology*, 6, 83–99.

Dorling, D. (2014) *All That Is Solid: How the Great Housing Disaster Defines Our Times, and What We Can Do About It* (London: Penguin).

Douglas, M. (1991) 'The Idea of Home: A Kind of Space', *Social Research*, 58:1, 287–307.

Dowling, R., R. Atkinson and P. M. McGuirk (2010) 'Privatism, Privatisation and Social Distinction in Master-Planned Residential Estates', *Urban Policy and Research*, 28:4, 391–410.

Duffy, B., R. Wake, T. Burrows and P. Bremner (2008) *Closing the Gap: Crime and Public Perceptions* (London: Ipsos Mori Social Research Institute).

Du Maurier, D. (1959) 'The Alibi', in *The Blue Lenses and Other Stories* (Harmondsworth: Penguin).

Duncan, J. and N. Duncan (2004) *Landscapes of Privilege* (New York: Routledge).

Dunstan, A. A. (1943) House of Assembly speech moving the second reading of *Housing Bill* (no. 2). *Victoria: Parliamentary* Debates (session), vol. 216.

Dupuis, A. and D. Thorns (1998) 'Home, Home Ownership and the Search for Ontological Security', *The Sociological Review*, 46:1, 24–47.

Dupuis, A. and D. Thorns (2008) 'Gated Communities as Exemplars of "Forting Up" Practices in a Risk Society', *Urban Policy and Research*, 26:2, 145–157.

Ellin, N. (ed.) (1997) *Architecture of Fear* (New York: Princeton Architectural Press).

Elliott, A. and C. Lemert (2006) *The New Individualism: The Emotional Costs of Globalization* (London: Routledge).

Entertainment Software Association (2015) *Essential Facts about the Computer and Video Game Industry*. [Online] Accessed 4 May 2016. Available at: www. theesa.com/wp-content/uploads/2015/04/ESA-Essential-Facts-2015.pdf.

Entick v Carrington (1795) 19 Howells State Trials 1029.

Fafinski, S. (2007) *UK Cybercrime Report*. [Online] Accessed 23 August 2015. Available at: www.garlik.com/press/Garlik_UK_Cybercrime_Report.pdf.

Farmer, L. (2006) 'Tony Martin and the Nightbreakers: Criminal Law, Victims, and the Power to Punish', in Sarah Armstrong and Lesley McAra (eds), *Perspectives on Punishment: The Contours of Control* (Oxford: Oxford University Press), pp. 49–68.

Farrall, S., J. Jackson and E. Gray (2009) *Social Order and the Fear of Crime in Contemporary Times*, Clarendon Studies in Criminology (Oxford: Oxford University Press).

Farrell, A. (2008) 'How to Keep a Billionaire Safe', *Forbes* magazine, 5 September 2008.

FBI (2013) *Murder*. [Online] Accessed 18 January 2016. Available at: www.fbi. gov/about-us/cjis/ucr/crime-in-the-u.s/2013/crime-in-the-u.s.-2013/violent-crime/murder-topic-page/murdermain_final.

Federal Bureau of Investigation (undated) *Cyber Crime*. [Online] Accessed 23 August 2015. Available at: www.fbi.gov/about-us/investigate/cyber.

Fennell, L. A. (2009) *The Unbounded Home: Property Values Beyond Property Lines* (New Haven, CT and London: Yale University Press).

Ferraro, K. F. (1995) *Fear of Crime: Interpreting Victimization Risk* (New York: SUNY Press).

Flint, J. (ed.) (2006) *Housing, Urban Governance and Anti-Social Behaviour: Perspectives, Policy and Practice* (Bristol: Policy Press).

Flusty, S. (2001) 'The Banality of Interdiction: Surveillance, Control and the Displacement of Diversity', *International Journal of Urban and Regional Research*, 25:3, 658–664.

Fogelson, R. (2007) *Bourgeois Nightmares: Suburbia, 1870–1930*. (New Haven, CT and London: Yale University Press).

Fowler, R. (1991) *Language in the News: Discourse and Ideology in the Press* (Routledge: London).

Freeman, E. A. (1873) *The History of the Norman Conquest of England* (Cambridge: Cambridge University Press).

Friedman, A. B. (1968) 'The Scatological Rites of Burglars', *Western Folklore*, 27:3, 171–179.

Freud, S. (1961) *Civilisation and its Discontents*, trans. J. Strachey (New York: W. W. Norton). First published in 1930 as *Das Unbehagen in der Kultur*.

Freud, S. (2003 [1919]) *The Uncanny*, trans. David McLintock (London: Penguin). First published as 'Das Unheimliche', *Imago*, 5:5–6 (1919).

Furedi, F. (2005) *Politics of Fear* (London: Bloomsbury Academic).

Galbraith, J. K. (1958) *The Affluent Society* (London: Hamish Hamilton).

Gardiner, S. (1976) *Evolution of the House* (St Albans: Paladin).

Gardner, D. (2009) 'Celebrity Obsessed Girl Gang Arrested Over Burglaries at Homes of Hollywood Stars', *Daily Mail* [Online] 25 October 2009. Accessed 24 August 2015. Available at: www.dailymail.co.uk/news/article-1223468/Wannabe-girl-gang-burgled-Hollywood-stars–1m-worth-designer-clothes-jewellery.html.

Garland, D. (2001) *The Culture of Control: Crime and Social Order in Late Modernity* (Oxford: Oxford University Press).

Geddes, A., G. Craig and S. Scott (2013) *Forced Labour in the UK* (York: Joseph Rowntree Foundation).

Genn, H. (1999) *Paths to Justice: What People Do and Think about Going to Law* (Oxford: Hart Publishing).

Gerth, H. H. and C. Wright Mills (eds) (1946) *From Max Weber: Essays in Sociology* (London: Routledge). [First published 1919 as *Politik als Beruf* (Politics as a Vocation)].

Getzler, J. (2005) 'Use of Force in Protecting Property', *Theoretical Inquiries in Law*, 7:1, 131–166.

Gibb, F. (2010) 'Fears of "Licence To Kill" as Tories Bid to Change Self-Defence Laws', *The Times*, 25 January 2010.

Giddens, A. (1990) *The Consequences of Modernity* (Stanford, CA: Stanford University Press).

Giddens, A. (1991) *Modernity and Self-identity: Self and Society in the Late Modern Age* (Cambridge: Polity).

Gill, M. and M. Hemming (2003) *The Causes of False Alarms* (Leicester: Perpetuity Press).

Gillow v UK [1986] 11 EHRR 335.

Glassner, B. (1999) *The Culture of Fear: Why Americans Are Afraid of the Wrong Things* (New York: Basic Books).

Goffman, E. (1971) [1956] *Relations in Public: Microstudies of the Public Order* (New York: Basic Books).

Goldberger, P. (1996) 'The Rise of the Private City', in J. Vitullo-Martin (ed.), *Breaking Away: The Future of Cities: Essays in Memory of Robert F. Wagner, Jr.* (New York: Twentieth Century Fund Book).

Graham, S. and S. Marvin (2001) *Splintering Urbanism: Networked Infrastructures, Technological Mobilities and the Urban Condition* (London: Routledge).

Gray, K. and S. F. Gray (1999) 'Private Property and Public Propriety', in J. McLean (ed.), *Property and the Constitution* (Oxford: Hart Publishing), pp. 11–39.

Gray, K. and S. F. Gray (2009) *Elements of Land Law*, 5th edn (London: Butterworths).

Great Dreams (2007) [Webpage] Accessed 18 January 2016. Available at: www.greatdreams.com/brown/ed-brown.htm.

Green, S. P. (1999) 'Castles and Carjackers: Proportionality and the Use of Deadly Force in Defence of Dwellings and Vehicles', *University of Illinois Law Review*, 1, 1–42.

Greenspan, A, (2003) Speech to Independent Community Bankers of America, Orlando, Florida, 4 March 2003. Accessed 4 May 2016. Available at: www.federalreserve.gov/BOARDDOCS/SPEECHES/2003/20030304/default.htm.

Greenspan, A. (2007) *The Age of Turbulence: Adventures in a New World* (London: Allen Lane, Penguin Books).

Gurney, C. M. (1999a) 'Lowering the Drawbridge: A Case Study of Analogy and Metaphor in the Social Construction of Home-ownership', *Urban Studies*, 36:10, 1705–1722.

Gurney, C. M. (1999b) 'Pride and Prejudice: Discourses of Normalisation in Public and Private Accounts of Home Ownership', *Housing Studies*, 14:2, 163–183.

Gurr, T., P. Grabosky and R. Hula (1976) *Rogues, Rebels, and Reformers: A Political History of Urban Crime and Conflict* (London: SAGE).

Hagemann-White, C. and S. Bohn (2007) *Protecting Women Against Violence* (Strasbourg: Council of Europe).

Hannigan, J. (1998) *Fantasy City: Pleasure and Profit in the Postmodern Metropolis* (London: Routledge).

Hansard (1980) 15 January 1980 [Online] Accessed 20 June 2016. Available at: http://hansard.millbanksystems.com/commons/1980/jan/15/housing-bill.

Harrow Community Support Limited v The Secretary of State for Defence (2012) EWHC 1921.

Harvey, D. (2005) *A Brief History of Neoliberalism* (Oxford: Oxford University Press).

Hauser, C. (2007) 'Actor and Neighbor Told to Stop Suing Each Other', *New York Times*. [Online] 29 December 2007. Accessed 23 August 2015. Available at: www.nytimes.com/2007/12/29/nyregion/29connery.html?_r=0.

Hay, J. (2006) 'Designing Homes to be the First Line of Defense: Safe Households, Mobilization, and the New Mobile Privatization', *Cultural Studies*, 20:4–5, 349–377.

Hegel, G. W. F. (1991) [1821] *Elements of the Philosophy of Right*, trans. H. B. Nisbet, ed. A. W. Wood (Cambridge: Cambridge University Press).

Helsley, R. W. and W. C. Strange (1999) 'Gated Communities and the Economic Geography Of Crime', *Journal of Urban Economics*, 46:1, 80–105.

Hepworth, M. (1999) 'Privacy, Security and Respectability: The Ideal Victorian Home', in T. Chapman and J. Hockey (eds), *Ideal Homes? Social Change and Domestic Life* (Abingdon: Routledge), pp. 17–29.

Herald Sun (2009) 'Man "Complained About Noise" Before Death', *Herald Sun* [Online] 22 November 2009. Accessed 4 May 2016. Available at: www. heraldsun.com.au/news/breaking-news/man-complained-about-noise -before-death/story-e6frf7kf-1225801797939.

Hildebrand, K. (2010) 'More Charges Filed in Burglary Ring', *Record-Courier* [Online] 2 October 2010. Accessed 24 August 2015. Available at: www.recordcourier.com/article/20101002/NEWS/101009985/1062 &ParentProfile=1049.

HM Inspectorate of Constabulary (2015) 'Targeting the Risk: An Inspection of the Efficiency and Effectiveness of Firearms Licensing in Police Forces in England and Wales'. [Online] Accessed 18 January 2016. Available at: www. justiceinspectorates.gov.uk/hmic/wp-content/uploads/firearms-licensing-targeting-the-risk.pdf.

Home Affairs Committee (2010) *Third Report: Firearms Control*. [Online] Accessed 4 May 2016. Available at: www.publications.parliament.uk/pa/ cm201011/cmselect/cmhaff/447/44705.htm.

Home Office (2009a) *Crime in England and Wales 2007/08 Findings from the British Crime Survey and Police Recorded Crime*, eds C. Kershaw, S. Nicholas and A. Walker (London: Home Office).

Home Office (2009b) *Local Crime Figures and Neighbourhood Police Details at the Touch of a Button* [Press Release] 20 October 2009. Accessed 20 August 2015. Available at: http://webarchive.nationalarchives.gov.uk/20100407182142/ press.homeoffice.gov.uk/press-releases/local-crime-figures.html.

Home Office (2013) *Crime in England and Wales 2010 to 2011* (London: HMSO).

Hope, T. (2000) 'Inequality and the Clubbing of Private Security', in T. Hope and R. Sparks (eds), *Crime, Risk and Insecurity: Law and Order in Everyday Life and Political Discourse* (London: Routledge), pp. 83–106.

Hope, T. (2001) 'Crime Victimization and Inequality in Risk Society', in R. Matthews and J. Pitts, *Crime, Disorder and Community Safety: A New Agenda* (London: Routledge), pp. 193–218.

Hotten, J. C. (1859) *Dictionary of Modern Slang, Cant and Vulgar Words* (London: John Camden Hotten).

HousePriceCrash (2015) 'Nationwide Average House Prices Adjusted For Inflation' [Online] Accessed 3 December 2015. Available at: www.housepricecrash.co.uk/indices-nationwide-national-inflation.php.

Hughes, M. (2008) 'Rumbled: Farmer Who Hid his Illegal Castle Behind the Hay', *Independent* [Online] 10 May 2008. Accessed 21 August 2015. Available at: www.independent.co.uk/news/uk/this-britain/rumbled-farmer-who-hid-his-illegal-castle-behind-the-hay-825416.html.

Ignoffo, M. J. (2010) *Captive of the Labyrinth: Sarah L. Winchester, Heiress to the Rifle Fortune* (Columbia, MO: University of Missouri Press).

Independent (2009) 'Joanne Harris: Life in the Middle of Nowhere', *Independent* [Online] 7 January 2009. Accessed 5 May 2016. Available at: www.independent.co.uk/news/people/news/joanne-harris-life-in-the-middle-of-nowhere-1229497.html.

Institute for Economics and Peace (2013) *UK Peace Index* (Sydney: Institute for Economics and Peace).

Jackson, S. (1962) *We Have Always Lived in the Castle* (London: Penguin).

Jacobs, M. (2009) *Law of Compulsory Land Acquisition* (Sydney: Thomson Reuters).

James, L. (2003) *Warrior Race: A History of the British at War* (New York: St Martin's Press).

Jamieson, S. (2015) 'The Invisible £4.5m Home: Underground Hampstead Heath House Up For Sale', *Telegraph*, 17 August 2015 [Online] Accessed 3 December 2015. Available at: www.telegraph.co.uk/finance/property/house-prices/11807991/The-invisible-4.5m-home-underground-Hampstead-Heath-house-up-for-sale.html.

Jansen, S. and M. E. Nugent-Borakove (2007) *Expansions to the Castle Doctrine: Implications for Policy and Practice* (Alexandria, VA: National District Attorneys Association). Available at: www.ndaa.org/pdf/Castle per cent-20Doctrine.pdf.

Johnson, D. (1990) 'Colorado Journal; "Make My Day": More Than a Threat', *The New York Times*, 1 June 1990. Accessed 18 January 2016. Available at: www.nytimes.com/1990/06/01/us/colorado-journal-make-my-day-more-than-a-threat.html.

Jones, D. (2009) 'Spending on Personal Security Perk for Ceos is Skyrocketing', *USA Today*, 7 July 2009. Accessed 18 January 2016. Available at: www.usatoday.com/money/companies/management/2009-09-07-CEO-security-spending_N.htm.

Jones, T. and T. Newburn (1999). 'Urban Change and Policing: Mass Private Property Re-Considered', *European Journal on Criminal Policy and Research*, 7:2, 225–244.

Jung, C. G. (1955) *Modern Man in Search of a Soul* (London: Routledge).

Jung, C. G. (1961) *Dreams, Memories, Reflections* (New York: Pantheon Books).

Katz, C. (2001) 'The State Goes Home: Local Hyper-Vigilance of Children and the Global Retreat from Social Reproduction', *Social Justice*, 28:3, 47–56.

Kelo v. City of New London (2005) 545 U.S. 469.

Kemeny, J. (1983) *The Great Australian Nightmare: A Critique of the Home-Ownership Ideology* (Melbourne: Georgian House).

King, A. (2007) 'Fortress and Fashion Statements: Gentry Castles in Fourteenth-Century Northumberland', *Journal of Medieval History*, 33, 372–397.

Kitchen, T. and R. H. Schneider (2001) *Planning for Crime Prevention: A Trans-atlantic Perspective* (London: Routledge).

Klauser, F. (2010) 'Splintering Spheres of Security: Peter Sloterdijk and the Contemporary Fortress City', *Environment and Planning D: Society and Space*, 28, 326–340.

Klein, M. (1975) *Envy and Gratitude and Other Works, 1946–1963* (London: The Hogarth Press).

Kluyev, V. and P. Mills (2010) 'Is Housing Wealth an "ATM"? International Trends', in Susan J. Smith and Beverley A. Searle (eds), *The Blackwell Companion to the Economics of Housing: The Housing Wealth of Nations* (Oxford: Blackwell), pp. 58–81.

Kostof, S. (1991) *The City Shaped: Urban Patterns and Meanings through History* (London: Thames and Hudson).

Kostof, S. (1992) *The City Assembled: The Elements of Urban Form through History* (London: Thames and Hudson).

Kumar, K. (1997) 'Home: The Promise and Predicament of Private Life at the End of the Twentieth Century', in J. Weintraub and K. Kumar (eds), *Public and Private in Thought and Practice: Perspectives on a Grand Dichotomy* (Chicago: University of Chicago Press), pp. 204–236.

Kunkle, F. (2008) 'Gun Sales Thriving Despite Tough Economy', *Washington Post*, 27 October 2008. Accessed 18 January 2016. Available at: www.cbsnews.com/stories/2008/10/27/politics/washingtonpost/main4547564.shtml.

Lakoff, G. and M. Johnson (1980) *Metaphors We Live By* (Chicago: University of Chicago Press).

Langton, L. (2011) *Identity Theft Reported by Households, 2005–2010 (NCJ 236245)*. [Online] Accessed 23 August 2015. Available at: www.bjs.gov/index.cfm?ty=pbdetail&iid=2207.

Lasch, C. (1995) *Haven in a Heartless World: The Family Besieged* (New York: W. W. Norton).

Law, P. (2006) 'Burglar Jailed for Life for Murdering Teacher'. [Online] Accessed 18 January 2016. Available at: www.thisislocallondon.co.uk/news/topstories/display.var.706463.0.burglar_guilty_of_murdering_teacher.php.

Law Commission (2004) *Partial Defences to Murder, Final Report* (London).

Law Commission (2006) *Murder, Manslaughter and Infanticide. Law Com No 304* (London).

Lee, M. (2007) *Inventing Fear of Crime: Criminology and the Politics of Anxiety* (Cullompton: Willan).

Lefebvre, H. (1991) [1974] *The Production of Space* (Oxford: Blackwell).

Library of Congress (2015) *Firearms-Control Legislation and Policy: Australia.* [Online] Accessed 18 August 2015. Available at: www.loc.gov/law/help/firearms-control/australia.php.

Liddiard, R. (2005) *Castles in Context: Power, Symbolism and Landscape, 1066 to 1500* (Macclesfield: Windgather Press).

Lipovetsky, G. (2005) *Hypermodern Times* (Cambridge: Polity Press).

Loader, I., E. Girling and R. Sparks (2000) 'After Success? Anxieties of Affluence in an English Village', in T. Hope and R. Sparks (eds), *Crime, Risk and Insecurity: Law and Order in Everyday Life and Political Discourse* (London: Routledge).

Locke, J. (1978) [1689] reprinted as 'Of Property', in Macpherson, C. B. (ed.), *Property: Mainstream and Critical Positions* (Toronto: University of Toronto Press), pp. 15–28.

Low, S. (2003) *Behind the Gates: Life, Security, and the Pursuit of Happiness in Fortress America* (London: Routledge).

Low, S. (2008) 'The New Emotions of Home: Fear, Insecurity, and Paranoia', in M. Sorkin (ed.), *Indefensible Space: The Architecture of the National Insecurity State* (New York: Routledge), pp. 233–257.

Low, S. and N. Smith (eds) (2006) *The Politics of Public Space* (New York: Routledge).

Lupton, D. and J. Tulloch (1999) 'Theorising Fear of Crime: Beyond the Rational/Irrational Opposition', *British Journal of Sociology*, 50:3, 507–523.

Macek, S. (2006) *Urban Nightmares: The Media, the Right, and the Moral Panic over the City* (Minneapolis, MN: University of Minnesota Press).

Macintyre, J. (2007) 'Council Condemns Man's "Ridiculous" Home Security', *Independent* [Online] 30 November 2007. Accessed 4 May 2016. Available at: www.independent.co.uk/news/uk/home-news/council-condemns-mans-ridiculous-home-security-761067.html.

Maguire, M. (1980) 'The Impact of Burglary on Victims', *British Journal of Criminology*, 20, 261–295.

Maher, K. (2003) 'Workers and Strangers: The Household Service Economy and the Landscape of Suburban Fear', *Urban Affairs Review*, 38:6, 751–786.

Maitland, J. (2007) 'Callous Conmen who Bled their Victims Dry', *International Express* [Online] 14 August 2007. Accessed 24 August 2015 [*electronic version* available by subscription only].

Malkin, B. (2009) 'Nicole Kidman's Neighbours Angry at Planting of Leylandii Trees', *Telegraph* [Online] 23 December 2009. Accessed 22 August 2015. Available at: www.telegraph.co.uk/news/celebritynews/6872641/Nicole -Kidmans-neighbours-angry-at-planting-of-leylandii-trees.html.

Mallett, S. (2004) 'Understanding Home: A Critical Review of the Literature', *The Sociological Review*, 52:1, 63–89.

Martin v R [2001] EWCA Crim 2245.

Massey, D. and N. Denton (1993) *American Apartheid: Segregation and the Making of the Underclass* (Boston, MA: Harvard University Press).

Mawby, R. (2013) *Burglary* (London: Routledge).

Mawby, R. I. and S. Walklate (1997) 'The Impact of Burglary: A Tale of Two Cities', *International Review of Victimology*, 4:4, 267–295.

McDonald v. Chicago (2010) 561 U.S. 742.

McKee, B. (2004) 'Fortress Home: Welcome Mat Bites', *New York Times* [Online] 22 January 2004. Accessed 24 August 2015. Available at: www.nytimes. com/2004/01/22/garden/fortress-home-welcome-mat-bites.html.

McMillan, P. (1990) 'Judge Rules That Madonna Can't Justify Her Hedge: Lawsuits: The Pop Star Must Cut Back Shrubbery and a Pine Tree at Her Hollywood Hills Home, Ending a Two-Year Battle with Neighbor', *Los Angeles Times* [Online] 7 December 1990. Accessed 22 August 2015. Available at: articles.latimes.com/1990-12-07/local/me-6072_1_hollywood-hills -home.

McSmith, A. (2010) 'Saatchi to Sell £36m Flat after Falling out with the Neighbours', *Independent* [Online] 20 October 2010. Accessed 23 August 2015. Available at: www.independent.co.uk/news/uk/home-news/saatchi -to-sell-16336m-flat-after-falling-out-with-the-neighbours-2111343.html.

Melossi, D. (2008) *Controlling Crime, Controlling Society: Thinking About Crime In Europe and America* (Cambridge: Polity).

Metropolitan Police (undated) *Security Alarms* [Online] Accessed 3 December 2015. Available at: http://content.met.police.uk/Article/Security-alarms/ 1400011145584/1400011145584.

Miller, D. (2008) *The Comfort of Things* (Cambridge: Polity).

Milner, G. R. (2000) 'Palisaded Settlements in Prehistoric Eastern North America', in J. D. Tracy (ed.), *City Walls: the Urban Enceinte in Global Perspective* (Cambridge: Cambridge University Press), pp. 46–70.

Ministry of Justice (2013) *Use of Force in Self Defence at Place of Residence*, Circular No. 2013/02 (London, Ministry of Justice).

Minton, A. (2012) *Ground Control: Fear and Happiness in the Twenty-First-Century City* (London: Penguin).

Mitchell, D. (2003) *The Right to the City: Social Justice and the Fight for Public Space* (London: Guilford Press).

Mitchell, D. (2005) 'The SUV Model of Citizenship: Floating Bubbles, Buffer Zones, and the Rise of the "Purely Atomic" Individual', *Political Geography*, 24:1, 77–100.

Mitchell, J. (2008) 'What Public Presence? Access, Commons and Property Rights', *Social and Legal Studies*, 18:3, 351–367.

Monahan, T. (2009) 'Identity Theft Vulnerability: Neoliberal Governance Through Crime Construction', *Theoretical Criminology*, 13:2, 155–176.

Monk, E. (2009) *Keys: Their History and Collection* (Princes Risborough: Shire).

Moore, J. (2000) 'Placing *Home* in Context', *Journal of Environmental Psychology*, XX, 207–217.

Morris, N. (1960–62) 'A New Qualified Defence to Murder', *Adelaide Law Review*, 23–52.

Muir, H. and R. Butt (2005) 'Freed Robber Obsessed with the Rich Guilty of Stabbing Financier To Death', *Guardian*, 16 December 2005 [Online] Accessed 18 January 2016. Available at: www.guardian.co.uk/uk/2005/dec/16/ukcrime.hughmuir.

Munzer, R. (1990) *A Theory of Property* (Cambridge: Cambridge University Press).

National Center for Missing and Abused Children (undated) *CyberTipline Fact Sheet* [Online] Accessed 23 August 2015. Available at: www.cybertipline.com/en_US/documents/CyberTiplineFactSheet.pdf.

National Research Council of the National Academies (2004) *Firearms and Violence: A Critical Review* (Washington) [Online] Accessed 18 January 2016. Available at: www.nap.edu/openbook.php?isbn=0309091241&page=1.

National Rifle Association – Institute for Legislative Action (2014) *2014 NRA-ILA Firearms Fact Card* [Online] Accessed 18 January 2016. Available at: www.nraila.org/articles/20140326/2014-nra-ila-firearms-fact-card.

NBC Miami (2015) 'Man Shot in Dispute Over Dog Poop Has Died', *NBC Miami* [Online] 30 June 2015. Accessed 30 August 2015. Available at: www.nbcmiami.com/news/local/Man-Shot-in-Dispute-over-Dog-Poop-Has-Died-310822351.html.

Newman, O. (1972) *Defensible Space: Crime Prevention Through Urban Design* (New York: Macmillan).

Nicolson, A. (2001) *Sea Room: An Island Life* (London: HarperCollins).

O'Donnell, A. (undated) *How Criminals Use Google Maps* [Online] Accessed 24 August 2015. Available at: netsecurity.about.com/od/perimetersecurity/a/How-Criminals-Use-Google-Maps-Street-View-To-Case-The-Joint.htm.

OECD Income Distribution Database (IDD [annual]) *Gini, poverty, income, Methods and Concepts* [Online] Accessed 18 January 2016. Available at: www.oecd.org/els/soc/income-distribution-database.htm.

Office of the Director for Public Prosecutions (NSW) (2013) *Media Release: Statement from the DPP, Decision in the Matter of Brookes* [Online] Accessed 3 December 2015. Available at: www.odpp.nsw.gov.au/docs/default-source/ recent-media-releases/06-12-2013-decision-in-the-matter-of-brookes -.pdf?sfvrsn=4.

Office for National Statistics (2007) *Social Trends, No.37* [Online] Accessed 4 May 2016. Available at: www.ons.gov.uk/ons/rel/social-trends-rd/social -trends/no–37-2007-edition/index.html.

Office for National Statistics (2013a) *A Century of Home Ownership and Renting in England and Wales.* Accessed 1 September 2015. Available at: www.ons.gov. uk/ons/rel/census/2011-census-analysis/a-century-of-home-ownership -and-renting-in-england-and-wales/short-story-on-housing.html.

Office for National Statistics (2013b) *Crime Statistics, Focus on Property Crime, 2011/12.* [Online] [Accessed 23 August 2015]. Available at: www.ons.gov. uk/ons/rel/crime-stats/crime-statistics/focus-on-property-crime—2011 –12/index.html

Office for National Statistics (2015a) *Improving Crime Statistics in England and Wales* [Online] Accessed 3 December 2015. Available at: www.ons.gov.uk/ ons/rel/crime-stats/crime-statistics/year-ending-june-2015/sty-fraud.html.

Office for National Statistics (2015b) *Statistical Bulletin: Crime in England and Wales, Year Ending March 2015, Chapter 2: Homicide.* Accessed 19 August 2015. Available at: www.ons.gov.uk/ons/rel/crime-stats/crime-statistics/focus-on -violent-crime-and-sexual-offences-2012-13/rpt—chapter-2—homicide. html.

O'Hagan, A. (2013) 'So Many Handbags, So Little Time', *London Review of Books*, 35:12, 19–20.

O'Neill, A. (2015) 'Billionaire's Beach Just Got a Lot Less Exclusive', *CNN* [Online] 17 July 2015. Accessed 4 May 2016. Available at: http://edition. cnn.com/2015/07/17/us/billionaires-beach-malibu-public-access/.

Palmer v R [1971] AC 814.

Parker, R. (1976) *The Common Stream* (London: Paladin).

Parkinson, S., B. A. Searle, S. J. Smith, A. Stoakes and G. Wood (2009) 'Mortgage Equity Withdrawal in Australia and Britain: Towards a Wealth-Fare State?', *European Journal of Housing Policy*, 9:4, 363–387.

Parks Associates (undated) *Home Systems: Home Security Update* [Online] Accessed 24 August 2015. Available at: www.parksassociates.com/report/ home-systems-home-security-update.

Parliament of Australia (2009) *Model Criminal Code* (Canberra: Parliament of Australia).

Paterson, M. (2000) 'Gardener is Shot Dead in Hedge Feud', *Telegraph* [Online] 7 July 2000. Accessed 22 August 2015. Available at: www.telegraph.co.uk/ news/uknews/1347205/Gardener-is-shot-dead-in-hedge-feud.html.

Pease, K. (1991) 'The Kirkholt Project: Preventing Burglary on a British Public Housing Estate', *Security Journal*, 2:2, 73–77.

Peck, J. (2010) *Constructions of Neoliberal Reason* (Oxford: Oxford University Press).

People v Tomlins [1914] 107 N.E. 496, 497 (NY).

Pet Food Manufacturer's Association (2013) *Pet Population 2013* [Online] Accessed 24 August 2015. Available at: www.pfma.org.uk/pet-population/.

Phillips, A. (1998) *The Beast in the Nursery: On Curiosity and Other Appetites* (New York: Pantheon Books).

Piketty, T. (2014) *Capital in the Twenty-First Century* (Cambridge, MA: Harvard University Press).

Planty, M. and J. L. Truman (2013) *Firearm Violence, 1993–2011* (Washington, DC: US Department of Justice) [Online] Accessed 18 January 2016. Available at: www.bjs.gov/content/pub/pdf/fv9311.pdf.

Plaut, P. O. (2011) 'The Characteristics and Tradeoffs of Households Choosing to Live in Gated Communities', *Environment and Planning B: Planning and Design*, 38:5, 757–775.

Pollinger, N. (2005) 'Meet the Burglar', *Daily Telegraph*, 8 January 2005.

Porteous, J. D. (1976) 'Home: The Territorial Core', *Geographical Review*, 66:4, 383–390.

Porter v Commissioner of Police for the Metropolis [1999] EWCA Civ 1055.

Pugh, T. (2008) 'Mother's "Horror Show" as Facebook Gatecrashers Invade Birthday Party', *Independent* [Online] 3 December 2008. Accessed: 23 August 2015. Available at: www.independent.co.uk/life-style/gadgets-and-tech/news/mothers-horror-show-as-facebook-gatecrashers-invade-birthday-party-1048845.html.

Pugin, A. (1836) *Contrasts, Or, A Parallel Between the Noble Edifices of the Fourteenth and Fifteenth Centuries and Similar Buildings of the Present Day* (London: Charles Dolman).

Putnam, R. D. (2000) *Bowling Alone: The Collapse and Revival of American Community* (New York, Simon & Schuster).

R (On the Application of Ashbrook) v East Sussex CC (2002) EWCA Civ 1701.

R (Fidler) v Secretary of State for Communities and Local Government and Reigate and Banstead BC [2011] EWCA Civ 1159.

R. v Dawes [2013] EWCA Crim 322.

R v McKay [1957] VR 560.

Radin, M. J. (1993) *Re-interpreting Property* (Chicago: University of Chicago Press).

Rainwater, E. (1966) 'Fear and the House-as-Haven in the Lower Class', *Journal of the American Institute of Planners*, 32:1, 23–31.

Rajan, A. (2008) 'Neighbour Shot Dog Dead to Stop Its "Incessant Barking"', *Independent* [Online] 28 November 2008. Accessed 23 August 2015.

Available at: www.independent.co.uk/news/uk/crime/neighbour-shot-dog -dead-to-stop-its-incessant-barking-1038870.html.

Rakoff, R. M. (1977) 'Ideology in Everyday Life: The Meaning of the House', *Politics and Society*, 7:1, 85–104.

Ramblers Organisation (2002) 'Victory For "Scum" Over Van Hoogstraten Path is Warning to All Councils', Ramblers Organisation [Online] 20 November 2002. Accessed 18 January 2016. Available at: www.ramblers.org.uk/news/ archive/2002/vanhoogstratensentecnenov02.htm.

Ramblers Organisation (2005) 'Ramblers Celebrate as "Van Hoogstraten Legal Loophole" Closes Today', Ramblers Organisation [Online] 14 January 2005. Accessed 18 January 2016. Available at: www.ramblers.org.uk/news/ archive/2005/vanhoogstratenloophole.htm.

RealtyTrac (2009) *Foreclosure Activity Increases 81 Percent in 2008* [Online] Accessed 27 February 2009. Available at: www.realtytrac.com/content/press -releases/foreclosure-activity-increases-81-percent-in-2008-4551?accnt =64847.

RealtyTrac (2010) *2009 Year End Foreclosure Report* [Online] Accessed 10 March 2010. Available at: www.realtytrac.com/landing/2009-year-end-foreclosure -report.html.

RealtyTrac (2015) *1.1 Million U.S. Properties with Foreclosure Filings in 2014, Down 18 Percent from 2013 to Lowest Level since 2006* [Online] Accessed 5 May 2016. Available at: www.realtytrac.com/news/foreclosure-trends/1-1 -million-u-s-properties-with-foreclosure-filings-in-2014-down-18 -percent-from-2013-to-lowest-level-since-2006/.

Reiner, R., E. Livingston and J. Allen (2000) 'No More Happy Endings? The Media and Popular Concern About Crime Since the Second World War', in T. Hope and R. Sparks (eds), *Crime, Risk and Insecurity: Law and Order in Everyday Life and Political Discourse* (London: Routledge), pp. 107–125.

Rheingold, H. (2002) *Smart Mobs: The Next Social Revolution* (Jackson, TN: Perseus Books).

Richards, L. (1990) *Nobody's Home: Dreams and Realties in a New Suburb* (Melbourne: Oxford University Press).

Robson and Another v Hallett (1967) 2 All E R 407.

Rodgers, D. (2004) '"Disembedding" the City: Crime, Insecurity and Spatial Organization in Managua, Nicaragua', *Environment and Urbanization*, 16:2, 113–124.

Rohe, W. M. and H. L. Watson (eds) (2007), *Chasing the American Dream: New Perspectives on Affordable Home ownership* (Ithaca, NY: Cornell University Press).

Ronald, R. (2008) *The Ideology of Home Ownership: Homeowner Societies and the Role of Housing* (Basingstoke: Palgrave Macmillan).

Rooth Law Group (undated) *Florida's 'Stand Your Ground' Law* [Online] Accessed 18 January 2016. Available at: www.roothlawgroup.com/library/st -petersburg-criminal-defense-attorney-fl-stand-your-ground-law.cfm.

Roots, G., M. Humphries, R. Fookes and J. Pereira (2008) *The Law of Compulsory Purchase* (London: Bloomsbury).

Rose, L. (2006) 'Platinum Protection', *Forbes* [Online] 9 December 2006. Accessed 24 August 2015. Available at: www.forbes.com/2006/09/11/ luxury-home-security_cx_lr_0912platinum.html.

Rose, N. (2000) 'Government and Control', *British Journal of Criminology*, 40:2, 321–339.

RSPCA Australia (2014) *How Many Pets are There in Australia?* [Online] Accessed 24 August 2015. Available at: kb.rspca.org.au/How-many-pets-are-there-in -Australia_58.html.

Ruskin, J. (2006) [1865] *Sesame and Lilies: Three Lectures* (Charleston, SC).

Rybczynski, W. (1986) *Home: A Short History of an Idea* (New York: Viking).

Rykwert, J. (1991) 'House and Home', *Social Research*, 58:1, 51–62.

Sacks, R. D. (1986) *Human Territoriality: Its theory and History* (Cambridge: Cambridge University Press).

Sales, N. J. (2013) *The Bling Ring* (London: HarperCollins).

Sampford, K. (1997) *Home Invasion Criminal Law Amendment Bill 1996; Legislation Bulletin no 2/97* (Brisbane: Queensland Parliamentary Library).

Sampson, R. (2007) *The Problem of False Burglar Alarms: Guide No. 5*, 2nd edn [Online] (Center for Problem-Oriented Policing). Accessed 26 August 2015. www.popcenter.org/problems/false_alarms/print/.

Sanchez, T. W., R. E Lang and D. Dhavale (2005) 'Security versus Status? A First Look at the Census's Gated Community Data', *Journal of Planning Education and Research*, 24, 281–291.

Sánchez-Pardo, E. (2003) *Cultures of the Death Drive: Melanie Klein and Modernist Melancholia* (Durham, NC: Duke University Press).

Sasson, T. (1995) *Crime Talk: How Citizens Construct a Social Problem* (Chicago: Aldine Transaction).

Saunders, P. (1990) *A Nation of Home Owners* (London: Unwin Hyman).

Saunders, P. and P. Williams (1988) 'The Meaning of "Home" in Contemporary English Culture', *Housing Studies*, III:2, 81–93.

Savage, M. (2008) 'Socialite Sues Landlord for Break-In at Mayfair Home', *Independent*, 13 August 2008.

Sayers, A. (1994) *Sidney Nolan: The Ned Kelly Story* (Sydney: MetPublications).

Schelzig, E. (2009a) 'Why It's Getting Easier to Carry a Gun in the US', *Independent on Sunday*, 13 December 2009, p. 39.

Schelzig, E. (2009b) 'NRA Quietly Winning Battles for Looser Gun Laws', *The Huffington Post*, 12 December 2009. Accessed 18 January 2016. Available at:

www.huffingtonpost.com/2009/12/12/nra-quietly-winning-loose_n_389684.html.

Schifferes, S. (2007) 'Foreclosure Wave Sweeps America', *BBC News* [Online] 5 November 2007. Accessed: 20 August 2015. Available at: news.bbc.co.uk/1/hi/business/7070935.stm.

Schoon, N. (2001) *The Chosen City* (London: Spon Press).

Schorr, D. B. (2009) 'How Blackstone Became a Blackstonian', *Theoretical Inquiries in Law*, 10:1, 103–126.

Security Sales & Integration (2014) *How Intruders Can Disable Home Security Systems*. [Online] Accessed 24 August 2015. Available at: www.securitysales.com/article/how_intruders_can_disable_home_security_systems.

Sedleigh-Denfield v O'Callaghan (1940) AC 880.

Semayne's Case (1604) 5 Co Rep 91a.

Sennett, R. (1974) *The Fall of Public Man* (New York: W. W. Norton).

Shearing, C. D. and P. C. Stenning (1981) 'Modern Private Security: Its Growth and Implications', *Crime and Justice*, 3:1, 193–245.

Sibley, D. (2005) 'Private/Public', in D. Atkinson, P. Jackson, D. Sibley and N. Washbourne (eds), *Cultural Geography: a Critical Dictionary of Key Concepts* (London: I.B. Tauris), pp. 155–160.

Simon, J. (2007) *Governing Through Crime: How the War on Crime Transformed American Democracy and Created a Culture of Fear* (Oxford: Oxford University Press).

Slater, P. (1990) *The Pursuit of Loneliness: American Culture at the Breaking Point* (Boston, MA: Beacon Press).

Spillett, R. (2015) 'Top Finance Lawyer Must Chop More Than 10 Metres Off the Leylandii at His £500,000 House After Neighbour Wins Legal Battle', *MailOnline*, 10 June 2015. Accessed 29 August 2015. Available at: www.dailymail.co.uk/news/article-3118323/Lawyer-chop-10-metres-trees-lengthy-legal-battle-neighbour.html#ixzz3kI2g93Dx.

Stamps, A. E. (2005) 'Enclosure and Safety in Urbanscapes', *Environment and Behaviour*, 37:1, 102–133.

Standing, G. (2011) *The Precariat: The New Dangerous Class* (London: Bloomsbury).

Stanko, E. (1990) *Everyday Violence: How Women and Men Experience Sexual and Physical Danger* (London: Harper Collins).

Stanko, E. (2000) 'Victims R Us: The Life History of "Fear Of Crime" and the Politicisation of Violence', in T. Hope and R. Sparks (eds), *Crime, Risk and Insecurity: Law and Order in Everyday Life and Political Discourse* (London: Routledge), pp. 13–30.

Stanley, J. (2001) 'Child Abuse and the Internet', *Child Abuse Prevention Issues*, 15 (Melbourne: National Child Protection Clearinghouse).

Stewart, A. (1981) *Housing Action in an Industrial Suburb* (London: Academic Press).

Stokoe, E. and J. Wallmark (2003) 'Space Invaders: The Moral Spatial Order in Neighbourhood Dispute Discourses', *British Journal of Social Psychology*, 42:4, 551–560.

Strider, J., A. Third, K. Locke and I. Richardson (2012) *Parental Approaches to Enhancing Young People's Online Safety: Literature Review* (Melbourne: Young and Well Cooperative Research Centre).

Suarez, G. *The Tactical Advantage: A Definitive Study of Personal Small-Arms Tactics*, Boulder, CO: Paladin Press, 1998).

Swinton Insurance (2015) 'Don't Lose Sleep Over Home Security' [Online] 23 February 2015. Accessed 18 January 2016. Available at: www.swinton. co.uk/home-insurance/guides/home-security-fears/.

Sydney Morning Herald (1998) 'Self-Defence in the Home', 10 September 1998.

Tasmania Law Reform Institute (2015) *Review of the Law Relating to Self-Defence; Final Report No 20* [Online] Accessed 3 December 2015. Available at: www.utas.edu.au/__data/assets/pdf_file/0003/756570/TLRI_Self-defence _FR_A4_06_Print.pdf.

Technavio (2015a) 'Interactive Residential Security Market in the US 2015–2019' [Online] Accessed 14 December 2015. Available at: www. industryreportstore.com/catalog/product/view/id/452327/s/interactive -residential-security-market-in-the-us-2015-2019/category/2120/.

Technavio (2015b) *Residential Security Market in Europe* [Online] Accessed 8 December 2015. Available at: www.industryreportstore.com/catalog/ product/view/id/450318/s/residential-security-market-in-europe-2015 -2019/category/2086/.

Telegraph (2008) 'Paint Your House or Face Action, Couple Told' [Online] 22 February 2008. Accessed 21 August 2015. Available at: www.telegraph .co.uk/news/uknews/1579500/Paint-your-house-or-face-action-couple -told.html.

Telegraph (2009) 'Son Killed Mother as Bailiffs Knocked on Door', 29 January 2009. Available at: www.telegraph.co.uk/news/uknews/law-and-order/ 4373992/Son-killed-mother-as-bailiffs-knocked-at-door.html.

The Economist (2009) 'Briefing: Home Ownership, Shelter or Burden?', 18 April 2009, pp. 76–78.

The Economist (2015) 'Bombing Along: A New Business Caters for London's Super-Rich And Super-Wary', *The Economist*, 1 August 2015.

The Guardian (2000) 'Even Nastier Nick' [Online] 8 September 2000. Accessed 21 August 2015. Available at: www.theguardian.com/g2/story/ 0,3604,365743,00.html.

The Statistics Portal (2015) 'Average Time Spent Gaming Weekly in Great Britain as of June 2014, by Age (in Hours)' [Online]. Accessed 18 January 2016. Available at: www.statista.com/statistics/323943/average-time-spent -gaming-weekly-uk.

Thompson, E.P. (1991) [1963] *The Making of the English Working Class* (Harmondsworth: Penguin).

Thornton, A., C. Hatton, C. Malone, T. Fryer, D. Walker, J. Cunningham and N. Durrani (2003) 'Distraction Burglary Amongst Older Adults and Ethnic Minority Communities' (London: Home Office).

Tracy, J. D. (ed.) (2000) *City Walls: The Urban Enceinte in Global Perspective* (Cambridge: Cambridge University Press).

Trahan, J. (2010) 'Teen Fatally Shoots Sister in Oak Cliff Home', *The Dallas Morning News*, 14 August 2010.

Treadwell, J. (2011) 'From The Car Boot to Booting It Up? Ebay, Online Counterfeit Crime and the Transformation of the Criminal Marketplace', *Criminology and Criminal Justice*, 12:2, 175–191.

Tuan, Y-F. (1975) 'Place: An Experimental Perspective', *American Geographical Society*, 65:2, 151–165.

UK Government (2016) *Mortgage and Landlord Possession Statistics.* [Online] Accessed 17 May 2016. Available at: www.gov.uk/government/collections/mortgage-and-landlord-possession-statistics.

UK Trade & Investment Defence and Security Organisation (UKTI DSO) and the Home Office (2014) *Increasing Our Security Exports: A New Government Approach* (London: UK Trade & Investment Defence and Security Organisation).

United Press International (2008) 'Deliverymen: Homeowner Brandished Gun' [Online] 25 March 2008. Accessed 22 August 2015.

United States Postal Service (2013) *National Dog Bite Prevention Week, May 19–25 2013.* [Online] Accessed 24 August 2015. Available at: about.usps.com/postal-bulletin/2013/pb22362/html/cover.htm.

US Census Bureau (2011) *Historical Census of Housing Tables: Home Ownership* [Online] Accessed 20 August 2015. Available at: www.census.gov/hhes/www/housing/census/historic/owner.html.

US Census Bureau (2012) *Historical Census of Housing Tables: Home Values* [Online] Accessed 20 August 2015. Available at: www.census.gov/hhes/www/housing/census/historic/values.html.

Uslaner, E. (2002) *The Moral Foundations of Trust* (Cambridge: Cambridge University Press).

Uslaner, E. M. (2012) *Segregation and Mistrust: Diversity, Isolation, and Social Cohesion* (Cambridge: Cambridge University Press).

Utratemp Ventures Ltd v Collins [2001] UKHL 43.

van Dijk, J. J. M., J. N. van Kesteren and P. Smit (2008) *Criminal Victimization in International Perspective: Key Findings From the 2004–05 ICVS and EU ICS* (The Hague: Boom Legal Publishers).

van Kesteren, J. N. (2014) 'Revisiting the Gun Ownership and Violence Link: A Multilevel Analysis of Victimization Survey Data', *British Journal of Criminology*, 54:1, 53–72.

Vanderbeck, R. M. (2003) 'Youth, Racism, and Place in the Tony Martin Affair', *Antipode*, 3, 376–384.

Vesselinov, E., M. Cazessus and W. Falk (2007) 'Gated Communities and Spatial Inequality', *Journal of Urban Affairs*, 29:2, 109–127.

Vesselinov, E. and R. Le Goix (2012) 'From Picket Fences to Iron Gates: Suburbanization and Gated Communities in Phoenix, Las Vegas and Seattle', *GeoJournal*, 77:2, 203–222.

Vickery, A. (2008) 'An Englishman's Home is His Castle? Thresholds, Boundaries and Privacies in the Eighteenth-Century London House', *Past and Present*, 199:1, 147–173.

Vulliamy, E. (2013) 'Scaffolding, Drills, Money … How the Super-Rich Ruined my Neighbourhood', *Observer* [Online] 22 September 2013. Accessed 23 August 2015. Available at: www.theguardian.com/uk-news/2013/sep/22/notting-hill-development-hell.

Waite, R. (2013) 'Witherford Watson Mann's Revamp of 12th Century Castle Wins 2013 Stirling Prize', *Architects Journal*, 26 September 2013. Accessed 26 August 2015. www.architectsjournal.co.uk/news/witherford-watson-manns-revamp-of-12th-century-castle-wins-2013-stirling-prize/8653560.article.

Walby, S., J. Allen and J. Simmons (2004) *Domestic Violence, Sexual Assault and Stalking: Findings from the British Crime Survey* (London: Home Office Research, Development and Statistics Directorate).

Walker, S. (2011) 'The Ukrainian, the £136m Flat – and the £60m Redecoration', *Independent* [Online] 20 April 2011. Accessed 20 August 2015. Available at: www.independent.co.uk/news/uk/home-news/the-ukrainian-the-163136m-flat-ndash-and-the-16360m-redecoration-2270073.html.

Walker, T. (2013) 'Obama Appeals for Calm as Trayvon's Killer is Cleared', *Independent*, 15 July 2015, pp. 5–6.

Wallace, A. (2008) 'Things Like That Don't Happen Here: Crime, Place and Real Estate in the News', *Crime, Media, Culture: An International Journal*, 4:3, 395–409.

Walters, W. (2004) 'Secure Borders, Safe Haven, Domopolitics', *Citizenship studies*, 8:3, 237–260.

Wang, B. (2005) 'Case of Feuding Neighbors Brings Rivalry into Court', *Concord Monitor* [Online] 7 October 2005. Accessed 22 August 2015. Available at: www.concordmonitor.com/article/case-of-feuding-neighbors-brings-rivalry-into-court.

Wellman, B. (1999) *Networks in the Global Village* (Boulder, CO: Westview Press).

Which? Advice (2010) 'Home CCTV'. Available at: www.which.co.uk/advice/home-cctv/index.jsp.

Wilbanks, W. (1990) *The Make My Day Law: Colorado's Experiment in Home Protection* (Lanham, MD: University Press of America).

Wilkes, D. (2009) 'Britain's Most Expensive Streets', *Daily Mail*, 30 December 2009.

Wilkinson, R. and K. Pickett (2009) *The Spirit Level: Why Equality is Better for Everyone* (London: Allen Lane: Penguin Books).

Willman, J. (2007) 'Knights of the Realm and Kings of their Castle', *Financial Times* [Online] 7 December 2007. Accessed 21 August 2015. Available at: http://www.ft.com/cms/s/0/21e7af52-a4ea-11dc-a93b-0000779fd2ac. html#axzz3jSZK9K59.

Wills, D. (undated) *Eric Bana – Biography* [Online] Accessed 24 August 2015. Available at: www.tiscali.co.uk/entertainment/film/biography/artist/eric -bana/biography/30.

Wilson, S. (2005) [1955] *The Man in the Gray Flannel Suit* (London: Penguin).

Wilson-Doenges, G. (2000) 'An Exploration of Sense of Community and Fear of Crime in Gated Communities', *Environment and Behavior*, 32:5, 597–611.

Winlow, S. and S. Hall (2013) *Rethinking Social Exclusion: The End of the Social?* (London: SAGE).

Winnicott, D. W. (1990). *Home is Where We Start From: Essays by a Psychoanalyst* (New York: Norton).

Wolak, J., D. Finkelhor, K. J. Mitchell and M. L. Ybarra (2008) 'Online "Predators" and Their Victims: Myths, Realities, and Implications for Prevention and Treatment', *American Psychologist*, 63:2, 111–128.

Woolsey, M. (2007) 'High-Security, High-End Homes', *Forbes* magazine [Online] 29 March 2007. Accessed 28 August 2015. www.forbes.com/ 2007/03/28/secure-tech-homes-forbeslife-cx_mw_0329securehomes.html.

Wright, G. (1991) 'Prescribing the Model Home', *Social Research*, 58:1, 213–225.

Wright, R. and S. Decker (1994) *Burglars on the Job: Streetlife and Residential Break-ins* (Lebanon, NH: Northeastern University Press).

Yates, R. (2001) [1961] *Revolutionary Road* (London: Methuen Publishing).

Young, A. (2009) 'The Screen of the Crime: Judging the Affect of Cinematic Violence', *Social and Legal Studies*, 18:1, 5–22.

Young, J. (1999) *The Exclusive Society: Social Exclusion, Crime and Difference in Late Modernity* (London: SAGE).

Young, J. (2007) *The Vertigo of Late Modernity* (London: SAGE).

Zecevic v Director of Public Prosecutions (Vic) (1987) 162 CLR 645.

Zedner, L. (2003) 'Too Much Security?', *International Journal of the Sociology of Law*, 31:3, 155–184.

Zillman, C. (2015) 'Which Fortune 100 CEO Has the Biggest Security Budget?', *Fortune*, 7 January.

Index

EU authorised representative for GPSR:
Easy Access System Europe, Mustamäe tee 50,
10621 Tallinn, Estonia
gpsr.requests@easproject.com